Sentential Negation in French

Sentential Negation in French

PAUL ROWLETT

New York   Oxford

Oxford University Press

1998

Oxford University Press

Oxford   New York
Athens   Auckland   Bangkok   Bogotá   Buenos Aires   Calcutta
Cape Town   Chennai   Dar es Salaam   Delhi   Florence   Hong Kong   Istanbul
Karachi   Kuala Lumpur   Madrid   Melbourne   Mexico City   Mumbai
Nairobi   Paris   São Paulo   Singapore   Taipei   Tokyo   Toronto   Warsaw

and associated companies in
Berlin   Ibadan

Published by Oxford University Press, Inc.
198 Madison Avenue, New York, New York 10016

Oxford is a registered trademark of Oxford University Press

Library of Congress Cataloging-in-Publication Data
Rowlett, Paul, 1966–
Sentential negation in French / Paul Rowlett
p.   cm.
Includes bibliographical references and index.
ISBN 0-19-511924-X; ISBN 0-19-512591-6 (pbk.)
1. French language—Negatives.   I. Title.
PC2359.N4R69   1998
445—dc21   98-18335

1 3 5 7 9 8 6 4 2
Printed in the United States of America
on acid-free paper

for Emma Vicky and Daniel Paul

Preface

Sentential negation has been of interest to linguists and philosophers for centuries. In this book, I propose an analysis of the principal phenomena in Modern French within the Principles-and-Parameters framework of generative syntax. (See Chomsky and Lasnik 1993 and Haegeman 1994a. For more recent versions of generative syntax, see Chomsky 1995b and Radford 1997. For introductions in French, see Pollock 1997a and Tellier 1995.) In so doing, I reconsider a number of the core issues that have been discussed in the literature: What items are truly negative in Modern French? Is Modern French a negative concord language? What is the status of *ne* and *pas*? What structural positions are they associated with? How is *ne* licensed? Why is *ne* excluded from nonsentential negation contexts? What is the theoretical significance of the controversial *pour ne pas que* construction? How are pseudopartitives licensed? Why does the distribution of *rien* typically follow that of *tout* rather than *personne*? Why can *jamais* readily follow a lexical infinitive while *pas* cannot? Why can items such as *jamais* and *rien* co-occur with each other without leading to logical double negation but not, generally, with *pas*? And why does the variety of French spoken in Quebec differ from Standard French in this respect? These and other questions are addressed in this book. In some cases, I come to the same conclusions as other researchers; in a number of cases, however, my conclusions differ.

Throughout the book, I follow a tradition initiated by Edward Klima more than thirty years ago and represented in current work by such linguists as Paolo Acquaviva, Adriana Belletti, Michel DeGraff, Viviane Déprez, Maria-Teresa Espinal, Liliane Haegeman, Paul Hirschbühler, Marie Labelle, Itziar Laka, Luc Moritz, Jamal Ouhalla, Elizabeth Pearce, Jean-Yves Pollock, Ljiljana Progovac, María-Luisa Rivero, Daniel Valois, and Raffaella Zanuttini. The work of these linguists will be referred to as the discussion progresses.

The fundamental assumption underlying the book is that clausal polarity is feature based. In particular, I assume, with Haegeman (1995: 107), that negative clauses are characterized by the presence of a feature, which I shall call [+NEG], on a functional head of the extended projection of V—that is, in the clausal domain. Consequently, most of my concern about sentential negation in Modern French revolves around how this feature specification is achieved. The data suggest that *ne*, which I assume, following work by Pollock (1989), is associated underlyingly with a functional head in the clausal domain, Neg°, is not in fact inherently negative; that is, it does not bear the abstract feature [+NEG] as a lexical property. Rather, it seems that the head Neg° hosting *ne* is endowed with the relevant [+NEG] feature by some dynamic agreement mechanism that transmits [+NEG] from a negative operator in specifier position. It seems further that this takes place at S-structure and not, as some have argued, at LF. This has far-reaching consequences for the analysis of the other "negative" elements–adverbs and arguments–associated with *ne*, some of which, I conclude, are not inherently negative.

In successive chapters, I consider various aspects of the empirical domain starting, in chapter 1, with an overview of the assumptions I shall be making, in particular concerning the extent of Verb Movement. I then give a syntactic characterization of the pre-verbal particle *ne*. Crucial to the analysis will be the idea that clausal polarity features are located within a functional projection NegP (Pollock 1989) and that negative markers such as French *ne* underlyingly head NegP. In the French case, I suggest that *ne* is never underlyingly negative in the modern language; rather, *ne* inherits negative features from a suitable operator in SpecNegP. As a prelude to later discussion, I introduce the notion of "affective" item (Klima 1964). I conclude that the distribution and interpretation of such items are determined by a wellformedness condition known as the AF-FECT criterion.

In chapter 2, I concentrate on the most salient aspect of negation in French, the adverbial negative marker *pas*, which I take to be the core overt lexical item in the modern language encoding negation. The discussion culminates in a syntactic analysis of this element that, following Pollock (1989), suggests that *pas* occupies SpecNegP (at S-structure). In contrast to Pollock's analysis, however, I argue that the S-structure position of *pas* in SpecNegP is the result of an application of Move-α that raises *pas* from a lower base position. Several empirical and theoretical arguments are given to motivate this revision of Pollock's original analysis. On the empirical front, such an analysis is argued to provide an elegant account of the contrast between the morphosyntactic properties of indefinite direct objects in positive clauses on the one hand and in negative clauses on the other, as well as otherwise problematic properties of imperative structures and the diachronic development of infinitival verb placement patterns. On the theoretical front, the approach follows naturally from the proposed analysis, inspired by Haegeman (1995), of sentential negation marking.

In many respects, chapter 3 is an excursus from the restricted domain of sentential negation in French. Predominantly cross-linguistic in outlook, the discussion addresses the distinction between negative concord (henceforth, NC) languages (e.g., Italian and Serbian/Croatian) and non-NC languages (e.g., Standard Modern English and Modern German). In very broad terms, NC languages are languages that allow multiple inherently negative constituents to co-occur within a single domain without their negative features being canceled out; non-NC languages do not. An account of the distinction between the two types of language is offered based on a reinterpretation of an observation made by Jespersen (1924), whereby the issue of whether or not a language is NC is determined by the nature of its regular negative marker. Languages whose regular negative marker is realized on Neg° are NC languages; those whose negative marker is associated with SpecNegP are not. I provide an explanation for this generalization that I term *Jespersen's Generalization*. The (un)availability of NC is attributed to the distinctive scope properties of Neg° and SpecNegP. Negative markers in SpecNegP take scope over negative XPs lower in the clause (via Generalized A'-binding); negative markers in Neg° do not. A negative marker in SpecNegP therefore cancels out the negative feature of a lower negative element (= Double Negation). Assuming that dynamic spec-head agreement is unidirectional (from SpecXP to X°) and does not therefore transfer [+NEG] from Neg° to SpecNegP, a negative marker in Neg° will not pass on its negative feature to its specifier and, further, will not cancel out the negative feature of a lower negative element (= NC).

Returning now to French, given that the regular negative marker in the modern language, *pas*, is syntactically aligned with English *not* and German *nicht* (in SpecNegP), rather than Italian *non* or Serbian/Croatian *ne* (generated under Neg°), Jespersen's Generalization predicts that Modern French is a non-NC language. At the end of chapter 3, I discuss why I believe that–despite appearances–this is in fact a reasonable conclusion to draw about Modern French.

Following the conclusions about negative concord in French made in chapters 2 and 3, I turn, in chapters 4 and 5, to more peripheral issues. In chapter 4, I consider "negative adverbs" other than *pas*, namely *plus* 'any/no more/longer', *jamais* '(n)ever', and *guère* 'hardly'. On the basis of the null hypothesis that these elements are in essence syntactically (if not semantically) identical to *pas*, I explore the ways in which their distribution departs from that of *pas*. A syntactic analysis is then proposed, taking into account the conclusion reached at the end of chapter 3–namely that Modern French is not an NC language.

In chapter 5, attention is turned to what might be termed "negative arguments", namely *rien* 'anything/nothing' and *personne* 'anyone/no-one'. My purpose here is to provide a syntactic analysis of the internal structure of these two nominal items that accounts for not only the similarities but also the differences between their respective distributions. Further, I relate the syntax of these items to the proposals for the "negative adverbs" in chapter 4. Given my contention that Modern French is a non-NC language, the "negative" items discussed in chapters 4 and 5 are not deemed to be inherently negative; rather than being the rough equivalents of Standard English *nothing*, *never*, and so on, these items are assumed to be more like *anything*, *ever*, and so on.

Some of the material in this book–a revised version of my doctoral dissertation (Rowlett 1996c)–has been presented to various audiences and/or has already appeared in print. Aspects of the analysis of *pas* detailed in chapter 2 have been presented to audiences in the United Kingdom in Cambridge, Edinburgh, Manchester, and York, as well as in Barcelona (Spain), Ferrara (Italy), and Girona (Spain) (Rowlett 1992a, b, 1993a–d). Jespersen's Generalization, discussed in chapter 3, has been presented to British audiences in Durham,

Manchester, Newcastle-upon-Tyne, Salford, and York, as well as in Geneva (Switzerland) and Ottawa (Canada) (Rowlett 1994c, 1995a, b, 1997). The material in chapter 4 on negative adverbs formed the basis of talks in Cambridge and York (Rowlett 1994a, b). Parts of the discussion of the negative arguments *rien* and *personne* in chapter 5 have been presented in Cambridge (Rowlett 1996a, b, e). My approach to non-overt operators has been presented in Utrecht (the Netherlands) (Rowlett 1996f, 1998b). Finally, an overview of a number of aspects of my analysis of sentential negation in French has been presented in Oxford (Rowlett 1996b) and Toulouse (France) (Rowlett 1998a). I am of course grateful to the members of all these audiences for their helpful comments and suggestions, as well as for the comments of anonymous reviewers of my published work. Thanks therefore go to Jacques Durand, Chris Lyons, and Leo Hickey for acting as editors of the University of Salford series of *Working Papers in Language and Linguistics*, to which articles containing some of this material have been submitted. Finally, the anonymous reviewers of the *Journal of French Language Studies*, the *Catalan Working Papers in Linguistics*, the *Journal of Linguistics*, *Linguistic Inquiry*, and *Probus* provided me with very detailed and helpful comments on a number of articles written on the basis of this material. The final version of my dissertation benefited from the comments of the examiners, Liliane Haegeman and Georges Tsoulas. The book manuscript was subjected to the careful eyes of two anonymous reviewers. Robert Brown and Odile Cyrille read through the final draft.

Writing this book—and the dissertation on which it is based—has been made possible by a number of people and bodies, all of whom deserve my thanks. John Green was my first linguistics teacher back in 1984 and gently encouraged me to consider linguistics at the postgraduate level. Later on, John was one of the first to consider offering me a job. Thanks for the confidence. Upon my arrival in York in 1989 as an M. A. student, Adrian Battye gave me initial guidance and support. He supervised my early work on French, as well as my dissertation. In autumn 1991, he began to supervise my doctorate. Adrian became a good friend and one I greatly miss. He died in March 1993. In September 1993, Bernadette Plunkett took over as my supervisor. Over the following two and a half years, she provided me with everything I could have needed as a research student. She offered the flexibility I required, given that I was living in Manchester—a ninety-minute train journey away—and given that I had to fit appointments in York around a full teaching and administration load at Salford. She provided discipline at times when I would rather have been doing other things and was an extremely valuable intellectual opponent to some of the conclusions I had drawn. I doubt I ever changed her mind, but it did me good having to try. My dissertation and this book are undoubtedly much the better for her critical eye.

I owe a lot to other linguists working specifically on negation. Paolo Acquaviva, Anastasia Giannakidou, Liliane Haegeman, Paul Hirschbühler, Marie Labelle, France Martineau, Claude Muller, Jamal Ouhalla, Hugues Péters, Ljiljana Progovac, Josep Quer, and Raffaella Zanuttini were particularly helpful in that they either provided comments on early versions of my ideas or discussed them in their own work. Others, such as David Adger, Bill Ashby, Adriana Belletti, Bob Borsley, Odile Cyrille, Viviane Déprez, Jacques Durand, John Green, Marie-Anne Hintze, Aafke Hulk, Ans van Kemenade, Bill Ladusaw, Richard Larson, Chris Lyons, Jean-Pierre Mailhac, John Payne, Liz Pearce, Carme Picallo, Jean-Yves Pollock, Ellen Prince, Ian Roberts, John-Charles Smith, Tim Stowell, and Nigel Vincent, were willing to discuss my work with me. For the information they provided about individual languages, thanks to Myriam Carr, Joe Cunningham, Odile Cyrille, Jacques Durand, Liliane Haegeman, Susan Hill, Sylvain Larose, Janet Lloyd, Jean-Pierre Mailhac, Jamal Ouhalla, Jean-Marc Pennetier, Ljiljana Progovac, Joëlle Riley, Ian Roberts, Philip Tomlinson, and Juliet Wigmore.

So much for individuals. As for the organizations whose help I have benefited from along the way, I should first of all acknowledge the British Academy, whose Post-graduate Studentship allowed me to go to York as a full-time M. A. student in the first place. Without them, I'd probably still be a (very unhappy) translator in Paris. They also offered me a further three years' Ph.D. funding (which I turned down) and provided part of the financial support–in the shape of an Overseas Conference Grant–that allowed me to accept an invitation to participate in the Negation: Syntax and Semantics conference in Ottawa (Canada) in 1995. I would like to extend my particular thanks to the Department of Modern Languages and the European Studies Research Institute, both at the University of Salford, for providing both the environment and the financial support that were essential in allowing me to carry out this work. The Department of Modern Languages funded my Ph.D. for four years, while the European Studies Research Institute financed most of my research travel. Both showed confidence in me early on, and I'm extremely grateful. The Department of Language and Linguistic Science at York–in particular Connie Cullen, Steve Harlow, and Anthony Warner–deserves my thanks for introducing me to the delights of theoretical syntax and for giving me the opportunity to prove myself as a teacher following Adrian Battye's death. Friends both within and without the UFR des Études du Monde Anglophone and the Équipe de Recherche en Syntaxe et Sémantique at the Université de Toulouse-Le Mirail made my 1998 stay in the South of France and completion of this book a most enjoyable experience.

On a personal note, thanks to Bev, Dr. Rob, Iain, Mad Maria, Marc, and Marietta for providing quality of life. Thanks finally to my mother and sister, whose love and respect were unconditional.

Toulouse, France   P. R.
June 1998

Contents

Abbreviations and Symbols

1, 2, 3	first, second, third person
A/A′	argument/nonargument
ACC	accusative (case)
Acc(P)	Accusative (Voice) (Phrase) (Sportiche 1992)
Adv(P)	Adverb (Phrase)
AGR	agreement
AgrO(P)	Object Agreement (Phrase)
Agr(P)	Agreement (Phrase)
AgrS(P)	Subject Agreement (Phrase)
Asp(P)	Aspect (Phrase)
Aux	auxiliary
BT	Binding Theory
C17Fr	Seventeenth-century French
CL	clitic
C(P)	Complementizer (Phrase)
DA	Dynamic Agreement (Rizzi 1996)
Dat(P)	Dative (Voice) (Phrase) (Sportiche 1992)
DN	(logical) Double Negation
D(P)	Determiner (Phrase)
ec	empty category
ECM	Exceptional Case Marking
ECP	Empty Category Principle
EMPH	emphatic
fn	footnote
F(P)	Functional (Phrase)
FUT	future
H&L	Hirschbühler and Labelle
HMC	Head Movement Constraint (Travis 1984)
H&Z	Haegeman and Zanuttini
IMP	imperfect/imperative
IND	indicative
INF	infinitive
Infl/INFL	inflection
Infn(P)	Infinitive (Phrase)

I(P)	Inflection (Phrase)
LF	Logical Form
LI	lexical infinitive
L-marking	lexical marking (Chomsky 1986b)
L-*tous*	leftward *tous* movement (Kayne 1975)
MI	modal infinitive
Mood(P)	Mood (Phrase)
M&V	Moritz and Valois
NC	negative concord
NEG	negative
Neg(P)	Negative (Phrase)
Nom(P)	Nominative (Voice) (Phrase) (Sportiche 1992)
N(P)	Noun (Phrase)
NPI	negative polarity item
NSE	Nonstandard English
Num(P)	Number (Phrase)
n-word	negative word (Laka 1990)
Op	non-overt operator
Op_{cont}	non-overt contentive operator (Haegeman 1995)
Op_{exp}	non-overt expletive operator (Haegeman 1995)
PL	plural
Pol(P)	Polarity (Phrase)
POS	positive
Pos(P)	Positive (Phrase)
pp.	pages
P(P)	Preposition (Phrase)
pro	non-overt pronominal
PRO	non-overt pronominal anaphor
PROG	progressive
PROS	prospective
PST	past
QàD	quantification at a distance (Obenauer 1983, 1984)
Q(P)	Quantifier (Phrase)
QR	Quantifier Raising
REFL	reflexive
SC	Serbian/Croatian
SE	Standard English
SG	singular
SOV	subject-object-verb
Spec	specifier
SUBJ	subjunctive
t	trace
T(P)	Tense (Phrase)
UG	Universal Grammar
V2	verb second

Vinf	infinitival verb
V(P)	Verb (Phrase)
V&W	Verrips and Weissenborn
WF	West Flemish
wh/WH	interrogative
x	variable over entities
X^{max}	XP
XP, YP, ZP	any maximal projection
φ	person, number, gender, etc.
θ	thematic
Δ	non-overt negative operator (Rowlett 1994a, b) (=Op[+NEG])
Σ(P)	Sigma (Phrase) (Laka 1990)
¬	logical operator of negation
∅	empty category
⋆	ungrammatical string
[*]	grammatical with a logical DN reading only
?/??	strings of increasingly questionable grammaticality
%	rejected by prescriptivists but acceptable to many speakers
∃	existential operator
∀	universal operator

Sentential Negation in French

1

Foundations

This is a study of the syntax of (sentential) negation, with particular reference to Modern French, and of the insight into Universal Grammar (henceforth, UG) it offers. The purpose of this first chapter is to set out my basic assumptions, which will be essential to the development of the study. Section 1.1 starts with my assumptions about the extent of Verb Movement, introducing the Split-Infl hypothesis. Section 1.2 turns to fundamental issues concerning the syntactic representation of sentential negation. In particular, I introduce and motivate NegP, a functional projection housing clausal polarity features. Section 1.3 introduces the notion of affective element; my conclusions are drawn together in section 1.4.

1.1   Verbal inflection and Verb Movement

1.1.1   Verb Movement versus Affix-Hopping

Since Emonds (1978: 163–8), it has generally been assumed that the mechanism linking French finite verb forms with inflectional morphology is (obligatorily) Verb Movement (see Koopman 1984). Within models of syntactic theory assumed in much work since the 1980s (Government and Binding, Principles-and-Parameters), this has meant that verbal roots are deemed to move out of their containing VP and incorporate into one or more successive c-commanding functional heads encoding verbal morphology. In English, in contrast, Affix-Hopping is deemed to lower the inflection onto the root of main verbs, which, consequently, do not need to raise out of VP. Only finite auxiliaries and modals are outside VP at S-structure in English, *à la française*.

The distinction between Verb Movement and Affix-Hopping is recast by Chomsky (1993) within Checking Theory as a distinction between pre-spell-out and post-spell-out checking. Within Checking Theory, morphologically complex words enter the derivation fully inflected, while functional heads are generated as bundles of formal features. Morphologically complex words are then "checked" by being matched with the features following cyclic head-to-head adjunction to the relevant c-commanding inflectional heads. The parametric difference between the "French" system and the "English" system centers around whether head-movement-cum-checking takes place before or after spell-out, that is, the input to the phonological component. This corresponds to the distinction between movement in the syntax as opposed to movement at LF in more traditional models. In French, movement/checking is pre-spell-out/overt; in English, movement/checking is post-spell-out/covert.

The difference between English and French is attributed by Pollock (1989) to the nature of agreement in the two languages. In French, it is strong, or transparent, and may be said to "attract" the verb; in English, in contrast, it is weak, or opaque. This parametric difference in the morphology of the two languages is claimed to be able to account for the following contrast:

(1) a.   Jean embrasse$_i$ souvent t_i Marie.   (French)
     b.   ★Jean   souvent embrasse Marie
          J.   (kisses)   often   (kisses) M.
          'J. often kisses M.'

(2) a.   ★John kisses$_i$ often t_i Mary.   (English)
     b.   John e$_i$ often kisses$_i$ Mary

(3)

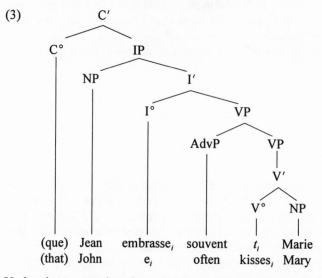

Under the assumption that adverbs of the same type—for example, *often* and *souvent* 'often'—are generated in the same position cross-linguistically,[1] Pollock (1989) argues that contrasts such as the one illustrated in (1) and (2) (his (4), p.

---

1. This assumption, shared by Belletti (1994a: 38fn13), is supported by Sportiche's (1988: 429) Adjunct Projection Principle that governs modification relations and Chomsky's (1986b: 16) general theory of adjunction. Taken together, these theories oblige "modifiers" such as adverbs to appear adjacent to their nonargument XP "modifiee" (or the head of their "modifiee"). Note that this assumption is challenged by Williams (1994a: 189), who rejects "the idea that there are universal 'slots' in which adverbs of various kinds can appear, one slot for each type of adverb"; neither does he think "that adverbs are distributed in the same way in different languages". In (3), I assume that *souvent/often* are VP-adjoined. I modify this assumption in sections 1.1.6 and 1.1.7.3.

367) strongly suggest that finite verbs in French move out of VP to the left of adverbs to an inflectional head such as I° to be associated with finiteness and φ-features, while finite verbs in English do not.

1.1.2 The Split-Infl hypothesis

Subsequent to Chomsky (1986b), Pollock (1989) has argued that the IP model fails to account for Verb Movement patterns in French. In short, a model of clause structure with a *single* inflectional head, such as I°, does not provide enough positions to allow an elegant account of word order. To resolve the problem, Pollock argues that the φ-feature and finiteness specification of I° should be associated with separate and independent heads which he labels T(ense) and Agr(eement), both of which project full phrasal categories within the X'-model.[2] Pollock motivates this "Split-Infl" model of clausal architecture on the basis of structures in French in which verbs undergo what he calls "short" Verb Movement as opposed to "long" Verb Movement. A model of clause structure in which there is just one inflectional head into which a verb either does or does not move is clearly not going to be able to account for such a fine-tuned distinction. In contrast, if IP is split into TP and AgrSP, with TP above AgrSP, the distinction between short and long movement can be represented as the distinction between movement from V° to AgrS° and movement from V° through AgrS° to T°.

Pollock's data involves the interplay of negative *pas*, adverbs such as *souvent*, and finite and nonfinite verbs. The data in (1) show that a finite verb in French moves to an inflectional head between the adverb and the subject. The data in (4) show that the distribution of negative *pas* resembles that of *souvent*. As a working hypothesis, one could assume that *souvent* and *pas* are both VP-adjoined.[3]

---

2. The separate treatment of tense and agreement, that is, in terms of distinct functional heads, is supported by the fact that some languages, such as the Mainland Scandinavian languages Danish, Norwegian, and Swedish, distinguish between finite and nonfinite but do not demonstrate subject-verb agreement (Platzack and Holmberg 1989). In a number of other languages, such as Arabic (Plunkett 1993), finite verbs appear with or without (subject) agreement morphology, depending on whether the subject is overt or not. In both cases, the verb is marked finite. This clearly suggests that agreement and tense are independent of each other. Pollock's Split-Infl hypothesis is one possible way of articulating that independence. Chomsky (1991) suggests that the Split-Infl hypothesis follows from an X'-theoretic condition on single-headedness proposed by Emonds (1976: 5). Anticipating later discussion, I relabel Pollock's AgrP *AgrSP*, that is, *subject* agreement phrase, to distinguish it from AgrOP, the *object* agreement phrase. For recent discussion of Agreement projections, see Chomsky (1995b).

3. This is only a provisional characterization of *pas* and adverbs like *souvent*. See section 1.2.1 and chapter 2 in particular for a detailed analysis of the syntactic properties of *pas*. For *souvent*, see section 1.1.6.

In most spoken varieties of Modern French, the pre-verbal negative marker *ne* is optional. See section 1.2.4 for discussion. This optionality is not explicitly indicated in the examples here. For discussion of "*ne*-drop", see Ashby (1976, 1981, 1991), Coveney (1989, 1990, 1996), Escure (1974), Pohl (1968, 1975), and Sankoff and Vincent (1977).

(4) a. Jean n' embrasse$_i$ pas t_i Marie.
     b. ⋆Jean ne   pas embrasse Marie.
         J. *ne* (kisses) *pas* (kisses) M.
         'J. doesn't kiss M.'

(5) a. Jean n' embrasse pas souvent Marie.
     b. ⋆Jean n' embrasse souvent pas Marie.
         J. *ne* kisses   *pas/souvent* M.
         'J. doesn't often kiss M.'

The data reviewed so far are perfectly compatible with the IP model of clause structure: in both (1) and (4), the finite verb can be argued to have raised out of VP into the IP domain, to the left of the adverb and negative *pas*. Note, though, that the examples in (5) show that the order of the adverb and the negation is fixed–the negation must precede the adverb. This would need to be stipulated if both elements were deemed to have the same status as VP-adverbs. (See footnote 4.)

However, the paradigms in (6) and (7), containing strings with infinitival auxiliaries rather than finite forms, are not compatible with this model of clause structure:

(6) a. J-P avoue n' être pas   souvent   à l' heure.
     b. J-P avoue ne   pas être souvent   à l' heure.
     c. J-P avoue ne   pas   souvent être à l' heure.
         J-P admits *ne* (be) *pas* (be) *souvent* (be) at the hour
         'J-P admits he isn't often on time.'

(7) a. Lucille prétend n' avoir pas   souvent   le temps.
     b. Lucille prétend ne   pas avoir souvent   le temps.
     c. Lucille prétend ne   pas   souvent avoir le temps.
         L.   claims *ne* (have) *pas* (have) *souvent* (have) the time
         'L. claims she doesn't often have the time.'

To account for (6a) and (7a), in which the adverb and negation are *post*-verbal, one could assume, as with the verbs in (1) and (4), that the infinitival auxiliaries move from V° over *souvent* and *pas* to a nonfinite I°. To account for (6c) and (7c), in which the adverb and negation are *pre*-verbal, one could assume, with Pollock (1989), that infinitivals (in contrast to finite forms) do not need to move out of VP and that, in these cases, the verb appears in situ in V°. In both cases, the IP model of clause structure can deal with the data. In contrast, (6b) and (7b) are a problem. Here, the verb appears *between* the negation and the adverb. Given that both these elements appear between I° and V°, the problem is that, within the IP model, there is no head position between the negation and the adverb for the verb to occupy:

(8) [$_{IP}$ [$_{I'}$ I° [$_{VP}$ pas ??? [$_{VP}$ souvent [$_{VP}$ *t*]]]]]

To account for these examples, Pollock (1989) uses his more articulated model of clause structure and suggests that the verbs in (6b) and (7b) have undergone short movement to AgrS°. In (6a) and (7a), in contrast, he claims that the verbs have undergone long movement through AgrS° to T°. In (6c) and (7c), the verbs are assumed to remain in situ in V°. Given the structure in (9), an infinitival auxiliary can occupy any one of the positions marked AUX, that is, V°, AgrS°, or T°:

(9) *Possible S-structure positions for infinitival auxiliaries in French (version 1)*:
$[_{TP} [_{T^\circ} \text{AUX}] [\text{pas} [_{AgrSP} [_{AgrS^\circ} \text{AUX}] [\text{souvent} [_{VP} [_{V^\circ} \text{AUX}]]]]]]$[4]

I therefore conclude that clause structure (in French, if not universally) is more intricate than the IP model would suggest; CP-IP-VP is to be translated into CP-TP-AgrSP-VP. Assuming the VP-internal subject hypothesis, such as that of Kitagawa (1986), a subject moves from its base position to SpecTP at S-structure, where it can be assigned nominative Case. In finite clauses in French (in contrast to English), the verb moves from its base position by a process of head-to-head movement through AgrS° to T°, whose [+FINITE] property allows nominative Case assignment to the subject in SpecTP.[5]

1.1.3 Support for the Split-Infl hypothesis from acquisition studies

The claim that there are two separate and independent syntactic heads associated with verbal inflection is supported not only by the word order patterns discussed in the previous section and the evidence referred to in footnote 1 but also by results from acquisition studies. Work reported in Verrips and Weissenborn (1992) (henceforth, V&W), on which the discussion in this section is based, suggests that L1 acquirers of French go through a stage during which morphologically finite verbs undergo short movement (rather than the long movement that finite verbs undergo in adult French grammars) and, consequently, appear to the right of the negation in the sequence: *pas + finite verb*.[6] Further, even

---

4. In the unified Infl model, negative *pas* and adverbs like *souvent* are both assumed to be adjoined to VP. Under such an analysis, we would expect the order of these items to be free. Yet, it is not, as shown in (5). The negative *pas* must precede the adverb *souvent*. In the structure in (9), in contrast, the negative *pas* and the adverb occupy distinct positions. The former occupies a position between T° and AgrS°, possibly adjoined to AgrSP (see also footnote 6); the latter occupies a position between AgrS° and V°. The Split-Infl model has the advantage then of predicting that the respective ordering of *pas* and *souvent* is fixed.

5. For further discussion of the issue of nominative Case assignment, see section 1.1.4. For further discussion of the VP-internal subject hypothesis, see Burton and Grimshaw (1992) and McNally (1992).

6. The fact that the verbs are clearly finite in their morphology suggests that they do not appear in situ in V°, but have raised at least as far as the lower functional head. For reasons why I reject a post-spell-out Checking Theory account of these data, see section 1.1.5. As in the previous section, I assume

after children appear to have acquired long Verb Movement of finite forms, they nevertheless persist in making errors (albeit rarely) that could be argued to be the result of failing to raise the verb as far as the adult grammar would require. Examples are given in (10) and (11):

(10) *Fabienne*:

    a.   pas joue le chat (2-0-13)   b.   pas compte (2-0-23)
         pas play the cat   *pas* count

(11) *Benjamin*:

    a.   pas chante moi (2-2-18)   c.   pas saute (2-3-1)
         pas sing   me   *pas* jump

    b.   pas met (2-2-18; 2-3-8)   d.   non, pas mange (2-3-8)
         pas put   no   *pas* eat

    While the rarity of these errors (two instances from Fabienne, five from Benjamin, none from Philippe during their respective periods of observation; see also the discussion in Déprez and Pierce 1993: 40; Pierce 1992: 65–7; Wexler 1994: 310) could be taken to indicate that these are examples of performance errors, V&W (pp. 308–9) venture that there are a number of aspects of the data that suggest, rather, that they reflect a principled process.[7]

    The first aspect that V&W mention is the fact that two of the three children studied go through an initial stage in which finite main verbs are *consistently* placed after the negation (rather than in front of it, as in the adult grammar). The interesting hypothesis that this observation might lead one to consider is that initial use of *pas* + *finite verb* may constitute a genuine milestone in the acquisition of Verb Movement in French prior to acquisition of the adult sequence *finite verb* + *pas*.[8] V&W refer to evidence that supports this hypothesis given by Choi (1988) and Boysson-Bardies (1976). Choi reports errors similar to the ones noted by V&W prior to the acquisition of the adult sequence. Furthermore, the transition from *pas* + *finite verb* to the adult *finite verb* + *pas* sequence took place at about the same point in the child considered by Choi as the two in V&W's study. While Boysson-Bardies does not note any errors of the type under discussion here, she does comment that at first only auxiliaries and modals appear with post-verbal negation. This implies that, like V&W's two subjects,

---

for the time being that *pas* is adjoined to AgrSP. I draw a different conclusion about the S-structure position of this element in section 1.2.3 and consider its base position in chapter 2.

    7. They also make the point (p. 327fn28) that, given that performance errors are generally assumed not to be random, these too must be accounted for on principled grounds. It seems to us that this is especially true in the present context, given that, according to Pierce's (1992: 66-7) statistics and discussion, although finite verbs in child French predominantly precede *pas* while nonfinite verbs follow *pas* (in other words the placement of the verb with respect to *pas* is far from arbitrary), finite verbs are nevertheless more likely to follow *pas* than nonfinite verbs are to precede *pas*.

    8. See also Pierce (1992) for important statistical evidence suggesting that "verbal inflection and the verb phrase, containing the subject, are divorced at an initial stage in S-structural representation, just as they are in the underlying syntactic structure" (p. 4).

Boysson-Bardies's subject also went through a stage characterized by an absence of finite lexical verbs appearing to the left of negation.[9]

The second point made by V&W with respect to these errors is that they do not involve the verbs *avoir* 'to have', *être* 'to be', or *aller* 'to go' despite the high frequency with which these particular verbs appear in the corpus. Fabienne used a finite main verb together with negation twice (between the ages of 1-5-11 and 2-0-23) and wrongly ordered the two elements on both occasions. (See (10).) During the same period of observation, she used finite forms of *être*, *avoir*, and *aller* together with negation on fifty-one occasions and got the order right every time. Meanwhile, Benjamin used a finite main verb together with negation five times (between the ages of 1-9-19 and 2-3-8) and wrongly ordered the two elements on all five occasions. (See (11).) During the same period of observation, he used finite forms of *être*, *avoir*, and *aller* together with negation on 140 occasions and got the order right every time. Clearly, then, there is something principled going on here.

The final aspect of V&W's data that, the authors suspect, suggests that the errors are the result of a principled process is the absence of pre-verbal subjects in the sequence *pas + finite verb*, on either side of the negation (cf. (10a)–(11a)).

These considerations taken together lead V&W to suggest that the erroneous *pas + finite verb* orderings might represent an initial stage in the acquisition of Verb Movement in French children, which they term *Partial Verb Raising*. In this respect, it may be the case that language development reflects the steps in the derivations posited in adult structures (V&W, p. 303).[10] In derivational terms, V&W (p. 312) analyze these sequences in terms of short Verb Movement to allow the verb to be marked for finiteness. Since, in Pollock's model in (9), the landing site for short Verb Movement is under the negation, the relative order of the two elements is accounted for. V&W (p. 311) suggest that these finite main verbs do not raise into the higher inflectional head because of a failure on the part of children to recognize that they have (subject) agreement features, a plausible claim when one considers that these main verbs mark agreement by a null inflection and do not appear with an overt pre-verbal subject and if, as believed by many (e.g., Hyams 1986), it is indeed the case that UG favors minimal derivations.[11] In contrast, the verbs *avoir*, *être*, and *aller*, which characteristically do not fail to raise to the left of the negation, morphologically mark person and number agreement by suppletion.

Of crucial importance to this analysis are (a) the morphological independence of finiteness and agreement on the one hand and (b) Pollock's (1989) Split-Infl hypothesis on the other. I therefore take these data to be further evidence in support of the hypothesis. However, what is odd about the details of

---

9. But see Pierce (1992: 65): "Finite verbs often appear in initial position, to the left of the negatives themselves. In short, French children as young as 20 months of age demonstrate knowledge and use of verb raising."

10. See also Lebeaux (1988) and Roeper (1991).

11. See also Chomsky (1986b): "The language learner assumes that there is syntactic movement only where there is overt evidence for it" (p. 50).

Pollock's formulation of the Split-Infl hypothesis is the respective order of the two inflectional heads T° and AgrS°: Pollock suggests TP is above AgrSP. Accordingly, in adult grammars, French finite verbs move from V° to AgrS° to T°. This analysis seems difficult to square with the discussion in the previous paragraph in which it was suggested that verbs move to the lower inflectional head (AgrS°) to be marked for finiteness and to the higher inflectional head (T°) where agreement features are identified. Why should a verb move to AgrS° to be marked for finiteness and to T° for agreement features? Would not the reverse be expected? This issue is discussed in the next section, where additional arguments are presented in favor of reversing the order of TP and AgrSP proposed by Pollock.

1.1.4   Relative order of T° and AgrS°

While accepting that I° needs to be split into component categories, a number of authors, including Belletti (1990), Chomsky (1991), and Ouhalla (1991), have suggested that Pollock's (1989) ordering of TP with respect to AgrSP should be reversed. In addition, in section 1.1.3, we saw that the data from acquisition studies discussed by V&W suggest that T° is closer to the verbal root than AgrS°.

Belletti's (1990) reason for wishing to reverse Pollock's (1989) order is morphological in nature. Observing the internal structure of finite verb forms in Italian, Belletti notes that the suffix corresponding to tense is closer to the verbal root than the suffix corresponding to agreement:

(12) *Italian*:   (from Belletti 1990: 28)

    a. Legg-eva-no.   b. Parl- er- ò.
        read- IMP-3PL   speak-FUT-1SG
        'They read (imperfect).'   'I will speak.'

Although overt verbal morphology is not as rich in French as it is in Italian, it is also the case in French that, where tense and agreement suffixes can be distinguished, tense is closer to the root than agreement:

(13) *French*:

    a. Arriv-ai- ent   b. Parl- ass-   es
        arrive-IMP-3PL   speak-IMP:SUBJ-2SG
        'arrived'   'might speak'

On the basis of Baker's (1985: 375 (4), 1988: 13 (25)) Mirror Principle of morphology given in (14), Belletti (1990) argues that a model of clause structure in which AgrSP is higher than TP more readily accounts for the internal morphological structure of these verb forms.[12]

---

12. But see Speas (1991a, b) for arguments that the Mirror Principle does not necessarily follow from Baker's incorporation theory. Belletti's (1990) argument with respect to Baker's Mirror Principle

(14) *The Mirror Principle*:
Morphological derivations must directly reflect syntactic derivations (and vice versa).

Given that the tense suffix is closer to the root than the agreement suffix, it is argued that S-structure incorporation (see section 1.1.1) of the verbal root into the features encoded under T° takes place before the resulting $[_{T°}\ [_{V°}\ V\ ] + T\ ]$ complex incorporates into the features under AgrS° to form a $[_{AgrS°}\ [_{T°}\ [_{V°}\ V\ ] + T\ ] + AgrS\ ]$ complex. This is most straightforwardly captured if AgrSP is positioned higher in clause structure than TP.

Working under standard incorporation assumptions, Chomsky (1991) also recognizes the morphological argument in favor of reversing Pollock's (1989) ordering of AgrSP and TP. In addition, Chomsky (1991) suggests that having AgrSP as the higher projection has welcome consequences within Case theory. With AgrSP in this position, the subject of a tensed clause in French appears in SpecAgrSP, the position in which it is assigned nominative Case. This result is welcomed by Chomsky since it fits in with his analysis in which structural Case assignment always takes place under spec-head agreement within an Agr projection (cf. objective Case assigned via spec-head agreement with AgrO°).[13]

Given the data from acquisition studies discussed in section 1.1.3, the morphological argument presented by Belletti (1990) and the theory-internal considerations discussed by Chomsky, I shall assume in what follows that AgrSP is in fact higher than TP. Consequently, (9) is modified as in (15):

(15) *Possible S-structure positions for infinitival auxiliaries in French (version 2)*:
$[_{AgrSP}\ [_{AgrS°}\ \text{AUX}\ ]\ [\ \text{pas}\ [_{TP}\ [_{T°}\ \text{AUX}\ ]\ [\ \text{souvent}\ [_{VP}\ [_{V°}\ \text{AUX}\ ]]]]]]$

1.1.5   An objection

To complicate matters further, if Checking Theory is to be adopted (see section 1.1.1), it could be argued that Pollock's (1989) original order of the inflectional projections TP and AgrSP *might* be required after all. Given that, within Checking Theory, Verb Movement checks the morphological features of fully inflected words, one might expect the word to pass through successive heads corresponding to the morphemes successively *furthest* away from the lexical root, rather than those successively *closest* to the root. So, in the case of the Romance verb forms discussed in the text, Pollock (1997b) argues that the verb moves *first* to AgrS° to check the outermost agreement feature(s) and *then* to T° to check the tense feature. While dealing with Belletti's morphological argument, this logic would, of course, singularly fail to deal with the acquisition evidence

is accepted by Pollock (1997b). However, Pollock maintains that Belletti's proposed ordering of TP with respect to AgrSP fails to link the [±OPAQUE] finite inflection parameter to any overt, that is, learnable, morphological property of the lower head, namely T° in Belletti's (1990) model.

13. But see Chomsky (1995b) for an alternative view of abstract Case.

discussed in section 1.1.3 and would deprive the framework of a uniform AgrP-based Case theory.

One way of solving the problem is to consider the extent to which Checking Theory as proposed by Chomsky (1993) needs to be adopted universally. The crucial issue, I suggest, is whether Checking Theory is adopted for languages with (relatively) rich verbal inflectional morphology like French and Italian. While Checking Theory seems attractive for languages such as English (with impoverished verbal morphology and no [lexical] Verb Movement), since it avoids the need to take recourse to a lowering operation like Affix-Hopping, it is not clear what is to be gained by generalizing the Checking Theory account of Verb Movement to languages like French and Italian. Instead of assuming (a) that *all* morphologically complex lexical items in *all* languages enter derivations fully inflected and (b) that parametric variation determines whether morphological features are checked pre- or post-spell-out, one could envisage the parametric variation being expressed in terms of whether or not lexical items enter derivations fully inflected. If this line of thinking were pursued, one could conclude that, in languages with (relatively) impoverished inflectional morphology, like English, lexical items enter derivations fully inflected and therefore do not need to check their features until after spell-out, that is, covertly at LF. Given principles of economy such as Procrastinate (Chomsky 1995b), movement will then *necessarily* be postponed until LF. In contrast, in languages like French and Italian, with (relatively) rich inflectional morphology, lexical roots could be argued to enter derivations uninflected, in which case movement would need to take place pre-spell-out, that is, overtly at S-structure, not to check morphological features but rather to ensure the lexical root is associated with its morphology in the conventional sense and to ensure that no stranded affixes remain. Consequently, overt Verb Movement in the traditional sense would be necessary in languages like French and Italian, and the relative order of AgrSP and TP proposed by Belletti (1990) and others would be required. This is the approach to the morphosyntax of French verbs I shall adopt in what follows.[14]

1.1.6   A third inflectional head?

In addition to the categories AgrS(P) and T(P), there is reason to believe that a third functional category (whose head encodes verbal inflectional morphology) is projected in French clausal architecture. Evidence in support of this claim has been presented in a number of articles by Kayne (e.g., 1990, 1991).[15] Consider the verb forms in (16):

14. See also Pierce's (1992: 13) distinction between languages such as Italian with morphologically rich verbal inflection, which, she suggests, is part of the core grammar, and languages such as English with morphologically impoverished verbal inflection that is peripheral to the grammar.

15. See also Pollock (1997b) and Pearce (1993).

(16) a. Frapp-er- ai- ent   b. Fin- ir- ai- s
         hit-   FUT-IMP-3PL   finish-FUT-IMP-1/2SG
         'would hit'   'would finish'

In each of these examples from the conditional paradigm, the verbal root is followed by a series of three inflectional affixes. The second and third suffixes run
parallel to those in (13), which I identified as realizations of T° and AgrS°, respectively. Between these two suffixes and the root is a further suffix, *-er* in
(16a), *-ir* in (16b), usually referred to as the infinitival ending:

(17) a. arriv- er   b. fin- ir
         arrive-INF   finish-INF
         'to arrive'   'to finish'

I assume that this additional affixal morpheme is generated as a syntactic head,
which I call Mood°, following Pollock (1997b).[16] Pollock describes the infinitival ending, which also appears in futures and conditionals, as "a [−REALIS]
mood marker".[17]
    The issue that then has to be addressed centers around how an infinitival
verb becomes associated with its morphology. Given the distinction between
French and English drawn in section 1.1.1, we envisage two possibilities: post-
spell-out movement (Affix-Hopping) or pre-spell-out movement (Verb Movement). Either the verb enters the derivation with its infinitival morphology (and
then does or does not raise into Mood° to check its features) or, alternatively, it
enters the derivation as a bare verbal root and necessarily raises at least as far as
Mood° in order to pick up its [−REALIS] mood marker. Given Emonds's (1978)
original characterization of Verb Movement patterns in French, the second option seems more likely. Since movement to T° and AgrS° to pick up tense and
agreement affixes is assumed to be overt in French, that is, pre-spell-out, it
would be odd to conclude that, in contrast, movement to Mood° can be postponed until LF, or post-spell-out.
    Furthermore, Haegeman (1994b) has presented syntactic evidence that sug-
gests that overt pre-spell-out movement is the correct analysis. Haegeman observes that an infinitival verb can appear with a clitic even when it appears to
the right of an adverb like *souvent*, supposedly VP-adjoined:

(18) Marie ne voulait pas souvent la   voir,   sa mère.
     M.   *ne* wanted *pas* often   her-CL see-INF her mother
     'M. didn't want to see her mother often.'

---

16. Kayne (1990, 1991) and Guasti (1991) use the terms Infn°/InfnP (Infinitive Phrase). In section
2.1.1, in the discussion of imperatives in French, I argue that Mood° is also the locus of (true) imperative morphology.
    17. I reject an analysis of the French infinitival ending along the lines of the one proposed by Rottet
(1992: 281–83) for the final [-e] segment that appears on verb forms in the French-based Louisiana
Creole for which no evidence of Verb Movement exists. Following a suggestion from Johan Rooryck,
Rottet analyses [-e] as a verb marker along similar lines to Harris's (1991) analysis of [-o] and [-a] as
noun markers in Spanish.

Given that the infinitive in (18) follows the adverb, we would, on the basis of (15), assume that it appears in situ in V°. How, then, does one account for the fact that an object clitic appears between the adverb and the infinitive? Without going into detailed discussion, current thinking suggests that clitics are realizations of functional heads.[18] One possible candidate host functional head for *la* in (18) is AgrO°, proposed in Chomsky (1991). Now, how can the clitic, as the realization of object agreement features, appear on the verb in (18) if the verb is in V° and if the clitic is to the right of an apparently VP-adjoined adverb? Is it necessary to posit some lowering transformation such as Affix-Hopping to lower the clitic over the adverb onto the verb? Such a solution is undesirable for a number of reasons. Not only would it have all the unattractive features of any lowering movement; it would also be out of place in a language like French in which nothing like lowering transformations seems to be necessary elsewhere in verb syntax. I therefore reject such an analysis and conclude, rather, that, even where infinitives appear to the right of adverbs like *souvent*, Verb Movement–albeit very short–to Mood° has taken place.

Assuming, with Pollock (1997b), that MoodP is present in clause structure even when Mood° is not overtly realized, the canonical clause structure I will therefore be assuming is (19):

(19) *Canonical French clause structure:*[19]

$[_{CP}$ C° $[_{AgrSP}$ AgrS° [pas $[_{TP}$ T° [souvent $[_{MoodP}$ Mood° $[_{VP}$ V°]]]]]]]

Note that this assumption entails analyzing some VP-adverbs such as *souvent* as MoodP-adverbs. I do not claim that VP-adverbs do not exist as such; rather, I am suggesting that not all adverbs traditionally labeled VP-adverbs are in fact adjoined to VP. Indeed, the contrast in (20) can be captured if it is assumed that the interpretation of an adverb such as *bien* 'well/indeed' is determined by its position:

(20) a. Le fait d' avoir bien parlé   ne suffit   pas.
         the fact of have *bien* spoken *ne* suffices *pas*
         'The fact that you spoke well isn't enough.'

     b. Le fait de bien avoir parlé   ne suffit   pas.
         the fact of *bien* have spoken *ne* suffices *pas*
         'The fact that you did indeed speak isn't enough.'

Here, the position of the adverb with respect to the infinitive determines its (most natural) interpretation. In (20a), the adverb *bien* is post-infinitival and is most naturally interpreted as 'well'; in (20b), it is pre-infinitival and means 'indeed'. Assuming that the position of the infinitive is constant in both examples, that is, no lower than Mood°, the adverb in (20a) is deemed to be VP-adjoined

18. See Sportiche (1992) for one possible implementation of this idea.
19. For the purposes of exposition, I abstract away from the issue of whether Chomsky's (1991) AgrOP is projected. It may be that Chomsky's AgrOP and our MoodP are in fact one and the same thing. I do not address this issue here.

while the adverb in (20b) is MoodP-adjoined (if not higher). This analysis is attractive for at least two reasons. First, it attributes adverb interpretation to adverb position (rather than to verb position). Second, it associates strict manner adverbs, as in (20a), with the VP-adjoined position, thus maintaining a traditional insight.[20]

1.1.7 Verb Movement patterns

Having determined a canonical clause structure for French within which Verb Movement can operate, it is useful now to bring together my assumptions about the way in which Verb Movement patterns are determined by such factors as the lexical (full, modal, auxiliary) and morphosyntactic (finite, nonfinite) properties of the verb in question.

1.1.7.1 Finite verbs

On the basis of (1) and (4), I conclude that finite lexical verbs move to the highest functional head encoding verbal inflection, that is, AgrS°. Given the data in (21)–(24) (and, of course, the provisional assumption that *pas* is TP-adjoined), this conclusion can be extended to cover finite auxiliaries and modal verbs, too.

(21) a.   Jean a   souvent   embrassé Marie.
     b.   ⋆Jean   souvent a   embrassé Marie.
         J.   (has) *souvent* (has) kissed   M.
         'J. often kissed M.'

(22) a.   Jean n' a   pas   embrassé Marie.
     b.   ⋆Jean ne   pas a   embrassé Marie.
         J.   *ne* (has) *pas* (has) kissed   M.
         'J. didn't kiss M.'

(23) a.   Jean doit   souvent   embrasser Marie.
     b.   ⋆Jean   souvent doit embrasser Marie.
         J.   (must) *souvent* (must) kiss   M.
         'J. often has to kiss M.'

(24) a.   Jean ne doit   pas   embrasser Marie.
     b.   ⋆Jean ne   pas doit   embrasser Marie.
         J.   *ne* (must) *pas* (must) kiss   M.
         'J. doesn't have to kiss M.'

(25) *Overt finite Verb Movement in French*:
     All finite verbs move to AgrS°.

---

20. My thanks to my colleagues Jean-Pierre Mailhac and Joëlle Riley for confirming the relevance of these data.

A D-structure such as the one in (26) therefore underlies the fully inflected S-structure representation in (27):

(26) *D-structure*:

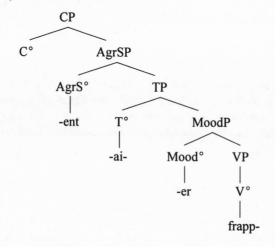

(27) *S-structure*:

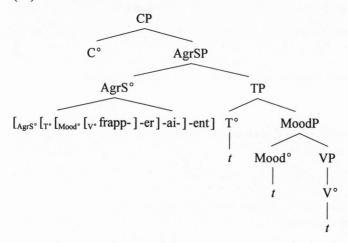

1.1.7.2 Infinitival auxiliaries

With nonfinite verbs, the picture is less clear. The general situation seems to be that infinitival lexical verbs do not move as far as, for example, infinitival auxiliaries or modals. The mobility of infinitival auxiliaries was illustrated in (6), and schematized in (19). These data, together with the assumption—made at the end of section 1.1.6—that even infinitivals have to move out of VP to be associated with their infinitival morphology, lead me to the conclusion that an infinitival auxiliary can occupy any one of the three inflectional heads identified in (19), namely AgrS°, T°, and Mood°.[21]

(28) *Overt movement of French infinitival auxiliaries*:
Infinitival auxiliaries (*être* 'to be', *avoir* 'to have') freely move to Mood° (short movement), T° (medium movement), or AgrS° (long movement).

1.1.7.3 Infinitival lexical verbs

If adverb placement can be taken as an indication of (the extent of) Verb Movement, as we have been assuming here, lexical infinitives seem to be the least mobile.

(29) a.   Souvent partir en vacances est un luxe   réservé à . . .
     b. Partir souvent   en vacances est un luxe   réservé à . . .
         (leave) *souvent* (leave) on holidays is   a   luxury reserved to
         'Often going on holiday is a luxury reserved for . . . '

(30) a. Ne   pas partir en France l' été,   c'est normal si . . .
     b. ⋆Ne partir pas   en France l' été,   c'est normal si . . .
         ne (leave) *pas* (leave) on France the summer it is   normal if
         'Not going to France in summer is normal if . . . '

Still assuming that infinitives minimally move to Mood°, as in (29a), the example in (29b) shows that a lexical infinitive can move from Mood° (over the top of the MoodP-adjoined adverb *souvent*) to T°. However, (30b) shows that it cannot move from T° over *pas* to AgrS°.

(31) *Overt movement of French infinitival lexical verbs*:
Infinitival lexical verbs move to Mood° (short movement) or T° (medium movement), but not as far as AgrS° (long movement).

1.1.7.4 Infinitival modal verbs

I turn finally to the movement of infinitival modals. This class of verb seems to be something of a halfway house between lexical infinitives (which cannot move to AgrS°) and infinitival auxiliaries (which freely move to AgrS°). Under the assumption that adverbs like *souvent* are adjoined to MoodP and that infinitives minimally move to Mood°, the string in (32a) shows that infinitival modals need move no further than Mood°. The string in (32b)—which is potentially synonymous with (32a)—shows nevertheless that infinitival modals *can* move beyond Mood°, that is, to T° and maybe even to AgrS°:

21. Hirschbühler and Labelle (1994b) suggest that the possible orderings of infinitival *être/avoir* and elements such as negative *pas* and VP-/MoodP-adverbs depend on whether the verb is used as an auxiliary or a copula.

(32) a.   Souvent devoir partir à l' étranger, c'est . . .
      b.   Devoir souvent   partir à l' étranger, c'est . . .
          (must) *souvent* (must) leave to the abroad   it is
          'Often having to travel abroad is . . . '

The data in (33) can be used to test whether infinitival modals can indeed reach AgrS°. Here, the modal is negated with *pas*. Recall that I have so far been assuming that *pas* is adjoined to TP. In (33a), the infinitival modal verb appears after the negation; I therefore assume the verb has not been raised into AgrS°. In (33b), the modal verb appears before the negation; I therefore assume the verb occupies AgrS°. The question mark against (33b) indicates that this ordering is only marginally acceptable. While the order in (33a) is the preferred order, the order in (33b) is not regarded as ungrammatical. Pollock (1989: 375, 1997b) judges strings similar to (33b) (Pollock's 1989: 375 (20)) to be "somewhat marginal" and "more exceptional", suggesting that they have "a very literary ring to them".[22]

(33) a.   Ne   pas devoir partir à l' étranger, c'est . . .
      b. ?Ne devoir pas   partir à l' étranger, c'est . . .
          ne (must) *pas* (must) leave to the abroad   it is . . .
          'Not having to travel abroad is . . . '

I conclude therefore that, in the modern language, infinitival modal verbs move minimally from V° to Mood°, optionally from Mood° to T°, but only marginally from T° to AgrS°.

(34) *Overt movement of French infinitival modal verbs*:
     Infinitival modal verbs move to Mood° (short movement) or T° (medium movement), *and only exceptionally to AgrS °* (long movement).

1.1.7.5 Summary

Summarizing, I conclude that Verb Movement patterns in French are as in (35):

(35) *Overt Verb Movement patterns in French*:
      a.   All finite verbs move to AgrS°.
      b'. Infinitival auxiliaries (*être, avoir*) freely move to Mood°, T°, or
          AgrS°.
      b". Infinitival modal verbs (e.g., *pouvoir, devoir*) move to Mood° or T°,
          and only exceptionally to AgrS °.
      b'''. Infinitival lexical verbs move to Mood° or T°, but not as far as AgrS°.

The three classes of infinitive can therefore be distinguished on the basis of their movement patterns to AgrS°. Infinitival auxiliaries move to AgrS° freely,

---

22. Hirschbühler and Labelle (1994b) report that speakers tend to reject orderings in which the modal infinitive is followed by *pas*, as in (33b).

modal infinitives move to AgrS° only exceptionally, while lexical infinitives cannot raise to AgrS° at all. These patterns are crucial in distinguishing between *pas* and the other "negative adverbs" in sections 4.2.2 and 4.4.1.

1.2   The syntax of sentential negation

Here, I set out my assumptions about sentential negation, which will be crucial in future chapters. Section 1.2.1 motivates a further functional projection, NegP, as the locus of clausal polarity features (Pollock 1989). I adopt the common assumption that SpecNegP is a suitable position for *pas* to occupy (rather than the TP-adjoined position we have assumed thus far). Section 1.2.2 discusses two problems for the general assumption that *ne* heads NegP. Section 1.2.3 discusses the position of NegP with respect to the other functional projections in clause structure. Sections 1.2.4 and 1.2.5 concentrate on the semantics and licensing conditions of *ne* in Modern French.

1.2.1   The locus of clausal polarity: NegP

In addition to the inflectional heads already discussed, the presence of a further functional head, encoding polarity features, has been posited.[23] It is assumed that negative markers such as those in italics in (36) are associated with this functional head.

(36) a.   Giovanni *non* è venuto.   (Italian)
          G.   *non* is come
          'G. didn't come.'

     b.   Milan *ne* poznaje Marij-u.   (Serbian/Croatian)
          Mi.   *ne* knows   Ma.- ACC
          'Mi. doesn't know Ma.'

     c.   *Ur* zrigh   Idir.   (Berber)
          ur saw-1SG I.
          'I didn't see I.'

     d.   Jean *ne* mange pas de chocolat.   (French)
          J.   *ne* eats   not of chocolate
          'J. doesn't eat chocolate.'

The claim that these negative markers are heads (rather than phrasal constituents) is supported by the fact that they have cliticized onto the finite verb in AgrS°, with which they form a syntactic unit. In the case of French, for example, *ne* moves with the verb in inversion contexts such as the interrogative:

---

23. See Haegeman (1995: 107), who assumes that negative clauses are clauses "which minimally have a NEG-feature associated with a functional head of the extended projection of V".

(37) Ne mange-t-il pas de chocolat?[24]
     ne eat   he *pas* of chocolate
     'Doesn't he eat chocolate?'

The XP to which this head projects has been variously labeled Neg(ative)P (Pollock 1989), Pol(arity)P (Ouhalla 1990; Belletti 1990; Culicover 1992), and ΣP (Sigma Phrase) (Laka 1990). Here, I use the label NegP. I assume that negative markers such as those italicized in (36) are generated as Neg°.

(38) *D-structure*:

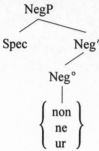

1.2.2   French *ne* as head of NegP?

Although I adopt the general assumption in the literature that French *ne* is generated under Neg°, two empirical facts could be taken to undermine this assumption. The data are problematic for the assumption that *ne* is Neg° because

---

24. In those varieties of French in which Neg° is phonologically null, I assume that it is nevertheless syntactically active and that, like its phonologically overt counterpart, it raises to AgrS°. This is clearly the null hypothesis given that I would not like to introduce any more differences between overt and non-overt Neg° than necessary. Haegeman (1995: 206, 226) assumes that, in Italian, the non-overt Neg° (which occurs with pre-verbal negative phrases) raises to AgrS° in the same way as its overt counterpart, *non*. In addition, Acquaviva (1994) discusses a possible semantic motivation for generalized Neg°-to-AgrS° raising:

(i) [S]uppose that a negative operator (corresponding to the classic Boolean connective ¬) is generated in NegP, and from there it merges with the existential closure, located under the topmost inflectional head. The merger of Boolean negation and existential closure is brought about in the syntax by the raising of the head Neg° to the topmost inflectional head, which I take to be Agr[S]°. . . . Neg° raises from its base position within NegP and is adjoined to the dominating inflectional head, giving rise to a complex operator analyzable as a negated existential.

This approach has the great advantage over previous analyses to provide an interpretive (as opposed to purely morphosyntactic) reason for the crosslinguistic generalization that negative markers tend to be incorporated into the topmost inflectional node, unless they can be analyzed as filling the specifier of NegP. (Acquaviva 1994: 113-14)

See also the discussion of negative imperatives in section 2.1.1 for empirical support for the claim that Neg° raises to AgrS° irrespective of whether Neg° is phonologically null or overt. For discussion of the semantics of *ne*, see section 1.2.4. For references to "*ne*-drop", see footnote 3.

they suggest that *ne* can appear in environments in which it is not immediately obvious that a NegP is available as a host.

First, the data in (39) show a nonstandard construction–*familière* according to Muller (1991: 125) (see footnote 26)–in which *ne* appears to be located, optionally, in the CP domain. The examples are taken from Muller (1991: 125, 149). (The construction is also discussed by Daoust-Blais and Kemp 1979, as well as Acquaviva 1995.)

(39) a. Il faut   que Luc rentre   pour *(ne)* pas que ses parents
        it is-necessary that L.   goes-home for   *ne pas* that his parents
        s'inquiètent.
        worry-SUBJ
        'L. should go home in order to prevent his parents from worrying.'

    b. Habillez-vous   bien, pour *(ne)* pas que vous preniez   froid.
        dress-   yourself well for   *ne pas* that you   take-SUBJ cold
        'Wrap up so you don't catch cold.'

Assuming that the purpose clauses in (39) are PPs headed by *pour* and, for the time being, that *que* heads a CP that is the complement of *pour*, as in (40), it is unclear how to account for the presence of *ne*:

(40)

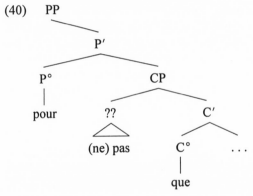

In cross-linguistic terms, this construction is extremely odd. Zanuttini (1996: 201fn7) notes the possibility but suggests that French *ne* is unique within its class of negative markers in appearing in the CP domain (inversion contexts such as (37) notwithstanding). The relevance of the construction is, however, unclear.[25] Rickard (1989: 147) claims that it is "incorrect" (*sic*) but common in "uneducated speech". In a review of Rickard's book, Gallagher (1993: 121) disagrees, claiming that *ne* is *always* omitted. In contrast, Muller (1991: 149) not only recognizes this construction as an exception to the generalization that *ne* is

25. See Rowlett (1994d) for brief discussion. Rizzi (1997) proposes a much more intricately articulated CP structure involving Focus Phrases and Topic Phrases. Such a structure might be able to accommodate the data discussed here.

restricted to verbal contexts but says that it is a *frequent* one no less.[26] It seems to me that the very fact that there is controversy surrounding the phenomenon suggests quite clearly that it exists and that some sort of explanation is required. Further, my own informants unanimously agree that *pour pas que* and *pour ne pas que* both exist in the modern language.

Hirschbühler and Labelle (1992/93: 34–7, section 1.1) envisage two syntactic approaches to the phenomenon. Either (a) the sequence *ne pas* is generated directly in CP or (b) it is generated lower (within the clause) and subsequently raised into CP. However, these authors arrive at no firm conclusions.

One might envisage dealing with this cross-linguistically highly marked and apparently hotly debated and controversial construction by exploiting the idea that it is analogous to the *pour ne pas Vinf* construction. (See Grevisse's 1986: 1489 §981 comment in footnote 26 and the comment in a footnote [p. 149] in Muller 1991. Muller suggests that *ne* might be adjoined at a late stage in the derivation by analogy with the infinitival construction *pour ne pas Vinf.*) One could entertain the possibility that the *pour (ne) pas que* construction (and possibly the *pour que* construction, too) contains a non-overt infinitival causative verb that can be negated by *(ne) pas* just like any other infinitive. While I know of no other proposal along these lines for this particular construction, it has marked similarities to recent proposals within the Minimalist Program of Chomsky (1995b) to posit phonologically null light verbs, labeled v and heading vP, to offer attractive accounts of a number of syntactic phenomena, for example, double-object constructions and causative/inchoative alternations. Within the terms of such a proposal, one might conclude that v appears within its own clausal domain between *pour* and CP in (40). It can then be negated by *ne pas* in the usual way. The negative head *ne* raises to AgrS°; v takes the CP headed by *que* as its complement:

(41) a.   ... pour [ne pas v [$_{CP}$ que ses parents s'inquiètent]]
    b.   ... pour [ne pas v [$_{CP}$ que vous preniez froid]]

Note that, although not particularly idiomatic, the examples in (42), in which the lexical causative verb *faire* is inserted between *pas* and *que*, are essentially synonymous with those in (39) and (41):

<hr/>

26. Prescriptive sources are far from unanimous on this point. The *Le Petit Robert 1* dictionary (1984, Paris: Le Robert, p. 1499) labels the *pour ne pas que* construction "fam" (familiar) and the *pour pas que* construction "pop" (popular). Grevisse (1986: 1489 §981) has the following to say: "La construction *pour ne pas que*, formée par analogie avec *pour ne pas* + infinitif, tend à passer de la langue populaire dans la langue littéraire, mais elle reste suspecte d'incorrection. . . . *Pour pas que* appartient à la langue populaire." (The *pour ne pas que* construction, formed by analogy with *pour ne pas Vinf*, is shifting from popular to literary language but is still suspected of being incorrect [*sic*]. . . . *Pour pas que* is popular.) According to Bénac (1976: 239): "Dans une proposition finale au subjonctif la négation *ne . . . pas* doit encadrer le verbe et non s'intercaler entre les deux éléments de la locution conjonctive: je lui ai écrit *pour* qu'il *ne* vienne *pas* (et non: ⋆pour ne pas qu'il vienne)." (In a purpose clause with subjunctive mood, *ne . . . pas* must straddle the verb and not appear between the two elements of the conjunction: je lui ai écrit *pour* qu'il *ne* vienne *pas* (and not: ⋆pour ne pas qu'il vienne).)

(42) a. ... pour ne pas *faire* (en sorte) que ses parents s'inquiètent.

　　b. ... pour ne pas *faire* (en sorte) que vous preniez froid.

Such an approach seems intuitively more attractive than proposals such as Acquaviva's (1995), for example. Acquaviva suggests that *ne* is a Q° taking the adverb *pas* as its complement. It seems to me that Acquaviva's proposal is untenable since it provides no structural position for the CP, [*que S*], which follows *pas* in this construction.[27]

A second problem for the assumption that *ne* is generated under Neg° comes in the form of data such as the examples in (43) from Muller (1991: 325):

(43) a. Je t' ordonne de *ne plus jamais ne rien* faire.
　　　　I you order of *ne plus jamais ne rien* do
　　　　'I order you never again not to do anything.'
　　　　(= 'I order you always to do something in future.')

　　b. - Il serait criminel de ne pas partir.
　　　　It be-COND criminal of *ne pas* leave
　　　　'It would be a crime not to leave.'

　　　　- Au contraire, il serait criminel de *ne pas ne pas* partir.
　　　　To-the contrary it be-COND criminal of *ne pas ne pas* leave
　　　　'On the contrary, it would be a crime not to not leave.'
　　　　(= 'On the contrary, it would be a crime not to stay.')

Here, within (what might appear to be?) a single infinitival clause, there are multiple instances of *ne*. These data are a problem for the current analysis in which *ne* heads NegP and each clause is assumed to contain maximally one instance of NegP. If these are indeed monoclausal structures, one would expect a single NegP to be projected and a single *ne* at most to be licensed. Yet the constituency of the examples as well as their interpretation suggest two fully fledged fully negative NegPs, one canceling out the other. Maybe, then, one should admit two instances of NegP in these clauses. In that case, there is still the issue of the surface position of *ne* to deal with; in section 1.2.1, it was assumed that *ne* is a clitic that raises to AgrS°. Clearly, this is not a possible analysis for both instances of *ne* in the examples in (43) (assuming a single AgrSP projection per clause). In the second part of (43b), the first *pas*, which, as I show later and in chapter 2, is a phrasal constituent, intervenes between the two instances of *ne*, casting serious doubt on any suggestion that both cases of *ne*

---

27. The approach proposed here for the *pour (ne) pas que* construction means that the contrast, noted by DeGraff (1993a: 74 (11)), illustrated here between French and Haitian Creole, remains a mystery.

(i) Bouki fait le clown pour pas qu' ils s'ennuient.　　　　　　　　　(French)
　　B. does the clown for *pas* that they get-bored
　　'Bouki's messing around so they don't get bored.'
(ii) Bouki ap fè komik pou (*pa) yo anniye.　　　　　　　　　(Haitian Creole)
　　B. PROG does comic for *pa* 3PL get-bored
　　(= (i))

have cliticized onto the same AgrS°. The same applies to the sequence *plus jamais* in (43a), which also intervenes between two instances of *ne*.

How, then, to account for the presence of two instances of *ne* in each case? Note that the second *ne* is crucial for the correct interpretation of (43a), which is reversed if the second *ne* is omitted.

(44) Je t'   ordonne de ne plus jamais rien faire.
    I you order   of *ne plus jamais rien* do
    'I order you never to do anything again.'
    (= the opposite of (43a))

Is one wrong to assume monoclausal structures for the infinitival clauses in (43)? Could each *ne* be generated under Neg° within its own clause and raised to its own AgrS°[28]? Such an analysis has a number of attractions in that it allows one to maintain these central assumptions: (a) that a single NegP is available per clause; (b) that *ne* is generated as Neg°; and (c) that *ne* cliticizes onto AgrS°.[29]

Furthermore, a biclausal approach is consistent with the approach adopted for the *pour ne pas que* construction discussed earlier. One might assume, for example, that the relevant part of (43a) actually has the structure in (45):

(45) . . . de [$_{IP}$ PRO ne plus jamais v [$_{IP}$ PRO ne rien faire]]

The double negation interpretation of example (43a) is then attributed to the presence of negation (and NegP) in two successive clauses, whereby one has scope over the other. The negative concord interpretation of (44) is due to the monoclausal nature of the example: a single clause having a single NegP (see chapters 4 and 5).

The proposal that the two problematic sets of data should be analyzed in terms of a null verb, v, is attractive in that v can, in terms of its selection properties, be aligned with a number of other French verbs. With the unified analysis in terms of v, the two problematic contexts are reduced to two c-selection frames. In (41), v selects a finite subjunctive clausal CP complement introduced by *que*; in (45), in contrast, v selects an infinitival IP complement without an overt complementizer. In this respect, v is analogous to a number of other semi-auxiliary verbs in French, for example, *vouloir* 'to want', as illustrated in (46).

---

28. Hirschbühler and Labelle (1992/93: 40 (18)) suggest an analysis in terms of NegP-recursion within the same clause. This proposal has the weakness of failing to account for the fact that the phenomenon in text examples (43) is restricted to infinitival contexts. If NegP-recursion is to be admitted by UG, a principled reason needs to be found to explain why similar effects are not attested in finite clauses.

29. DeGraff (1993b: 65fn4 (ii), 71fn12) suggests that the Haitian Creole example in (i) can be analyzed in terms of two NegP projections:
(i)   Jan pa -p   pa vini.
      J.   NEG IRREAL NEG come
      'J. wouldn't (won't) come.'

(46) a. Nous voulons que vous restiez.
     we   want   that you stay-SUBJ
     'We want you to stay.'

    b. Nous voulons rester.
     we   want   stay-INF
     'We want to stay.'

The biclausal analysis opens the way, finally, to an explanation for the perhaps unexpected grammaticality of (47):[30]

(47) Je te   conseille de ne plus jamais ne pas être à l' heure.
    I you advise   of *ne plus jamais ne pas* be   to the hour
    'I advise you never again not to be on time.'

My assumption of a biclausal structure for this example accounts for the double negation interpretation. Consider now what happens when the second *ne* is removed. When this operation was performed in (43a), the double negation turned into negative concord, as in (44). In the case of (47), though, the result is ungrammaticality, as in (48):

(48) ★Je te conseille de ne plus jamais pas être à l'heure.

A straightforward account for the ungrammaticality of (48) can be given on the basis of the presence, within a single clause, of *plus/jamais* and *pas*. This is known independently not to be possible in French (see chapters 4 and 5 for an account). The problem, then, becomes (47): why is this example fine? If I had maintained a monoclausal analysis of (47), I would not have had an answer. Yet, if the relevant part of (47) is deemed to be biclausal, as illustrated in (49), the acceptability and interpretation of the example are expected: the co-occurrence of *pas* and *plus/jamais* is acceptable because they are not clausemates; the double negation interpretation is predicted because each nonfinite clause contains a fully negative NegP.

(49) Je te conseille de [$_{IP}$ ne plus jamais *v* [$_{IP}$ ne pas être à l'heure]]

I therefore conclude that the data reviewed in this section do not pose a problem for the assumption that *ne* is uniquely generated as the head of NegP and that clauses contain maximally one NegP.

1.2.3 The position of NegP

I now turn to the location of NegP within clause structure. Ouhalla (1990) suggests that there is no universally applicable ordering (see also Zanuttini 1991 and Pollock 1997b). Rather, hierarchical ordering of NegP in relation to other

---

30. For discussion of this example and the others in this section, I am grateful to my colleague Joëlle Riley.

functional projections is argued by Ouhalla to be subject to parametric variation, determined by what he terms the *Neg Parameter*. With respect to French, for example, in which the negative marker generated under Neg°, *ne*, is a clitic, its surface position does not reflect the underlying position of NegP since the marker cliticizes onto AgrS° (see section 1.2.1). Consequently, it is the position of *pas*, which, following Pollock (1989), I assume occupies SpecNegP (at S-structure), that indicates the location of NegP in clause structure. Given that *pas* immediately follows tensed verbs, I conclude that NegP is the complement of AgrS°. The clause structure given in (19), and repeated here for convenience as (50) is therefore revised as in (51).

(50) *Canonical French clause structure*:

$[_{CP} [_{AgrSP} \text{AgrS}° [\text{pas} [_{TP} \text{T}° [\text{souvent} [_{MoodP} \text{Mood}° [_{VP} \text{V}°]]]]]]]$

(51) *Canonical French clause structure (revised)*:

$[_{CP} [_{AgrSP} \text{AgrS}° [_{NegP} [_{Spec} \text{pas}] \text{Neg}° [_{TP} \text{T}° [\text{souvent} [_{MoodP} \text{Mood}° [_{VP} \text{V}°]]]]]]]$

Within the framework of (51), *ne* is generated under Neg° and subsequently cliticizes onto AgrS°. The semantics and licensing conditions of *ne* in the modern language are discussed in the next two sections. As for the other negative markers in French, *pas* is dealt with in chapter 2. Consideration of the "negative adverbs" (*plus* 'no/any more/longer', *jamais* '(n)ever', and *guère* 'hardly') and the "negative" arguments (*rien* 'anything/nothing' and *personne* 'anyone/no-one') is postponed until chapters 4 and 5, respectively.

1.2.4   French *ne* as inherently negative?

In this section and the next, I turn to the properties of the lexical item that, in some varieties of Modern French, is the realization of Neg°, that is, *ne*. A number of facts relating to *ne* point to the conclusion that this element is not inherently negative in the modern language.[31] First, pre-verbal *ne* is insufficient to mark negation, as in (52), except with a very restricted set of pseudomodal verbs such as *savoir* 'to know', *oser* 'to dare', and *pouvoir* 'to be able', as in (53),[32] frozen archaic expressions or proverbs, as in (54), or, as pointed out by a reviewer, certain restricted embedded contexts such as (55):

31. Of course, this has not always been the case. See sections 3.1.1, 3.1.2, and 3.5.2 and the references in chapter 3, footnote 3, for discussion of the history of negation in French. In a recent study, Acquaviva (1995) addresses the issue of whether Modern French *ne* is or is not inherently negative but does not come to a firm conclusion one way or the other.

32. Note that these verbs can be negated by *ne* alone only if they take an infinitival complement. The examples in (i)–(iii), in which this condition is not met, are ungrammatical:

(i)   ★Pierre ne sait   la réponse.
       P.   *ne* knows the answer
(ii)   ★On ne le peut.
       one *ne* it can
(iii) ★Je n' osais.
       I *ne* dared

(52) ⋆Je *ne* fais mon travail.
     I *ne* do my work

(53) a. Pierre *ne* savait que faire.
        P.   *ne* knew what do
        'P. didn't know what to do.'

     b. Je *n'* osais venir.
        I *ne* dared come
        'I didn't dare come.'

     c. On *ne* peut vous aider.
        one *ne* can you help
        'We cannot help you.'

(54) a. *Ne* vous en déplaise.
        ne you of-it displease
        'If you will.'

     b. Il *n'* est pire eau que l' eau qui dort.
        it *ne* is worse water than the water which sleeps
        'Still waters run deep.'

     c. *N'* ayez crainte!
        ne have fear
        'Fear not!'

(55) Cela fait dix ans qu' elle *n'* a chanté Carmen.
     It   does ten years that she *ne* has sung Carmen
     'It's ten years since she last sang Carmen.'

Second, as pointed out in footnote 3, *ne* can be omitted from negative utterances in most spoken varieties of French. Indeed, in Québécois, *ne* is almost never overt (Sankoff and Vincent 1977). The pre-verbal element *ne* is therefore not essential to the expression of negation. Alongside (56a), (56b) is also acceptable in the spoken language.

(56) a. Je n' ai   pas faim.
     b. J'   ai   pas faim
        I *(ne)* have *pas* hunger
        'I'm not hungry.'

Third, *ne* has an "expletive" use. Here, *ne* appears in the complement of adversative predicates and comparatives, for example, in which it does not have negative force, as in (57a, b). In (58), note that the object of the fear expressed in the complement clause in (58a) is the opposite of the object of the fear expressed in (58b), even though both contain *ne*. The significant expression of negation is clearly *pas*, absent from (58a) but present in (58b), rather than *ne*, which can freely be omitted in both and seems only to indicate register. Further, as pointed out by a reviewer, expletive *ne* can be used for rhetorical effect in some interrogative contexts, as in (57c).

(57) a.   Je doute qu' il *ne* soit   là.
         I   doubt that he *ne* be-SUBJ there
         'I doubt he's there.'

     b.   Marie est plus grande que *n'* est son frère.
         M.   is more tall   than *ne* is her brother
         'M. is taller than her brother is.'

     c.   Qui *ne* souhaite partir en vacances?
         Who *ne* wishes   leave on holidays
         'Who (on earth) doesn't want to go on holiday?'

(58) a.   Elle a   peur que tu *ne* sois   là.
         She has fear that you *ne* be-SUBJ there
         'She's worried you might be there.'

     b.   Elle a   peur que tu *ne* sois   *pas* là.
         She has fear that you *ne* be-SUBJ *pas* there
         'She's worried you might *not* be there.'

The contrast between (56a) and (57) could be taken as evidence to suggest that there are in fact two homophonous lexical items *ne* in the modern language: one negative, one nonnegative. I reject this possibility. Instead, I suggest that there is a single *ne* in Modern French and that it is not inherently negative. Where *ne* is overt and is interpreted negatively, as, for example, in (56a), it does so by virtue of its relationship with a negative operator, for example, *pas* in SpecNegP. I assume that Rizzi's (1996: 76) mechanism of Dynamic Agreement (henceforth, DA) is responsible for endowing the negative head–and, hence, the whole clause (Haegeman 1995: 107)–with the [+NEG] feature of the specifier.

DA is used by Rizzi (1996) within the context of *wh*-movement. Rizzi assumes that, where *wh*-expressions are fronted, as in typical *wh*-questions, the *wh*-XP in SpecCP and C° itself agree with respect to the feature [+WH].

(59)

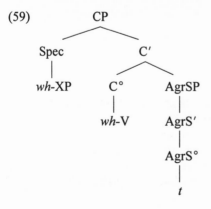

Of course, fronting of a *wh*-XP is often accompanied by movement of the finite verb from AgrS° to C°, as in (59). Indeed, subject-auxiliary inversion can be motivated if it is assumed that (the finite verb in) AgrS° bears the feature [+WH] and moves into C° in order for C° and SpecCP to agree.

AgrS°-to-C° movement cannot be motivated on the basis of the distribution of *wh*-features alone. One might imagine, for example, that the verb bearing *wh*-features could happily remain in AgrS°, while the *wh*-XP occupies SpecCP. To motivate the movement of the verb to the C° position, Rizzi further assumes a wellformedness condition on *wh*-constituents with wide scope, known as the *wh*-criterion (cf. May 1985: 17):

(60) *The* wh-*criterion*:
    a.   Each *wh*-X° must be in a spec-head relationship with a *wh*-operator.
    b.   Each *wh*-operator must be in a spec-head relationship with a *wh*-X°.

(61) a.   When are you coming?
    b.   ★When you are coming?

Indeed, the obligatory nature of subject-auxiliary inversion in matrix *wh*-questions in English, as illustrated in (61), is attributed to (60): the verb, marked [+WH], moves to C° to produce the required configuration. I return to the *wh*-criterion in section 1.3.

In some languages, however, subject-auxiliary inversion is not required in *wh*-questions. One such language is French. In French, subject-auxiliary inversion is possible—but not necessary—in matrix *wh*-questions, as shown in (62), in which the *wh*-XP has fronted (to SpecCP, I assume), but the verb has not inverted to C°.

(62) Où   tu   vas?
    where you go
    'Where are you going?'

(63) [$_{CP}$ Où [$_{C'}$ C° [$_{AgrSP}$ tu vas]]]

Rather than assuming that, in such cases, the *wh*-criterion fails to apply, Rizzi suggests that DA allows the [+WH] feature to be transmitted from the *wh*-expression in SpecCP to the non-overt C°. He schematizes DA as in (64):

(64) *Dynamic Agreement*:   (Rizzi 1996: 76)
    Op X ⇒ Op X
    WH   WH WH

DA is therefore a mechanism for endowing a syntactic head with the relevant feature(s) of its specifier.[33] The availability of DA is deemed to be subject to parametric variation. Thus, it is available in French but not in English; hence the contrast between (62) and (61b).

---

33. Note that DA is unidirectional, passing features from specifier to head but not vice versa. This will be important in section 3.3.2.

I propose that the same mechanism that endows the C° head with the feature [+WH] in (62) is also responsible for endowing the Neg° head with the feature [+NEG] in a negative clause such as (56a):

(65)

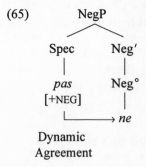

Turning now to the cases in (53), in which *ne* is the sole overt marker of sentential negation, one might wonder where the [+NEG] feature comes from, given that *ne* itself is not inherently negative. To account for these data, I propose the existence of a non-overt operator, Op, which bears the feature [+NEG], occupies SpecNegP in these examples, and, by virtue of DA, can transmit its negative feature to *ne* in Neg°:[34]

(66)

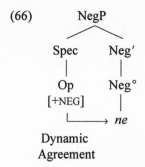

Op in (66) can be regarded as the negative equivalent of the non-overt *wh*-operator (Haegeman 1995: 98–100), OP[+WH], assumed to occupy SpecCP in yes-no questions such as (67) and whose presence triggers subject-auxiliary inversion:[35]

34. Op[+NEG] is what Haegeman (1995) labels Op$_{cont}$, that is, the non-overt contentive negative operator. In Rowlett (1994a, b), I used the label Δ. I assume that Op[+NEG] also provides a key to the interpretation of the French *ne ... que* construction:
(i)   Jean ne voit que Marie.
      J.   *ne* sees *que* M.
      'J. can see only M.'
I assume that Op[+NEG] raises to SpecNegP and is responsible for the (absolute) negation to which [*que* ...] provides the exception. Such an approach avoids the need to assume that *ne* is inherently negative (Acquaviva 1995). Op[+NEG] is central to my analysis of the "negative" adverbs and arguments in chapters 4 and 5. See also Rowlett (1996f; 1998b) for discussion of the *ne ... que* construction.
35. See the discussion of (86) later in this chapter.

(67) a. Have you finished?

   b. [$_{CP}$ OP[+WH] [$_{C'}$ have$_i$[+WH] [$_{AgrSP}$ you t_i finished]]]

The full array of overt and non-overt negative (French) and interrogative (English) operators that such an approach posits is illustrated in the table in (68):

(68) *Operators*:

	overt	non-overt	
[+WH]	whether	OP[+WH]	(English)
[+NEG]	pas	Op[+NEG]	(French)

Evidence to support the claim that SpecNegP is occupied by a non-overt operator in the examples in (53) comes from inner island opacity effects. These effects are illustrated in (69) and are commonly attributed to Relativized Minimality violations (Rizzi 1990). Consider the contrast between (69a) and (69b). In (69a), the fronted *wh*-expression can be associated with either the matrix or the embedded predicate; in (69b), it cannot. In (69b), it can be associated only with the matrix predicate. Assuming that a *wh*-XP such as *pourquoi* 'why' is generated AgrSP-adjoined, the unavailability of the second interpretation in the case of (69b) can be explained in the following way: the operator *pas* in the matrix SpecNegP counts as a potential antecedent A'-governor for the trace of the *wh*-expression extracted from the embedded clause. The second reading is therefore unavailable because of Relativized Minimality.

(69) a. Pourquoi avez-vous dit   que Jean était absent?
         Why   have you said that J.   was absent
         'Why did you say J. was absent?'

   b. Pourquoi n' avez-vous pas dit   que Jean était absent?
       Why   *ne* have you *pas* said that J.   was absent
       'Why didn't you say that J. was absent?'

Now, consider (70a). Once again, this *wh*-question is ambiguous. The fronted *wh*-expression can be associated with either the matrix or the embedded predicate.

(70) a. Pour quelle raison osais- tu   lui   téléphoner?
         For what   reason dared you to-him call
         EITHER: ≈ 'What was it that made you dare phone him?'
         OR: ≈ 'What was the reason for the phone call you dared to make to
             him?'

   b. Pour quelle raison *n'* osais- tu   lui   téléphoner?
       For what   reason *ne* dared you to-him call
       'Why didn't you dare call him?'
       ≠ 'What was the reason for the phone call to him you didn't dare
         make?'

In contrast, the second reading is unavailable in (70b). Given the absence of *pas*, we assume that the Relativized Minimality effects are to be attributed to the presence of a non-overt operator in SpecNegP. In our terms, this non-overt operator is negative Op, the source of the [+NEG] feature transmitted to Neg° by DA.[36]

Inner island effects—or, rather, the lack of them—can also be used as evidence to support the claim that expletive *ne* in (57) and (58a) does not co-occur with a non-overt negative operator, a welcome outcome since, as its name suggests, expletive *ne* is not interpreted negatively. Generally, I have been assuming that, where *ne* in interpreted negatively at all, this can be attributed to its relationship with an operator, *pas* or Op[+NEG], in SpecNegP. In addition, this operator has been argued to be responsible for the inner island effects discussed earlier. What is significant about expletive *ne* is that inner island effects are not in fact attested, as shown by the example in (71). It would, of course, be nice to be able to attribute both the lack of inner island effects and the expletive interpretation of *ne* to one and the same fact, and this is indeed what I would like to do. In (71), the *wh*-expression can be associated with any of the predicates in the clause. Most significant for my purposes, it can be associated with the most deeply embedded verb, despite the presence of *ne* in the immediately superior clause. The fact that extraction of *pourquoi* from the most embedded clause to the matrix SpecCP does not lead to a Relativized Minimality violation suggests that there is no intervening A'-operator in SpecNegP in the middle clause to count as a closer potential antecedent for the trace of *pourquoi* in the embedded clause. The nonnegative expletive interpretation of *ne* and the absence of inner island effects are then reduced to the absence of any (negative) operator in SpecNegP.

(71) Pourquoi crains-tu   qu' elle *ne* dise   qu' elle t'   aime?
      Why   fear   you that she *ne* say-SUBJ that she you loves
      'Why are you afraid she might say she loves you?'

The same point is made by the example in (72), taken from Haegeman (1995: 161 (5b)):

(72) Comment crains-tu   qu' il   ne se   comporte?
      How   fear   you that he *ne* REFL behaves
      'How do you fear he will behave?'

Here, *comment* 'how' is a manner adverb that can be construed with the predicate in the embedded clause; expletive *ne* does not give rise to a blocking effect.

---

36. Of course, and as one of the reviewers of this book pointed out, the next question to be addressed is why it is that, when used in this way (see footnote 32), these verbs allow *ne* to be licensed by a non-overt operator while, in the absence of elements such as *jamais* or *rien*, "normal" verbs require *ne* to be licensed by overt *pas*. It seems to me that this phenomenon must be related to the modal properties of this use of the verbs concerned.

Given the assumptions I am making here, I therefore conclude that no non-overt operator occupies SpecNegP in the embedded clause.

One final piece of evidence I shall use to support my claim that expletive *ne* is not accompanied by a non-overt operator in SpecNegP concerns the licensing of partitive and pseudopartitive indefinite direct objects.[37] I postpone detailed discussion of the licensing of these structures until section 2.2.1, and content myself here with pointing out the empirical contrast. The indefinite direct object in (73a) has what I term a partitive structure; the pseudopartitive direct object in (73b) is ungrammatical:

(73) a. J'ai   acheté *des   livres.*
         I have bought of-the books
         'I bought some books.'

     b. ★J'ai   acheté *de livres.*
         I have bought of books

Pseudopartitive direct objects can be licensed in a number of ways, such as by a quantifier like *beaucoup* 'lots' in (74a), negative *pas* in (74b), or the non-overt negative operator assumed to be present (in SpecNegP) in (74c, d).

(74) a. J'ai   *beaucoup* acheté *de livres.*
         I have lots   bought of books
         'I bought lots of books.'

     b. Je n' ai   *pas* acheté *de livres.*
         I *ne* have *pas* bought of books
         'I didn't buy any books.'

     c. Je ne peux *Op* acheter *de livres.*
         I *ne* can   buy   of books
         'I can't buy any books.'

     d. Cela fait dix ans   qu' elle n' a   *Op* eu *d' amant(s).*
         It   does ten years that she *ne* has   had of lover(s)
         'It's ten years since she last had a lover.'

The generalization (which is explored in more detail in section 2.2.1) seems to be that pseudopartitive direct objects are licensed in the presence of a c-commanding operator. Crucially, though, pseudopartitive direct objects are not licensed by expletive *ne*:

(75) a. ★Je crains qu' il n' ait   acheté *de livres.*
         I fear   that he *ne* have-SUBJ bought of books

     b. Je crains qu' il n' ait   acheté *des   livres.*
         I fear   that he *ne* have-SUBJ bought of-the books
         'I'm worried he might have bought some books.'

---

37. The terms partitive and pseudopartitive come from Selkirk (1977: 302ff).

(76) a. ⋆Qui ne souhaite gagner *de prix*?
         Who *ne* wishes win   of prizes

    b. Qui ne souhaite gagner *des   prix*?
         Who *ne* wishes win   of-the prizes
         'Who (on earth) doesn't want to win prizes?'

I take this as further evidence to suggest that expletive *ne* is not accompanied by a non-overt operator in SpecNegP. Of course, such a conclusion allows a unified account of a number of phenomena and is therefore welcome. While *ne* is assumed to be nonnegative underlyingly, it can be endowed with the negative feature of a negative operator in SpecNegP (*pas* or Op[+NEG]), which leads to inner island effects and licenses pseudopartitives. The absence of such an operator therefore has a number of consequences: first, *ne* will not be interpreted negatively; second, inner island effects will not be produced; third, pseudopartitive objects will not be licensed. Having considered the semantics of *ne* and concluded that this element is not inherently negative, I now turn to consider its licensing conditions.

1.2.5 Licensing *ne*

In the modern language, pre-verbal *ne* cannot freely occur in a clause. I attribute this to licensing conditions.

(77) ⋆Marie n' aime Paul.
     M.   *ne* likes P.

I suggest that *ne* can be licensed in either (or both) of the two following ways. On the one hand, it is licensed by (indirect) selection (i.e., government); on the other, it can be licensed by spec-head agreement. The first possibility is exemplified by expletive *ne*, already discussed. What is particular about expletive *ne* is that its availability is determined by the immediately superior predicate. (In (57c), expletive *ne* seems to be licensed by the contents of the CP level.) Thus, in (78) (= (58a)), expletive *ne* is licensed in the embedded clause because of the presence of the adversative predicate *avoir peur* 'to fear' in the matrix clause.

(78) Elle a   peur que tu *ne* sois   là.
     She has fear that you *ne* be-SUBJ there
     'She's worried you might be there.'

I assume that there is some indirect selection relationship between the matrix predicate and the embedded Neg° (mediated by C° at the very least) and that it is this relationship that licenses expletive *ne* in the embedded clause.[38] The ma-

---

38. The same extended selection relationship can also be seen to license the subjunctive morphology on the verb. For discussion of the relationship between negation and subjunctive mood in French, see Kampers-Manhe (1992).

trix predicate selects a CP whose head C° bears a specific feature that ensures that a specific kind of AgrSP is selected, and so on down to Neg°, at which point expletive *ne* is licensed.

The second way in which *ne* can be licensed, namely by S-structure spec-head agreement, can be exemplified by straightforward examples of clauses negated by *pas*, as in (79) (= (56a)).

(79) Je n' ai   pas faim.
     I *ne* have *pas* hunger
     'I'm not hungry.'

Assuming, as in section 1.2.3, and following standard assumptions since Pollock (1989), that *pas* occupies SpecNegP at S-structure, I conclude that DA is responsible for transmitting the feature [+NEG] to Neg°, as in (65), thereby licensing *ne*. Note that, where *pas* occupies a position *below* SpecNegP, *ne* is not licensed. See, for example, the data in chapter 2, footnote 36.

In (80) (= (58b)), I assume that *ne* is in fact "doubly" licensed, that is, by selection (by the matrix predicate *avoir peur* 'to fear') and by spec-head agreement (with *pas*):

(80) Elle a   peur que tu *ne* sois   *pas* là.
     She has fear that you *ne* be-SUBJ *pas* there
     'She's worried you might *not* be there.'

Crucially, licensing is required one way or another. This assumption is necessary to explain the ungrammaticality of (77) and is an important consideration in the discussion of "negative" adverbs and arguments in chapters 4 and 5.

The important difference between the licensing mechanisms proposed for expletive *ne* in (78) and negative *ne* in (79) is that expletive *ne* does not require the presence of an operator in SpecNegP in order to be licensed. In fact, in the previous section, I offered a number of reasons to conclude that no non-overt operator occupies SpecNegP in the context of expletive *ne*. Under the generally accepted assumption that the type of inner island effect that excludes one of the feasible interpretations of (69b) and (70b) is due to a Relativized Minimality violation, that is, the fact that the A'-operator in SpecNegP prevents proper government of the trace of the extracted A'-operator by its antecedent by counting as a closer potential A'-governor, I assume that the availability in (71) of all feasible interpretations means that no such A'-operator occupies SpecNegP. Were such an operator to occupy this position, one would expect the same inner island effects, contrary to fact. So, expletive *ne* cannot in fact be deemed to be licensed by spec-head agreement with an operator in SpecNegP, because no such operator is present in that position. Such a conclusion supports my analysis of the licensing mechanism of expletive *ne*, that is, by extended selection.

Having presented my assumptions about the syntactic representation of sentential negation and my conclusions regarding the semantics and licensing conditions of *ne* in Modern French, I now turn to the AFFECT criterion, a wellformedness condition deemed to determine the distribution and interpretation, not only of *wh*-expressions but of negative expressions, too.

1.3 The AFFECT criterion

In section 1.2.4, I showed that the *wh*-criterion in (60) can account for the type of subject-auxiliary inversion attested in matrix *wh*-questions in English and to explain the contrast between (61a) and (61b). In fact, interrogative structures are not the only ones that, in English, for example, trigger subject-auxiliary inversion. Compare (81) with (82):

(81) a.   *Not for a million dollars* would Adam be unfaithful.
    b.   ⋆*Not for a million dollars* Adam would be unfaithful.

(82) a.   ⋆*Not long afterwards* did Susan die.
    b.   *Not long afterwards* Susan died.

In (81), the italicized preposed negative constituent triggers inversion, what Rizzi (1996) refers to as residual V2; in (82), in contrast, it does not. The essential difference between the two grammatical sentences is that (81a) is a negative sentence (marked, we assume, by an abstract feature [+NEG] on the verb), while (82b) is not. This can be verified by means of a simple test, namely tag question formation (see Lakoff 1969). English statements can be continued with a tag question when the speaker is looking for confirmation, for example, from the hearer. Examples are given in (83):

(83) a.   Susan's pregnant, isn't she?
    b.   Bob can't come, can he?

Tag questions with this function are formed by repeating the auxiliary verb from the antecedent, reversing its polarity and pronominalizing the subject. The crucial aspect of these tag questions is the necessary polarity reversal. In (83a), the antecedent is positive, so the tag is negative, and vice versa in (83b). If the polarity is not reversed, the tag question fails to fulfill the same function.[39] Now, consider (81a) and (82b) again, repeated complete with (confirmation-seeking) tag questions:

(84) a.   *Not for a million dollars* would Adam be unfaithful, WOULD he?
    b.   *Not long afterwards* Susan died, DIDN'T she?

The fact that (81a) is a negative sentence is shown by the positive polarity of the tag in (84a); the fact that the tag in (84b) is negative indicates that (82b) is posi-

---

39. Consider (i), in which the polarity of the tag matches that of the statement. Here, the function of the tag is to express doubt or disbelief.
(i)   Susan's pregnant, is she?
For some reason, such tags are not possible in negative clauses:
(ii)   ⋆Bob can't come, can't he?

tive. In (81a), then, the preposed negative constituent is a negative operator that takes sentential scope, endowing a functional head in clause structure with the feature [+NEG] and producing a negative sentence. In (82b), in contrast, the scope of negation is restricted to the sentence-initial constituent; negation does not take scope over the entire clause.[40]

I am not interested here in determining how it is that the negative constituent in (81) counts as an operator while the one in (82) does not (see Haegeman 1996a for discussion). I assume, for the sake of concreteness, that the [+NEG] feature manages to percolate up to the highest node of the preposed constituent in (81) but fails to do so in (82) and that the constituent *not long afterwards* in (82b) is not negative in any relevant sense.

Under the assumption that negative operators such as the one in (81a) move to SpecCP in the syntax as a reflex of the LF property that A'-specifier positions are canonical scope positions (Rizzi 1990: 20), what I am interested in here is why the presence in sentence-initial position of a negative operator in (81a) triggers subject-auxiliary inversion (i.e., AgrS°-to-C° movement). In the earliest generative work in this area (Klima 1964: 313), an "attraction" transformation for "affective" (but not factive) operators was posited, pulling the verb to the operator over the subject. More recently, Rizzi (1996) has suggested that affective operators are subject to a licensing requirement expressed in terms of spec-head agreement: "affective operators must be in a spec-head configuration with a head marked with the relevant affective feature". This wellformedness condition was formulated in Haegeman (1992b) as the AFFECT criterion:[41]

(85) *The AFFECT criterion*:
   a.   Each AFFECTIVE X° must be in a spec-head relationship with an AF-
        FECTIVE operator.
   b.   Each AFFECTIVE operator must be in a spec-head relationship with an
        AFFECTIVE X°.

Rizzi (1996) defines an operator as an XP (bearing the relevant feature[s]) occupying a left-peripheral A'-position, that is, an adjoined position or a specifier position.

The AFFECT criterion in (85) obliges an XP of a certain type to be in a spec-head configuration with an X° of a certain type and provides an explanation for the inversion witnessed in sentences with initial negative operators, such as

---

40. The operator/nonoperator distinction between the two preposed constituents in (81) and (82) is probably why, in the first case, preposing is obligatory while, in the second case, it is not:
(i)   a.   ★Adam would be unfaithful not for a million dollars.
      b.   Susan died not long afterwards.

41. With respect to the level of representation at which the AFFECT criterion must be met, there is some debate in the literature. In his adoption of the *wh*-criterion, of which the AFFECT criterion is deemed to be a more general formulation, Rizzi (1990, 1996) assumes that it applies at LF universally but that it may, in some languages, be met as early as S-structure. The possibility that the criterion could be met in the base, that is, at D-structure, is not explicitly considered. Haegeman (1995), following suggestions made by Brody (1995), argues that the Neg Criterion applies universally at S-structure.

(81a). Suppose that the sentence-initial negative constituent in (81a) bears the AFFECTIVE feature [+NEG]. Given that (81a)–in contrast to (82b)–is in fact a negative sentence, suppose, further, following Haegeman (1995: 107), that the AFFECTIVE feature [+NEG] is also borne by AgrS°, realized on the verb. What the AFFECT criterion in (85) does given such assumptions is to oblige the finite verb and negative operator to be in a spec-head configuration. The domain in which this can be achieved is above the traditional AgrSP domain, and I assume it to be within CP (see Rizzi 1997). The operator occupies SpecCP by virtue of the scope properties of this A'-specifier position, as discussed earlier, and the finite verb raises to C° in order to satisfy the AFFECT criterion, resulting in the attested inversion.

I assume that the same reason underlies inversion in root non-*wh*-interrogatives in languages like English:

(86) a.   Have you done your homework?

Here, I assume a phonologically null but syntactically active *wh*-operator that has moved into SpecCP for the reasons already outlined (see (67)).[42] Once in that position, the AFFECT criterion will oblige the finite [+WH] verb to raise into C°. I therefore assume that (86a) can be represented as (86b):

(86) b. $[_{CP}$ OP[+WH] $[_{C'}$ have[+WH]$_i$ $[_{AgrSP}$ you t_i done your homework]]]

Thus, the AFFECT criterion can be seen to be doing the work, that is, be a more general version, of the *wh*-criterion and the Neg Criterion.

(87)   *The Neg Criterion*:
   a.   Each Neg X° must be in a spec-head relationship with a Neg operator.
   b.   Each Neg operator must be in a spec-head relationship with a Neg X°.

(88)   *The* wh-*criterion*:
   a.   Each *wh*-X° must be in a spec-head relationship with a *wh*-operator.
   b.   Each *wh*-operator must be in a spec-head relationship with a *wh*-X°.

Despite the fact that the two criteria in (87) and (88) are nothing more than construction-specific versions of the same principle, in subsequent chapters, I often refer to the individual criteria rather than to the more general AFFECT criterion. The Neg Criterion in particular is mentioned at various points.

1.4   Summary

In this chapter, I have set out my assumptions about Verb Movement and sentential negation in Modern French. Having argued in favor of an "exploded" Infl, a model of clause structure recognizing a number of functional categories

---

42. Acquaviva (1993: 11) suggests this null operator is probably responsible for the opacity effects triggered by *if* in (i):
(i)   ★How do you wonder if John behaved?

associated with verbal inflectional morphology ((CP-)AgrSP-TP-MoodP(-VP)), I concluded that Verb Movement patterns are determined (a) by the finiteness of the verb (all finite verbs in French raise to AgrS°; not all infinitives do) and (b) by the nature of the verb (auxiliary, modal, and lexical infinitives have divergent Verb Movement patterns in French). The conclusions set out in (35) are repeated as (89) here:

(89) *Overt Verb Movement patterns in French*:
    a.   All finite verbs move to AgrS°.
    b'. Infinitival auxiliaries (*être, avoir*) freely move to Mood°, T°, or AgrS°.
    b". Infinitival modal verbs (e.g., *pouvoir, devoir*) move to Mood° or T°, *and only exceptionally to AgrS* °.
    b'''. Infinitival lexical verbs move to Mood° or T°, but not as far as AgrS°.

I then argued for a further functional projection in clause structure, namely NegP, whose head is the locus of features determining clausal polarity. In French, it was concluded that NegP is located between AgrSP and TP. Following Pollock (1989), I assume that SpecNegP can be occupied at S-structure by *pas*. Further, it was argued that Neg° is the base position of pre-verbal *ne* (in those varieties in which this element is overt). The element *ne* itself was not concluded to be inherently negative. As for the licensing mechanisms of *ne*, I concluded that this element can be licensed in one (or both) of two ways. First, negative *ne* is licensed by spec-head agreement with an inherently negative operator, overt *pas* or non-overt Op, in SpecNegP. Rizzi's DA then ensures that the feature [+NEG] is transmitted to *ne* in Neg°, guaranteeing a negative interpretation for the clause. Second, expletive *ne*–which can appear only in embedded contexts–is licensed by extended selection from the superordinate predicate or an interrogative C°. In this case, there is no operator in SpecNegP (a conclusion supported by the lack of inner island effects and the unavailability of pseudopartitive objects), no DA, and no negative interpretation for *ne* or for the clause.

Finally, I addressed the syntax of affective elements in general, not just negative elements. Here, I concluded that the distribution and interpretation of affective elements such as negatives and interrogatives is governed by a universal principle, the AFFECT criterion, which, following Haegeman (1995), I assume to apply at S-structure.

(90) *The AFFECT criterion*:
    a. Each AFFECTIVE X° must be in a spec-head relationship with an AFFECTIVE operator.
    b. Each AFFECTIVE operator must be in a spec-head relationship with an AFFECTIVE X°.

These conclusions form the basis of the rest of this book.

2

The Negative Marker

In this chapter, I consider the element *pas*, which, in contrast to *ne*, is inherently negative. Indeed, I have already observed that *pas* is one of the elements that can occupy SpecNegP and license *ne* by transmitting its [+NEG] feature to Neg°. The central idea behind the analysis proposed here is that, in the context of sentential negation, SpecNegP is in fact the *derived* position of *pas*, which does not occupy the same position at both D-structure and S-structure. It is argued that, underlyingly, the position of *pas* is determined by its scope as a lexical negator: typically, *pas* is adjoined to VP, which, given the VP-internal subject hypothesis of, for example, Kitagawa (1986), is the minimal domain containing the verb and all its arguments; a VP-adjoined adverb therefore takes scope over all verbal arguments. This is explored in section 2.1. Alternatively, *pas* can function as a quantifier similar to *beaucoup* 'lots' and can, consequently, be generated within an indefinite nominal expression. This is explored in section 2.2.

In both cases, the *superficial* position occupied by *pas* is determined by those properties of the grammar that govern the syntax of sentential negation, that is, the need for a functional head in clausal hierarchy to bear the feature [+NEG] at S-structure (Haegeman 1995: 107). Given that French $[_{Neg°}$ ne] is not inherently negative, the only way for this feature specification to be achieved is by DA with a negative operator in a functional specifier position or, in the more general case, with a negative operator chain that involves a functional specifier. In other words, either *pas* itself raises at S-structure or, alternatively, *pas* is bound, in situ, by an expletive negative operator (in the sense of Haegeman 1995) occupying a suitable position. In either scenario, the scope of the negation is widened to the clause. The evidence considered in section 1.2.5 clearly suggests that, in order to mark sentential negation, *pas* needs to raise *overtly* to a position that I identified as SpecNegP. I interpret this empirical fact as indicating, in theoretical terms, that no expletive negative operator is available in French. Given the unavailability of such an operator, overt raising (followed by DA) is the only way *pas* is able to mark sentential negation. Following Pollock (1989), I assume that the landing site of raising is SpecNegP. Once *pas* occupies SpecNegP, DA and the spec-head configuration created between *pas* and (the trace of) *ne* ensures that Neg° bears the feature [+NEG]; *ne* is consequently licensed, and the clause is interpreted negatively. The relevant configuration is illustrated in (1):

(1)

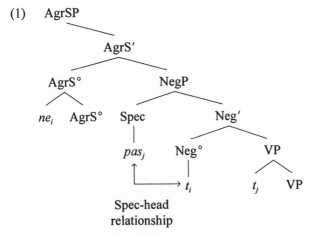

Spec-head
relationship

The claim that *pas* occupies SpecNegP at S-structure is, of course, not new. In his seminal comparative work on negation in French and English in the tradition of Emonds (1978), Pollock (1989) concludes that *pas* is generated in Spec-NegP. While I agree that *pas* occupies SpecNegP at S-structure, my analysis differs from Pollock's with respect to the base position of *pas*. For him, it is SpecNegP; for me, it is a lower position, one that reflects the fundamental relationship between negation and the predicate.

As already detailed, overt movement of *pas* from its base position into Spec-NegP is motivated by the need for a negative operator to occupy an S-structure position from which it can endow a functional head in the clausal domain with the feature [+NEG]. The issue arises as to whether raising of *pas* into SpecNegP should be attributed to either or both clauses of the Neg Criterion, repeated here as (2).

(2) *The Neg Criterion*:
   a.   Each Neg X° must be in a spec-head relationship with a Neg operator.
   b.   Each Neg operator must be in a spec-head relationship with a Neg X°.

Consider first clause (a). Given our conclusion in section 1.2.4 that there is just one *ne* in Modern French and that it is *not* underlyingly negative, it is not possible to motivate raising of *pas* to SpecNegP on the basis of the features of *ne* in Neg°.[1] Given that *ne* is nonnegative, it cannot trigger movement of an operator to its specifier position on the basis of clause (a) of the Neg Criterion. Further, in the discussion in section 1.2.4 of inner island effects induced by non-overt operators in SpecNegP, I noted that expletive *ne* does not trigger such effects, suggesting that there is no operator in SpecNegP. In short, it seems that clause (a) of the Neg Criterion is irrelevant to the raising of *pas* to SpecNegP.

---

1. Note further that the principle of Greed prevents one constituent from moving in order to satisfy the licensing requirements of another.

Consider, then, clause (b), which states that negative operators need to be in a spec-head configuration with negative heads. On the surface, this approach seems more promising, given that *pas* is indeed underlyingly negative. Yet, this is not entirely unproblematic, either. The discussion of "true" imperatives in section 2.1.1, in which *pas* does not raise to SpecNegP, as well as other, non-sentential uses of *pas* (e.g., the examples in (3)) suggest that *pas* does not, in fact, *have* to occupy SpecNegP in order to be licensed.[2] The discussion seems, therefore, to have come to a dead end. The head *ne* can be licensed without an operator, suggesting that clause (a) of the Neg Criterion does not apply to it; further, the negative adverb *pas* can appear in positions other than SpecNegP, suggesting that clause (b) does not apply to it.[3] How, then, can one motivate *pas*-raising to SpecNegP? An important feature of the contexts in which *pas* has to raise to SpecNegP is the nature and/or the scope of the negation: sentential rather than constituent.[4] *Pas* raises to SpecNegP to endow the clause with the negative feature, rather than to license *ne*. *Ne* is licensed as a consequence of the presence of the feature [+NEG] on Neg°. It seems, then, that *pas*-raising to SpecNegP occurs for scope reasons.

Alternatively, *pas*-raising to SpecNegP could be motivated within some version of Checking Theory on the assumption that *ne* is "weak" in some intuitive sense and needs to be "identified" or "supported" by virtue of its relationship with its specifier. I do not deal with this issue any further here since it would take me too far afield. However, I return to the Neg Criterion in section 3.3.1 and chapter 3, footnote 39, where I ultimately conclude that the Neg Criterion, as least inasmuch as it is seen as a configurational constraint, is in fact warranted by the data. I shall, therefore, continue to assume an approach to the empirical domain based on the Neg Criterion, although I recognize that there are some important questions to be answered. (The issue of the necessity of the Neg Criterion is briefly discussed in my review, Rowlett 1996d, of Haegeman 1995.)

2.1   Configuration 1: *pas* as an adverb

This section pursues a syntactic analysis of *pas* that sheds light on the fact that this element is used in contexts of both sentential and constituent negation. Negative *pas* is an adverb, that is, it serves to modify something. In fact, Pollock (1989), in the context of his analysis of *pas* in sentential negation, notices the distributional parallels between *pas* and adverbs. He notes (1989: 370, 377) that there is "a significant correlation in French between the placement of negation

2. But see Kampers-Manhe (1992), who follows Rizzi (1990) in assuming that *pas* occupies a specifier position even when it is used as a constituent negator. Under such an approach, *pas* might be deemed to satisfy clause (b) of the Neg Criterion in situ.

3. Plunkett (1996) in fact argues that clause (b) of the *wh*-criterion could be abandoned. See footnote 2.

4. Note, though, that Haegeman (1996b: 9) argues that scope properties are insufficient in explaining the distribution of negative words such as Modern French *pas*.

and that of adverbs" in both tensed and infinitival clauses. Cardinaletti and Guasti (1992) also observe that *pas* may function as an adverbial projection. Furthermore, as the examples in (3) illustrate, the adverbial/modifier function of *pas* is not restricted to sentential contexts:

(3) a. A: Ça va?   How are you?
         B: *Pas* mal.   Not bad.

     b. A: Qui est-ce qui veut un café? Who's for coffee?
         B: *Pas* moi.   Not me.

     c. *Pas* vrai!   Never!

     d. *Pas* possible!   Impossible!

     e. A: T'as du fric?   Got any money?
         B: *Pas* un sou!   Not a penny.

Zanuttini (1996: 184) notes further that the distribution of the equivalent of *pas* in other Romance varieties (e.g., Piedmontese *nen* and Milanese *minga*) also overlaps with some adverbs. She concludes that all these items are lexical adverbial elements generated in an adjoined position lower than NegP. (See footnote 2.) (See Zanuttini 1997a for a more recent and articulated analysis.)

In the context of a sentence (negated with *pas*) that contains either an intransitive verb or a transitive verb governing a definite direct object,[5] I suggest that negative *pas* is generated adjoined to the lexical projection it modifies, that is, VP, as in (4).[6] This reflects the fundamental relationship between *pas* and the predicate; *pas* is a negative predicate adverb. (Sportiche's Adjunct Projection Principle and Chomsky's general theory of adjunction, together, oblige "modifiers" to appear adjacent to their nonargument XP "modifiee" or the head of their "modifiee".)

(4) $[_{VP}$ pas $[_{VP}$]]

While this analysis of *pas* is conceptually attractive, it has one major problem that is avoided within Pollock's model, namely the fairly convincing evidence discussed in sections 1.1.2, 1.1.6, and 1.2.1, that, superficially, *pas* occupies SpecNegP, that is, above the VP-adjoined position. I take this to suggest that *pas* raises from its VP-adjoined base position to SpecNegP in order to convert constituent negation into sentential negation; by raising to SpecNegP, *pas* endows Neg° with the feature [+NEG]. (See the discussion in the previous section.)

5. For contexts in which *pas* negates a sentence containing a transitive verb governing an *in*definite direct object, see section 2.2.
6. In her discussion of bipartite sentential negation in Navajo, Speas (1991b: 394–95) suggests that the post-verbal *da* marker is the overt realisation of Neg° while *doo*, which canonically appears immediately before the direct object, occupies either SpecNegP or an adverbial position.

2.1.1   Synchronic evidence: negative imperatives

In this section, I present synchronic data that, I argue, are incompatible with a syntactic analysis of *pas* such as the one proposed by Pollock (1989), in which the element is assumed to be generated in SpecNegP. It is argued that, in cross-linguistic terms, the morphologically truncated structures of so-called true imperatives suggest that such paradigms project truncated syntactic structures in which no functional structure above and including NegP is projected. The fact that such imperatives in French are nevertheless compatible with *pas* but not *ne* (as well as the fact that such true imperatives in numerous other languages are compatible with adverbial negative markers but not head negative markers) undermines the claim that *pas* is uniquely associated with SpecNegP in verbal contexts.

The analysis hinges on the assumption that there are two kinds of (negative) imperative in French and is based on the data in the next section and on recent work by María-Luisa Rivero (1994) and Raffaella Zanuttini (1990, 1991, 1994a, 1996). Following these authors, I assume that the difference between the two kinds of imperative is position: one kind of imperative occupies one position, while the other kind occupies another. In the two subsequent sections, I discuss theoretical approaches to the distinction proposed by Rivero and Zanuttini, respectively. While I ultimately reject Rivero's analysis, I show that Zanuttini's offers interesting insights into the morphological and syntactic properties of imperatives. Finally, I show how the syntax of negative imperatives suggests that *pas* in French is not uniquely associated with SpecNegP.

2.1.1.1   The data

Negative imperatives in French appear with *either* tonic *or* atonic complement pronouns: tonic forms are post-verbal, as in (5); atonic ones are pre-verbal, as in (6).[7] I assume that the nature of complement pronouns (tonic/post-verbal versus atonic/pre-verbal) is determined by the syntactic properties of the imperative verb, more specifically the position of the verb. This approach is supported by the fact that pre-verbal complement pronouns cannot co-occur with post-verbal ones. If the pre-verbal atonic pronouns are licensed by virtue of the imperative occupying one position, while the post-verbal tonic ones are licensed by virtue of the imperative occupying a different position, then I expect pre- and post-verbal pronouns to be mutually incompatible; the imperative cannot occupy both positions simultaneously. I conclude, then, that the choice of pronoun is determined by the position of the verb.

Another feature associated with negative imperatives that seems to be determined by the position of the verb (and therefore co-varies with pronoun posi-

---

7. In some cases, corresponding tonic and atonic pronouns are homophonous. I assume that this is a matter of coincidence and does not detract from the conclusion that there are two independent sets of pronouns, with their own distinct properties.

tion) is the (un)availability of "negative" *ne*. French imperatives can always be negated by *pas* alone, but they cannot always be negated by bipartite *ne . . . pas*. Significantly, the (un)availability of bipartite *ne . . . pas* patterns identically with the choice of complement pronouns: imperatives that license post-verbal tonic pronouns are incompatible with *ne*, as in (5c), while no such incompatibility prevents imperatives that license pre-verbal atonic pronouns from co-occurring with *ne*, as in (6c). Given that the pre-/post-verbal position of the pronouns is deemed to be determined by verb position, this suggests that the (un)availability of *ne* is also determined by verb position. (The patterns in (5) and (6) are based on Muller 1991: 142):

(5) a. Regarde- moi. / Donne- le lui.
        watch-IMP me   / give-IMP it to-him
        'Look at me.'   / 'Give it to him.'

     b. Regarde- moi pas. / Donne- le lui   pas.
        watch-IMP me *pas* / give-IMP it to-him *pas*
        'Don't look at me.' / 'Don't give it to him.'

     c. ⋆Ne regarde- moi pas. / ⋆Ne donne- le lui   pas.
        ne watch-IMP me *pas* / *ne* give-IMP it to-him *pas*
        (= (5b))

(6) a. ⋆Me regarde. / ⋆Le lui   donne.
        me watch-IMP / it to-him give-IMP
        (= (5a))

     b. Me regarde   pas. / Le lui   donne   pas.
        me watch-IMP *pas* / it to-him give-IMP *pas*
        (= (5b))

     c. Ne me regarde   pas. / Ne le lui   donne   pas.
        ne me watch-IMP *pas* / *ne* it to-him give-IMP *pas*
        (= (5c))

Observe that the pre-verbal pronouns are incompatible with positive imperatives: compare the grammatical (5a) with the ungrammatical (6a). I assume that this restriction is purely syntactic: the position necessarily occupied by a positive imperative is not the one that licenses pre-verbal pronouns. The inability of the verb to occupy the necessary position to license pre-verbal pronouns could be attributed to economy if the derivation of (5a) is less costly than (6a), for example, if (6a) involves (gratuitously) generating more functional structure than (5a) and if Hyams (1986) is right that UG favors minimal derivations. (See section 2.1.1.3 for details.) In contrast, the examples in (6b) could be argued to be fine for the simple reason that, as examples of sentential negation, NegP is non-empty; generating the required structure is not therefore deemed to be gratuitous.

Consider now negative imperatives. Where the verb is negated by *pas* alone (without *ne*), it can be accompanied by either tonic or atonic pronouns (but not both–see my earlier discussion): (5b) and (6b) are both grammatical. I assume that the same position is occupied by the verbs in (5a, b) and that this is reflected in the position of the pronouns. In (6b), I assume that the atonic pre-verbal pronouns are licensed because the verb occupies a different position from the verb in (5a, b). Where the imperative is negated by bipartite *ne . . . pas*, the accompanying pronouns must be atonic and pre-verbal: compare the ungrammatical (5c) with the grammatical (6c). I assume that the unavailability of the tonic post-verbal pronouns together with *ne* in (5c) can be explained in terms of incompatible requirements on the imperative: the verb needs to be in one position to license the post-verbal pronoun(s) and in another to licence *ne*. Given that the two constraints cannot be met simultaneously, the string is ungrammatical. In summary, then, the imperatives in (5) are compatible with neither *ne* nor pre-verbal complement pronouns, while the imperatives in (6) are compatible with both.

I assume that the absence of pre-verbal *ne* in (6b) is due to optional "*ne*-drop", discussed in chapter 1, footnote 3. The acceptability of (6c) shows that *ne* is possible in such a structure. In (5b), in contrast, I assume that the absence of *ne* is the result of some deeper grammatical incompatibility; hence the ungrammaticality of (5c).

These and similar data from other Romance languages have been considered by Zanuttini (1990, 1991, 1994a, b, 1996, 1997a, b) and Rivero (1994). Both authors exploit the distinction drawn by Joseph and Philippaki-Warburton (1987) between "true" imperatives (e.g., (5)) and "surrogate" imperatives (e.g., (6)). Informally speaking, true imperatives represent a distinct verbal paradigm, while surrogate imperatives are verb forms taken from another morphological paradigm, for example, the subjunctive or the infinitive, used with imperative force.[8] True imperatives have distinctive structural properties; surrogate imperatives adopt the structural properties of their source morphological paradigms. In the next two sections, I consider first Rivero's then Zanuttini's analyses of the distinction between true and surrogate imperatives.

2.1.1.2 Rivero's analysis

Rivero (1994) pursues an analysis of the distinction between true and surrogate imperatives in terms of verb position (see also Rivero and Terzi 1995). For Rivero, true imperatives occupy a higher position than surrogate imperatives. To be precise, while surrogate imperatives occupy whatever position one would expect their source forms to occupy, typically AgrS° in the case of surrogate

---

8. Where infinitives are used with imperative force, as in (i), we assume they share the syntax of infinitives used in other contexts. Note that *ne* is present and that *pas* is pre-verbal.
(i)   Ne pas marcher sur la pelouse.
        ne pas walk-INF on the lawn
        'Keep off the grass!'

imperatives borrowed from finite paradigms, true imperatives occupy C°. Rivero suggests that raising into C° is triggered by the presence of some non-overt imperative operator base-generated within CP. Rivero suggests that this explains the root nature of true imperatives and the fact that pronouns follow true imperatives.

I have two criticisms of Rivero's (1994) analysis. First, the model fails to account for the cross-linguistically significant fact that true imperatives typically witness impoverished morphological makeup, often no more than a verbal stem. If, as Rivero suggests, the extent of Verb Movement undergone by true imperatives is a superset of the Verb Movement undergone by, for example, finite verbs (and assuming that Verb Movement is driven by morphology; see section 1.1), why should true imperatives not witness at least comparable morphological complexity? If the morphological properties of true imperatives make any predictions about Verb Movement at all, it is that true imperatives move less far than finite forms. While in French there is admittedly no overt morphological difference between true and surrogate imperatives, there is clear cross-linguistic evidence to suggest that true imperatives are morphologically impoverished forms, unlike surrogate imperatives.

Second, Rivero's (1994) analysis fails to account for the fact that, in a large number of languages, including the Romance languages she discusses explicitly, true imperatives are incompatible with pre-verbal negative markers and pre-verbal complement pronouns. The phenomenon is witnessed in French in (5c).[9] Rivero does, however, address this issue. Assuming a CP-NegP-IP-VP model of clause structure, Rivero accounts for the cross-linguistic tendency by suggesting that a nonincorporating Neg° blocks movement of the imperative verb from I° to C°. The absence of true negative imperatives is thus reduced to the HMC (Travis 1984), that is, Relativized Minimality. This account is problematic for a number of reasons. First, contrast the Neg° negative markers in Spanish (explicitly mentioned by Rivero) and French. Rivero assumes that Spanish *no* does not incorporate and that this fact accounts for the absence of true negative imperatives. Given the incompatibility of French *ne* with true imperatives, one would naturally want to assume that *ne* does not incorporate, either. This seems, however, an unwelcome conclusion to have to draw, given the discussion in chapter

---

9. The incompatibility between the pre-verbal negative marker *ne* and true imperatives (but not between the post-verbal negative marker *pas* and true imperatives) is common among Romance languages. In Spanish and Italian, for example, pre-verbal *no/non* are incompatible with true imperatives. In Piedmontese and Milanese, in contrast, post-verbal *nen/minga* are compatible with true imperatives. (See the work of Zanuttini, especially 1991, 1997b, for discussion of negation in a number of Romance varieties. See also Parry 1996 for discussion of sentential negation in the dialects of Italy.) Rivero (1994) points out, though, that while Zanuttini's generalization holds also for Modern Greek, it does not appear to hold for Bulgarian, Slovak, Serbian/Croatian, and Breton, in which true imperatives can be negated by a pre-verbal Neg° negative marker. It may well be desirable to deal with this contrast in terms of Ouhalla's (1990) *Neg Parameter*, his assumed parametric variation with respect to the position in clausal architecture of NegP. In those languages in which NegP is generated relatively low in clausal hierarchy, NegP may be oblivious to the truncated structures of true imperatives.

1 and the grammaticality of (7), in which the verb and negative marker have inverted to C°:[10]

(7) Qui n' avez-vous pas vu?
     Who *ne* have you *pas* seen
     'Who didn't you see?'

Second, consider again (7). Here, raising of verb + negative marker to C° is accounted for by the *wh*-criterion, an instantiation of the AFFECT criterion, as discussed in section 1.3; the [+WH] verb raises to be in the required spec-head configuration with the [+WH] operator in SpecCP, arguably in parallel to the way Rivero suggests that true imperatives raise to C°. Given that a combined verb + negative marker can be drawn into C° by [+WH] features, as in (7), it is implausible to suggest that the same is not true in the case of imperative force features. Rivero fails to address this issue.

Given these considerations, I reject Rivero's (1994) analysis of the distinction between true and surrogate imperatives and turn, in the next section, to an alternative proposal from Zanuttini.

2.1.1.3 Zanuttini's analysis

Zanuttini (1994a) agrees with Rivero (1994) inasmuch as she argues that true imperatives occupy a different position from surrogate imperatives. In contrast to Rivero, though, it is the surrogate imperatives that are typically higher than the true imperatives in Zanuttini's model. If Zanuttini's analysis is adapted to the CP-AgrSP-NegP-TP-(MoodP-)VP ordering of functional projections assumed here, it can be deemed to share with Rivero's the assumption that the position occupied by the surrogate imperatives in (6) is the position occupied by any finite verb, that is, AgrS°. In French, given the verb's position in AgrS°, the pronouns are pre-verbal (as in finite clauses), and *ne* is available, as in (6c), but frequently omitted, as in (6b).

Considering the true imperatives in (5), Zanuttini assumes, *contra* Rivero, that, rather than C° (above AgrS°), the verb occupies a position *below* AgrS°. Within my terms, this position could be T° or, more probably, some lower functional head above VP, such as Mood° (Pollock 1997b), encoding whatever formal feature(s) is/are associated with imperatives.[11] Indeed, if Zanuttini's (1994a) and Kayne's (1992) conclusion for Italian, namely that TP and the functional structure above TP are not projected in the context of true imperatives, can be adopted for the closely related French, then Mood° will in fact be the highest functional head available to host the imperative verb. If this analysis is along the

10. A possible solution to this problem with an analysis along the lines of the one proposed by Rivero might be envisaged by distinguishing between incorporation and cliticisation. I do not pursue this here.

11. Rottet (1992: 272, 275, 279) argues that the equivalent of true imperatives in the French-lexifier and heavily decreolized Louisiana Creole raises to Mood°.

right lines, an immediate explanation suggests itself for the unavailability of pre-verbal atonic pronouns: if no structure above MoodP is projected, then no suitable head is available for the pronouns to cliticize onto, for example, AgrS° or an infinitival Mood°. The post-verbal tonic pronouns that *are* licensed by true imperatives are then presumably enclitic on the verb in Mood° or proclitic on some lower null functional head, possibly AgrO°. Note that the true imperative and the post-verbal pronouns are inseparable.

(8)   MoodP/AgrOP

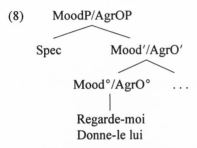

Spec   Mood'/AgrO'

        Mood°/AgrO°   . . .

        Regarde-moi
        Donne-le lui

Zanuttini's analysis has certain explanatory potential:

a. It explains the root nature of true imperatives. Given that these verb forms do not project to CP and given that certain embedded contexts are characterized by their dependence on CP, the absence of embedded true imperatives can be attributed to the fact that CP is not projected.

b. It explains the morphological poverty of true imperatives cross-linguistically when contrasted with surrogate imperatives and other verbal paradigms more generally. (On this issue, see Rivero's analysis discussed in section 2.1.1.2.)[12]

c. It explains why the complement pronouns in (5a) are post-verbal, that is, tonic. Pre-verbal *a*tonic pronouns are pro-clitic on some suitable inflectional head. Since inflectional categories above MoodP fail to project in positive imperatives, and assuming that an imperative Mood° is not a

---

12. Admittedly, a weakness of any analysis of the distinction between the French imperatives in (5) and those in (6) based on movement to AgrS° versus no movement to AgrS° is the fact that the verb morphology is identical in both cases. This is all the more surprising since, in a number of the languages described by Zanuttini (1991) and numerous others, there are clear morphological differences between true and surrogate imperatives. The French imperatives in (5) and (6) are morphologically reduced, the verb arguably comprising nothing more than a stem. This fact could be taken to indicate the lack of movement to T° or AgrS°. This conclusion could be challenged by the second person *plural* imperatives in (i):
(i)   a.   Regardez-moi pas. / Donnez-le lui pas.
       b.   Me regardez pas. / Le lui donnez pas.
             (= (5b) and (6b) but second person *plural* rather than *singular*)
However, in the context of parallel number marking distinctions on Spanish imperatives, Zanuttini (1996) suggests that it is in fact debatable whether the plural marking should be considered an agreement morpheme. The distinction between the examples in (i) and text examples (5b) and (6b) might not therefore imply movement to AgrS°.

suitable host for clitics,[13] there is no pre-verbal position for the pronouns to pro-cliticize onto; hence the ungrammaticality of (6a) and the obligatory post-verbal position of the complement pronouns with positive imperatives.

d. It explains why, in (6), the properties of the pronouns and *ne* correspond to their properties in finite clauses. In structural terms, at least, the strings in (6) are AgrSPs, just like finite clauses. Pronouns are therefore pre-verbal, and *ne* is available but not compulsory.

e. It explains why bipartite sentential negation using *ne . . . pas* cannot occur in (5c): since *ne* and, according to Pollock (1989), *pas* are generated as head and specifier of NegP, respectively, and if we accept Zanuttini's suggestion that NegP is not projected in the context of true imperatives, the unavailability of bipartite negation in (5c) is predicted.

Yet there is a problem:

f. If Pollock's analysis of *ne* and *pas* as head and specifier of NegP underlyingly is adopted, Zanuttini's model fails to account for the grammaticality of the negated true imperative in (5b). I assume that (5b) is a true imperative on the basis of the position of the pronouns: they are post-verbal, as in (5a); the unavailability of *ne* also suggests the verbs in (5) are true imperatives. Zanuttini's model therefore predicts that NegP is not projected in (5b). Nevertheless, the verb is negated with *pas*. If *pas* is generated in SpecNegP, how can *pas* occur in (5b) where NegP is not projected? Do we reject Zanuttini's characterization of the difference between true and surrogate imperatives? Or do we reconsider Pollock's analysis of *pas* base-generated in SpecNegP?

I suggest that the latter option is better motivated, given (a) the otherwise attractive explanatory power of Zanuttini's model of (negative) true imperatives, (b) the reasons already given for suspecting that *pas* is generated lower than SpecNegP and, in the specific context of sentential negation, subsequently raised into SpecNegP, and (c) the discussion in section 2.1.2. If we abandon Pollock's (1989) claim that *pas* originates in SpecNegP, the presence of *pas* in the negative imperatives in (5)—in which we have reason to believe no NegP is in fact generated—ceases to be a problem. I suggest, rather, that, in (5b), *pas* occupies its base position, namely adjoined to VP. Crucially, the VP-adjoined position is lower than MoodP and therefore indifferent to the presence or absence of (TP and) NegP. The absence of these two functional projections is then not expected to prevent the appearance of *pas*.

In fact, the problem outlined in (f) was recognized by Zanuttini herself. To solve it, she too assumes that the position occupied by *pas* in (5b) is lower than

13. Why imperative Mood° should be an unsuitable host for pre-verbal clitic pronouns should be investigated.

TP/NegP. To be precise, she suggests that post-verbal negative markers such as *pas* in French should be analyzed as specifiers of a second NegP projection, NegP-2, which is distinct from NegP(-1) in that it is below TP (and, presumably, MoodP) and therefore insensitive to the presence or absence of TP. (In Zanuttini 1994b: 430, NegP-1 and NegP-2 are renamed PolP and NegP, respectively; in Zanuttini 1997a, there are four NegPs.) In French, then, according to Zanuttini (1991), *ne* occupies Neg°-1, while *pas* occupies SpecNegP-2. In true (negative) imperatives, NegP-1 fails to be projected (due, according to Zanuttini 1991 and the conception of clausal hierarchy in terms of strict selection, to the absence of TP); hence the unavailability of *ne* in (5c). In contrast, NegP-2 can be projected in true imperatives (since it is independent of TP); hence the availability of *pas* in (5b).

I suggest this proposal has at least two weaknesses. First, on an empirical footing, the hypothesis that there are two NegP projections implies that overt negative markers occupying Neg°-2 and SpecNegP-1 should be attested, that is, head negative markers located in the lower NegP and phrasal negative markers in the higher NegP, both in isolation and in combination. However, the predicted multiplicity of negative markers (and combinations of negative markers) seems not to be a characteristic of natural language. In other words, while Zanuttini's model leads one to expect to find the familiar pre-verbal X° and post-verbal XP negative markers co-occurring with post-verbal X° and pre-verbal XP negative markers, in fact one does not, a fact that casts doubt on Zanuttini's suggestion that NegP-1 and NegP-2 are both available to UG in the first place (see also Robbers 1992).[14]

Second, and more conceptually, in a model admitting co-occurring NegP-1 and NegP-2, one might wonder what the respective contributions of each NegP projection are. Quite apart from the strangeness of an analysis in which a unique semanticosyntactic feature is encoded in two distinct functional projections within clausal structure, if each were independently to be headed by a negative feature, one would expect the two to cancel each other out (as in the Modern French examples discussed in section 1.2.2). However, co-occurring *ne* and *pas* do not and never have resulted in logical Double Negation in French. Yet if the two NegPs do not each contribute a polarity feature to the clause, it is difficult to see how one could motivate them both in the first place, at least in conceptual terms.

The alternative proposed here, namely that post-verbal negative markers such as *pas* are base-generated neither as the specifier of NegP-1 nor as the specifier of NegP-2 (the very existence of which I reject anyway) but rather as adjoined adverbs, is better motivated in that it avoids both problems raised in the previous paragraphs. First, it explains why the full range of (four) overt negative markers do not co-occur cross-linguistically. Zanuttini's SpecNegP-2 is in fact

---

14. Note that, even in Navajo (see footnote 6) and Fɔn (see chapter 3, footnote 10), in which a pre-verbal XP negative marker co-occurs with a post-verbal X° negative marker, the predicted pattern of co-occurrence is not attested.

analyzed as an adverb in an adjoined position. The absence of Neg°-2, which Zanuttini's model fails to predict, is a direct consequence of my proposal, because NegP-2 is not posited. Second, the absence of logical Double Negation in varieties with bipartite negation (analyzed by Zanuttini in terms of NegP-1 co-occurring with NegP-2) also follows from my model, since bipartite negation is not accounted for in terms of two distinct NegP projections. In conclusion, then, if I assume that *pas* is generated as an adverb, I may be able to hang on to Zanuttini's analysis of the distinction between true and surrogate imperatives in Romance, including French, even though there are no morphological differences between the two sets of imperative. (See footnote 12.)

Note that this analysis also goes some way to explaining why the imperative in (9) is interpreted as being negative, even though it contains no overt negative marker. The imperative verb appears with a pre-verbal pronoun, which, as already discussed, is incompatible with a positive imperative. The negative interpretation is therefore imposed on the utterance as a consequence of word order, and the overt negative marker(s) (*ne*) . . . *pas* are redundant.

(9) T' inquiète!
     You worry
     'Don't worry!'

To reiterate the conclusions of these sections, I have adopted a syntactic analysis of true imperatives in which these verb forms occupy a functional head very low in clause structure. Crucially, true imperatives are characterized by a truncated tree structure; in my model, CP, AgrSP, NegP, and TP fail to project. This analysis, while attractive for a number of reasons, is problematic when confronted with the assumption that *pas* is generated in SpecNegP, since the failure of NegP to project should entail the incompatibility of true imperatives and *pas*, contrary to fact. I have interpreted this state of affairs as evidence to support my claim that *pas* is not in fact generated in SpecNegP and that, rather, this element is generated in an adjoined position reflecting its fundamental modifying function.

A few comments are in order about the contribution of *pas* in the true imperatives discussed earlier. I have previously assumed that *pas* raises into SpecNegP to mark sentential negation (and license *ne*). In the case of the true negative imperative in (5b), *pas* does not raise to SpecNegP; indeed, NegP is not projected. The absence of *ne* is therefore expected. The issue remains whether or not (5b) is an instance of sentential negation. Recall that I have been assuming Haegeman's (1995) characterization of negative clauses in terms of the appearance of the feature [+NEG] on a functional head in the extended domain of V. In the discussion of (5b), I suggested that *pas* remains VP-adjoined, a position from which it has not so far been able to mark sentential negation. One might therefore want to conclude that (6b) contrasts with (5b) in that, while (6b) is an instance of sentential negation, (5b) is not.

2.1.2 Diachronic evidence: *pas*-placement relative to lexical infinitives

In this section, I argue that the analysis of the syntax of *pas* proposed in section 2.1 immediately lends itself to an account of the historical development of the distribution of *pas* with respect to lexical infinitives.[15] The data in this section come largely from recent work by such authors as Paul Hirschbühler and Marie Labelle (henceforth, H&L) (1992a, b, 1993, 1994a, b), France Martineau (1990, 1994), and Elizabeth Pearce (1990, 1991, 1993), who have looked at the diachronic development of the syntax of *pas*, in particular its position with respect to infinitives, especially lexical infinitives. (See also Pollock 1997a: chapter 13.)

From a diachronic perspective, there are two clear pieces of evidence that suggest that *pas* has not always occupied SpecNegP at S-structure and that consequently cast some doubt on the claim that this element originates in SpecNegP in the modern language. Prior to its advent as main sentential negator, the position of *pas* relative to infinitival verbs and the fact that *pas* could be fronted for emphatic purposes both suggest this element is best analyzed in the same way as a number of other adverbs, rather than as an element uniquely associated with (Spec)NegP. I suggest that an analysis of the syntax of *pas* in terms of adjunction in the base followed from about the seventeenth century by increasingly compulsory raising into SpecNegP is well placed to account for not only the synchronic facts but also the diachronic development.

The first piece of evidence concerns the relative order of *pas* and lexical infinitives. While, in the modern language, *pas* obligatorily precedes a lexical infinitive (see section 1.1.7.3), this has not always been the case. Prior to the seventeenth century (when *ne* was capable of marking sentential negation on its own, that is, when the appearance of *pas* in negative clauses was optional[16]), the two orderings illustrated in (10) (H&L's 1993: 1 (1)) were attested (Pearce 1993: 3–4), although the *ne V pas* order illustrated in (10a) was more common than the *ne pas V* order–obligatory in the modern language–illustrated in (10b) (H&L 1993: 3). During the seventeenth century, there was a clear shift from the *ne V pas* order in (10a) to the *ne pas V* order in (10b).

(10) a. ... c'est de NE S' ABANDONNER PAS au plaisir de les suivre.
   it is of *ne* REFL abandon *pas* to-the pleasure of them follow
  ' ... is not giving in to the pleasure of following them.'

---

15. During the periods in the history of French that are relevant to the discussion in this section, *pas* competed with *point* as an "intensifier" for negative *ne* in the absence of "negative" pronouns and adverbs such as the ones discussed in chapters 4 and 5. Consequently, the observations made here about word order apply to both *pas* and *point*, even where explicit reference is only made to *pas*. (See Price 1984: 252–57, chapter 19, for discussion of an initial difference between *pas* and *point*.) Note that, contrary to the comments in Yaeger-Dror (1997: 27fn3), *pas* is not a reduced form of *point*. See footnote 25.

16. See sections 3.1.1, 3.1.2, and 3.5.2, as well as section 4.3.2, for discussion of the diachronic development of the system of sentential negation in French.

b. Nous fûmes bien malheureux de NE PAS T'   EMMENER . . .
    we   were well unhappy   of *ne pas* you take
    'We were very unhappy not taking you (with us) . . . '

H&L's (1993: 4, 1994a, b) statistical data suggest that the "modern" construction, that is, the *ne pas V* order in (10b), was used just 30 to 40 percent of the time at the beginning of the seventeenth century, but 80 to 90 percent of the time by the end of the seventeenth century.[17]

Under the assumption (on which see my later discussion) that Verb Movement patterns remained constant during this time, that is, that lexical infinitives occupy a position below NegP throughout (as argued for the modern language in section 1.1.7.3), the earlier order clearly suggests that *pas* does not occupy SpecNegP in (10a). The shift from (10a) to (10b) can therefore be attributed to a progressive development whereby *pas* is increasingly obliged to raise to SpecNegP (at S-structure). Given that I have so far motivated *pas*-raising to SpecNegP by the need to mark sentential negation, namely to endow Neg° with the feature [+NEG], the shift from the order in (10a) to the one in (10b) can be interpreted in association with the progressive weakening or "denegativization" of *ne* and the concomitant "negativization" of *pas*. This conclusion, as well as the association of *ne* "denegativization" with *pas* "negativization", is supported by the coincidence of two developments with the shift from (10a) to (10b), namely (a) the loss of the ability of *ne* to function as the sole overt marker of sentential negation and (b) the shift in the interpretation of *pas* from an emphatic item to a negative item, according to Price (1993) and Posner (1985).[18]

The second piece of evidence relevant to the base position of *pas* comes from a third possible—albeit marked—order alongside (10a, b), illustrated in (11) ((11a) is taken from Martineau 1994: 59 (14), and H&L 1993: 15 (9a); (11b) is from H&L 1993: 16 (9c)), in which *pas/poin(c)t* actually precede the main negative marker *ne*:[19]

---

17. Given that the data on which these statistics are based are literary in nature, they are of course unlikely to be an accurate reflection (in terms of absolute percentages) of vernacular usage. However, the clear shift in literary usage represented by these figures is likely to reflect a parallel (possibly earlier) shift, in relative terms, in vernacular usage. Given the conservatism of written language, these shifts in absolute terms undoubtedly predated the seventeenth century. See footnote 20.

18. The issue arises as to the cause-and-effect relationship between the "denegativization" of *ne* and the "negativization" of *pas*. It seems to me that further study is needed on this issue, and I hope to be able to address it in future work. What seems clear is that the relationship between X° and XP negative markers is often mediated by non-overt operators. I suspect, therefore, that any causality as might exist between the "denegativization" of *ne* and the "negativization" of *pas* is likely to be indirect, that is, mediated by such a non-overt operator.

19. Yvon (1948: 22) gives the following Old French examples from finite clauses:
(i)   Pas ne vus esmaiez!   (*Vie de Saint Alexis*, v 681)
      pas ne you dismay
      'Don't fret!'
(ii) Ço est Climborins qui pas ne fut produme.   (*Chanson de Roland*, v 1528)
      It is C.   who *pas ne* was worthy
      'He is C. and he was not a man of worth.'

(11) a.   ... affin   de ..., PAS NE TRAVAILLER, POINCT NE ME SOUCIER.
           in-order of   *pas ne* work-INF   *point   ne* me worry-INF
           ' ... so as to ..., not to work, not to worry.'

     b.   Il nous faut ...   partir,   et   POINT N' ATTENDRE ici   nos
           it to-us is-necessary leave-INF and *point ne* wait-INF   here our
           ennemis.
           enemies
           'It is necessary for us ... to leave, and not wait here for our enemies.'

Once again, assuming constant Verb Movement patterns and cliticization of *ne*
to AgrS°, these data suggest that *pas/poin(c)t* do not occupy SpecNegP.

Recent accounts of these historical facts with a view to relating them to the
situation in the modern language by H&L (1992a, b), Martineau (1990), Pearce
(1990, 1991), and Pollock (1997a) have argued that the contrast between (10a)
and (10b) can be attributed to differences in infinitival Verb Movement patterns. However, the fact that *pas* was the only negative adverb affected by the
shift from (10a) to (10b) during the seventeenth century (H&L 1993: 2fn3, 13)
suggests that Verb Movement is unlikely to have been responsible for the
change. Note also that differing infinitival Verb Movement patterns alone are
insufficient to account for the possibility of the examples in (11) or the finite
examples in footnote 19.

In contrast, I suggest, following H&L (1993, 1994a, b) and Pearce (1993),
that, instead of being the result of differing Verb Movement patterns, the contrast is due, rather, to a change in the (surface) position of the negative *pas*. As
H&L (1993: 5) put it: "We now favor the idea that the change from *ne V pas* to
ne pas V in the case of lexical verbs reflects a change in the position of the p-
negative adverbs [i.e., *pas/point*] and not in the extent of [infinitival, PR] Verb
Movement." In the "old" system, illustrated in (10a), Neg° can be endowed
with the feature [+NEG] without the negative operator *pas* raising to SpecNegP.
Consequently, *pas* was able to appear in situ in the VP-adjoined position. Given
V-raising out of VP, minimally to Mood°, *pas* then follows the verb. In contrast, in the "new" system, illustrated in (10b), Neg° *cannot* be endowed with
the feature [+NEG] without a negative operator raising to SpecNegP. For the
reasons detailed at the start of this chapter, this has the consequence that, in
(10b), *pas* raises to SpecNegP and precedes the infinitive.

The discussion in the previous paragraph does not in fact follow H&L's
(1993, 1994a, b) analysis fully. For me, the contrast between (10a) and (10b)
revolves around the *superficial* position of *pas*; it is generated adjoined to VP in
both cases and either does or doesn't raise to SpecNegP. In contrast, H&L suggest that it is the *base* position of *pas* that changes; although generated in an
adjoined position in (10a), *pas* is generated directly in SpecNegP in (10b), as in
Pollock's (1989) analysis of Modern French. In section 2.1, raising of *pas* into
SpecNegP in the modern language was motivated by the need to mark sentential
negation: given that, in Modern French, *pas* is inherently negative, it bears the
feature [+NEG] and can endow Neg° with that feature via DA after raising into

the specifier position. The fact that this movement seems once to have been un-necessary/unavailable/optional can be explained if *ne* is deemed formerly to have been inherently negative, an approach supported by the facts that *ne* could mark sentential negation on its own and *pas* was interpreted as an emphatic item. Within the terms of an analysis along these lines, obligatory raising of *pas* from its base position to SpecNegP and, hence, the shift from *ne V pas* to *ne pas V* in the context of lexical infinitives is seen as a consequence of the process by which *pas* increasingly took over the role of primary sentence negator from *ne*. This approach is supported by the following related facts (H&L 1993: 15): first, the loss of (10a) and (11) coincides with the loss of the ability of *ne* to mark negation on its own; second, the loss of (10a) and (11) coincides with the shift in the interpretation of *pas* from an emphatic/polarity item to a strictly negative element. According to H&L's (1993: 15) interpretation of the statistical data, the critical period is the beginning of the seventeenth century.[20]

In summary, H&L's idea that the change from *ne V pas* to *ne pas V* in the context of lexical infinitives is the consequence of a change in the *base* position of the negative requires assumptions in addition to those required by the analy-sis proposed here in which the change in relative position of the two items is seen as a consequence of increasingly obligatory raising to SpecNegP, that is, a change in *surface* position only. H&L's analysis requires reanalysis of *pas/point* from an adverb to a SpecNegP-associated element. In addition, given that the shift from (10a) to (10b) is progressive, that is, given that two orders exist si-multaneously during an intermediate period, H&L's analysis assumes a period of dual classification. In contrast, my proposed analysis assumes nothing more than the increasing "negativization" of *pas* (and *point*) and "denegativization" of *ne*. The need for a functional head in clausal structure to bear the feature [+NEG] to mark sentential negation (Haegeman 1995) does the rest, in that, in the absence of an inherently negative marker in Neg° and a suitable non-overt operator, an overt [+NEG] XP will be obliged to raise into specifier position. The shift from (10a) to (10b) then falls out directly. The period during which *pas/point* appear to have had a dual classification can then be viewed as an ambiva-lence with respect to the status of *ne* ([+NEG] or not) and *pas* (negative quantifi-er or emphatic NPI) (H&L 1993: 17; Price 1993), rather than ambivalence with respect to the position in which *pas* is generated. I therefore conclude that the diachronic developments discussed in this section are best analyzed in terms of increasingly compulsory *pas*-raising to SpecNegP and that, as claimed in section 2.1, *pas* is generated in an adjoined adverbial position throughout.

---

20. Posner (1985: 184) agrees that the changes coincide but suggests a critical period two centuries earlier: "The obligatory intercalation of the 'forclusif' between the auxiliary or modal and the non-finite lexical verb dates from the late fourteenth century: before then its position was freer and it had emphatic import." See footnote 17.

2.2   Configuration 2: *pas* and indefinite direct objects

Here I consider a syntactic context representing an exception to the analysis of *pas* proposed and supported so far. Where the clause (negated by *pas*) contains a transitive verb that governs an *indefinite* direct object, it is argued that, exceptionally, *pas* is not generated in an adjoined position. Rather, in this context, *pas* functions as what Adrian Battye termed a "nominal quantifier".

2.2.1   Preliminaries: partitive and pseudopartitive direct objects

Indefinite nominal expressions can take on one of three forms: either they contain a singular indefinite article, or they exhibit a partitive or pseudopartitive structure, as illustrated in small capitals in (12a–c), respectively:

(12) a.   Marie achète UN LIVRE.   (singular indefinite)
           M.   buys   a   book
           'M. is buying a book.'

     b.   Marie achète DES   LIVRES.   (partitive)
           M.   buys   of-the books
           'M. is buying (some) books.'

     c.   Marie a   beaucoup acheté DE LIVRES.   (pseudopartitive)
           M.   has lots   bought of books
           'M. has bought lots of books.'

Ignoring the irrelevant (12a), I concentrate on the contrast between the partitive in (12b) and the pseudopartitive in (12c). The partitive structure in (12b) is fairly unanimously analyzed as being (at least) the syntactic combination of the preposition *de* 'of' and a definite nominal expression. In contrast, the pseudopartitive structure illustrated in (12c) has generated considerable debate within the literature.[21]

Battye (1991: 38) assumes that partitives have the structure in (13). These indefinites are introduced by a non-overt D° and N°;[22] the complement of the latter is a PP headed by *de* 'of' which, in turn, selects a definite DP. I assume that a partitive structure does not have particular licensing conditions since its distribution is generally unrestricted. A partitive structure can appear in subject position (14a), direct (12b) and indirect (14b) object positions, and as the complement of a preposition (14c).

---

21. See Englebert (1993) for review and discussion.
22. In section 2.2.3 and footnote 28, I consider the possibility, following Lyons (1994a), that, as indefinites, partitives lack a DP shell altogether. The exact nature of the non-overt N° is not relevant for my purposes, but see Battye (1991) for a proposal and Rowlett (1993a) for discussion. See also Kornfilt (1990) for discussion of partitives with non-overt heads in Turkish.

(13)

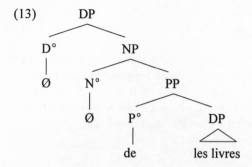

(14) a. DES   ÉTUDIANTS viennent souvent me voir.
         of-the students   come   often   me see
         'Students often come to see me.'

     b. Cette voiture, je l' ai   donnée à DES   AMIS.
         that car   I it have given   to of-the friends
         'I gave that car to friends.'

     c. Le pain se   mange avec DU   FROMAGE.
         the bread REFL eats   with of-the cheese
         'Bread is eaten with cheese.'

In contrast, pseudopartitive structures have a restricted distribution. They can appear only when licensed by another element. In (12c), for example, the pseudopartitive structure is licensed by *beaucoup* 'lots'. Witness the ungrammaticality of (15), which is identical to (12c) modulo *beaucoup*.

(15) ★Marie a   acheté DE LIVRES.
       M.   has bought of books

I leave discussion of the internal structure of pseudopartitives until section 2.2.3. In the next section, I consider in some detail their licensing conditions and their relevance to negation.

2.2.2   Obenauer's quantification at a distance
      and Battye's nominal quantification

Work by Obenauer (1983, 1984) and Battye (1987, 1989, 1990, 1991, 1995) suggests that *pas* and a number of other quantificational items, such as *peu* 'a little', *trop* 'too much', *beaucoup* 'lots', and *assez* 'enough', have a dual function in Modern French. In addition to being adverbs, as in (16), these items can appear as quantifiers within indefinite nominal expressions, as in (17).

(16) J'aime $\left\{\begin{array}{l}\text{beaucoup}\\\text{trop}\\\text{peu}\\\text{assez}\end{array}\right\}$ les films d'horreur.

'I like horror films a lot/too much/not much/enough.'

(17) Le bouquiniste a vendu [$\left\{\begin{array}{l}\text{beaucoup}\\\text{trop}\\\text{peu}\\\text{assez}\end{array}\right\}$ de romans]

'The secondhand-bookseller has sold lots of/too many/few/enough novels.'

In addition to the word order in (17), these quantifiers can (generally speaking—see the restrictions discussed in section 2.2.4.1) also be used with an alternative word order, as in (18), in which the quantifier is separated from the rest of the indefinite nominal, leaving a pseudopartitive structure behind:

(18) Le bouquiniste a $\left\{\begin{array}{l}\text{beaucoup}\\\text{trop}\\\text{peu}\\\text{assez}\end{array}\right\}$ vendu [de romans]

(≈ (17)—see the next paragraph)

In (17) and (18), which are taken from Obenauer, *beaucoup* and the other quantifiers can be said, intuitively, to quantify the noun *romans* 'novels', irrespective of the fact that the scope of the quantification might be thought to differ in (17) and (18). In (17), the scope of the quantifier is restricted to the direct object of which it forms a part ([beaucoup [de romans]]), while in (18), labeled "quantification at a distance" (henceforth, QàD) by Obenauer (1984), where the quantifier appears in some left-peripheral position, the scope of the quantifier extends to the entire predicate. The position of the quantifier reflects the semantic contrast.[23]

The structure for (18) assumed by Battye, partially following Obenauer, is given in (18'):

(18') Le bouquiniste a beaucoup vendu [*t* de romans]

etc.

(= (18))

As Battye (1991: 23) puts it, "the position marked *t* is that with which the quantifier . . . *beaucoup* . . . [is] associated". Essentially, both Obenauer (working within an earlier model of generative grammar) and Battye posit that, in (18), where *beaucoup* and the other quantifiers do not appear within the direct object, the position that these quantifiers would otherwise occupy within the direct object is filled by some null element. Thus, both researchers suggest that the direct

---

23. Obenauer (1983: 68, 1984: 156) suggests that QàD structures are regarded as somewhat *relâché* 'loose' by purists.

object in (18) has the structure in (19) where *ec* represents an empty category of some kind.

(19) [*ec* [de romans]]

Further, both Battye and Obenauer assume that, in QàD structures such as (18), *beaucoup* and the other quantifiers and the empty category, *ec*, are "linked" within the terms of Binding Theory, that is, that the empty category is (A'-) bound by *beaucoup*, and so on. In Obenauer's (1983: 68–69) terms, the empty position is "localement lié par le quantifieur lexical qui . . . se trouve en position A'" ("locally bound by the lexical quantifier in A'-position").

With respect to whether or not the binding relationship between the quantifier and the empty category is the result of movement, Obenauer does not commit himself one way or the other; neither does he express any interest in the issue. Kayne (1975: 29ff), Battye (1991: 23ff), and Kampers-Manhe (1992), in contrast, are bolder on the question. In the case of Kayne and Kampers-Manhe, no movement is invoked in the relationship between *beaucoup* and the empty category (but see Milner 1978: 690–92 for a critique of Kayne 1975: 29ff). In the case of Battye, the association between *beaucoup* and the empty category in these constructions is the relationship between an antecedent and its trace *t*.[24] For my part, I endorse the movement approach. A detailed discussion of how QàD can be derived from nominal quantification appears in section 2.2.3. In section 2.2.4, I suggest that *pas* should be included in the list of nominal quantifiers.

A necessary corollary of Battye's (movement) analysis (according to Battye 1995) is that the quantifier that appears, on the surface, either attached to or detached from the nominal it intuitively quantifies over must also be able to function independently as an adverbial. Informally speaking, nominal quantification and QàD are parasitic on VP-adjunction: an element cannot function as a nominal quantifier unless it can also function as a VP-adverb. The possibility of (16) is a necessary (although not sufficient) prerequisite for the possibility of (17) and (18). This is not to say that the implicature/corollary is bidirectional. As Milner (1978: 690–92) illustrates, it is not the case that all adverbial elements that can function as in (16) can also function in association with the indefinite direct object of a transitive verb as in (17) and (18).[25] In the modern language, although both *énormément* and *abondamment* 'a lot' can appear as VP-adverbs,

---

24. What Battye (1991: 23) actually says with respect to QàD structures is that the quantifiers "seemingly 'float' backwards off the noun phrase in direct object position". I have interpreted this as a movement approach to QàD, although Battye himself does not propose any structural analysis of the mechanics involved.

25. In section 2.2.4, I suggest that *pas* should be included in the class of nominal quantifier. While *pas* could, from relatively early in the development of French, function as a generalized negative adverb, its association with indefinite direct objects was a later development. Rickard (1989: 75) claims that *pas* could not be used in pseudopartitive structures until the sixteenth century, and then only rarely. In similar vein, Price (1986: 574–75) points out that, while pseudopartitive structures involving the negative marker *point* are found in the earliest texts, similar constructions using *pas* are not found until much later. In contrast, even in early texts, *pas* could function as an adverbial negator.

as in (20), the former can appear in association with an indefinite direct object (both QàD and non-QàD), as in (21), while the latter cannot, as in (22), (taken from Milner 1978: 691 (53)):

(20) a. J'ai énormément lu.
    b. J'ai abondamment lu.
       I have a-lot   read
       'I have read a lot.'

(21) a. J'ai   lu énormément de livres.   (non-QàD)
    b. J'ai énormément lu   de livres.   (QàD)
       I have (a-lot)   read (a-lot)   of books
       'I have read lots of books.'

(22) a. ★J'ai lu abondamment de livres.   (non-QàD)
    b. ★J'ai abondamment lu de livres.   (QàD)
       (= (21))

Indeed, Milner uses these distributions to argue, *contra* Kayne (1975), that QàD structures are derived from non-QàD structures. His argument centers on the ungrammaticality of (22b), which contrasts with the acceptability of (20b). Kayne (1975) argues that elements like *énormément* and *abondamment* are base-generated in VP-initial position not only in (20) but also in (21b) and in (the ungrammatical) (22b). If this is indeed the case, we have no way of accounting for why (20a), (20b), and (21b) are grammatical while (22b) alone is not. If, alternatively, and as Milner proposes, the QàD strings in (21b) and (22b) are derived from the non-QàD strings in (21a) and (22a), then the unacceptability of the QàD example in (22b) containing *abondamment* can be accounted for in straightforward fashion. This particular element cannot appear in a (derived) QàD structure for the simple reason that it cannot appear in the (almost) equivalent (base-generated) non-QàD structure. So, in Kayne's analysis, (22a) and (22b) have to be explained independent of each another; in an analysis in which (22b) is derived from (22a), only one explanation is required. I take this as strong evidence to suggest that QàD is a derived word order in French.

2.2.3 Analysis

With respect to the syntactic category of quantifiers such as *beaucoup*, Battye (1991) claims that, unlike other quantifiers in French (whereby the term "quantifier" represents an intuitively functional rather than a strictly syntactic characterization), *beaucoup* and so on are neither adjectives (cf. *quelques* 'some') nor determiners (cf. *plusieurs* 'several'). Rather, Battye (1991) exploits Abney's (1987) DP hypothesis to argue that these elements are in fact nominals, generated as the head N° within an indefinite DP, as in (23):

(23) $[_{DP} [_{D'} \emptyset [_{NP} [_{N'} [_{N} \text{beaucoup}] [(de) NP]]]]]$

As nominals, *beaucoup* and the other terms absorb the Case assigned to the indefinite DP. Consequently, while they take an NP complement, the Case-marking preposition *de* 'of' must be inserted to avoid a Case filter violation. The structure in (23) seems not to pose any problems for the non-QàD configurations in (17). How, then, can the QàD configurations in (18) be derived from a structure such as (23)? While Battye assumes (or, rather, implies—see footnote 24) that examples such as those in (18) are derived from those in (17), he offers no concrete analysis of how the derivation might proceed. In Rowlett (1993a: 58–63), I address the issue, and I present the essential points of that analysis here.

There is a major difference between the underlying structure assumed by Battye, that is, (23), and the one assumed by Obenauer. Obenauer assumes the structure in (24):

(24) $[_{NP} [_{QP}$ beaucoup, etc. $]$ $[$ de N' $]]$

The major difference concerns the status, in X'-theoretic terms, of the quantifier. In (23), it is a head; in (24), it is a maximal projection. The difference is significant if one is to pursue an analysis in which (18) is derived from (17), that is, if QàD is to be derived from non-QàD in terms of Move-α, the versatility of which is determined in part by principles of X'-syntax: head movement is more restricted than XP movement. Crucially, head movement is subject to the HMC (Travis 1984), while XP movement is not.[26]

In Rowlett (1993a), I followed Battye in assuming an underlying structure such as (23) in which the quantifier is the head of the construction. This left me with the problem of deriving QàD from non-QàD. In concrete terms, the quantifier, under N°, cannot be extracted directly from its containing maximal projection to its final left-peripheral position. To solve this problem, I suggested that the complement of the nominal quantifier, that is, the adnominal NP preceded by *de* 'of', should first be extraposed, or right-adjoined to VP, as in (25) (after Rowlett 1993a: 60 (31)). Once the adnominal NP has been extraposed, I suggested that the indefinite DP containing the quantifier itself is free to move independently. I assumed that the DP moves to the left-peripheral A' scope position, as in (26), (after Rowlett 1993a: 61 (32)). I further assumed that the extraposed NP (NP_i) can properly bind its trace (t_i) by reconstruction of DP_j.

The obvious weakness in this structural analysis is the (rather inelegant) need to extrapose the NP complement of *beaucoup* prior to raising the nominal quantifier itself. In addition to its lack of elegance, though, it could be argued that the proposed analysis makes an incorrect prediction. More precisely, one might expect the extraposed constituent, NP_i in (25) and (26), to be an island for extraction. Yet this is not the case, as witnessed by the grammaticality of the QàD example in (27), derived from (28), in which the topic has been extracted from what, in my analysis, would be an extraposed constituent, NP_i, as illustrated in

---

26. A second significant difference between (23) and (24) concerns the nature of the lexical head of the nominal construction. In (23), it is the quantifier; in (24), it is the quantified noun.

the simplified structure in (29). Hence, there are good reasons to doubt the validity of this analysis of QàD.

(25)

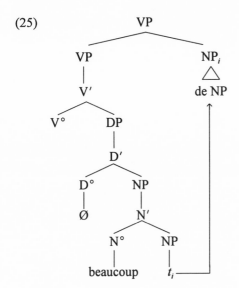

(26)

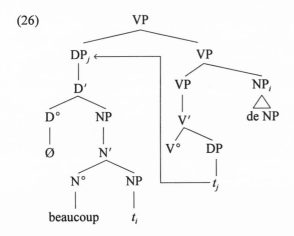

(27) C'est de Zola Op que Jean a   beaucoup lu   de livres.
     It is of Z.   that J.   have lots   read of books
     'Z.'s the one J. has read lots of books by.'

(28) . . . Jean a beaucoup lu [de livres Op]

(29)

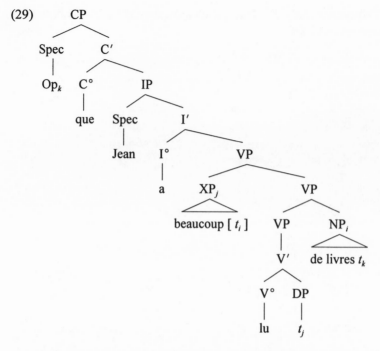

As an alternative to the underlying structure assumed by Battye, one might maintain Obenauer's assumption that the nominal quantifier is a full XP constituent, even where it quantifies over an indefinite direct object, i.e., even in (17).[27] To capture this, one could assume that—rather than being generated as the head N in an indefinite DP–*beaucoup* is generated in a specifier position within the indefinite nominal. This analysis is, in fact, more in line with Battye's own original (1987, 1995) work on nominal quantification. Working prior to the widespread awareness of Abney's DP hypothesis, Battye suggests that nominal quantifiers appear in SpecNP. It was only later that he modified his analysis by placing these elements in N°. Given the profusion of functional projections currently being proposed in the literature and not just in the context of clauses, it may well be the case that nominal quantifiers occupy an extended specifier position of NP (in the sense of Grimshaw 1993), rather that SpecNP itself. An immediately obvious candidate would be the specifier of a number phrase: SpecNumP. With nominal quantifiers such as *beaucoup* in SpecNumP, the obligatory indefinite nature of such nominal expressions might be attributed to the spec-head relationship between the quantifier and the non-overt head Num° (see Lyons 1994a). SpecDP would not be a possible position for these nominal quantifiers in a model such as the one proposed by Lyons, since he assumes that DP is not projected in indefinite nominal expressions.

27. I am grateful to David Adger for discussing these issues with me.

The Case-theoretic features of pseudopartitives, that is, the obligatory insertion of the prepositional Case-marker *de* 'of' before the adnominal NP, could receive an explanation almost identical to the previous analysis. With *beaucoup* in specifier position (such as SpecNumP) absorbing the Case assigned by the transitive verb under government,[28] *de* 'of' is still required to see that the (otherwise Case-less) adnominal NP does not violate the Case filter.

The attraction of such an analysis in which the nominal quantifier is an XP in SpecNumP is that initial extraposition of the adnominal NP is not required to allow extraction of the nominal quantifier from within the direct object to the left-peripheral A' scope position. Instead, extraction can proceed as in (30):

(30)

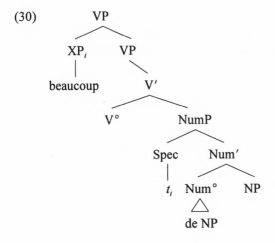

The analysis of *beaucoup* and similar terms as syntactic specifiers rather than heads has the added advantage of tying their syntax to their semantics.

---

28. It is interesting to compare this proposal with traditional analyses of Exceptional Case Marking (ECM), illustrated in (i):

(i)   The villagers believed John to be a liar.

Examples of ECM such as (i) are often assumed to have a number of properties. The complement of the ECM verb *believe* is a nonfinite clause; the subject of that clause, *John*, is (consequently) not assigned nominative Case by the embedded AgrS°. Rather, it is "exceptionally" assigned accusative Case by the ECM verb under government. Government is deemed to be possible because, first, CP is not assumed to be projected by the embedded nonfinite clause and, second, the embedded AgrSP fails to count as a barrier against outside government due to the defective status of (nonfinite) AgrS°.

Compare this with the proposed analysis of nominal quantification. The nominal quantifier to be Case-marked is in SpecNumP, yet Case-marked by an external governor. This could be argued to be possible given, first, that DP is not assumed to be projected by the indefinite nominal expression and, second, that NumP fails to count as a barrier given the defective status of the indefinite NumP.

This proposal is supported by work by Lyons (1994a), who suggests that indefinites are characterized by their failure to project to the DP level. Further, the parallel between (non)finiteness/nominative Case assignment and (in)definiteness/genitive Case assignment is attested in English nominals. In English, only definite D° can assign genitive Case to its "subject", arguably in the same way that only finite AgrS° can assign nominative Case to its "subject". Pushed to its logical conclusion, one would also have to conclude that, like nominative Case, genitive Case is structural rather than inherent.

Semantically, *beaucoup* and other quantifiers fulfill a specific *function* with respect to the indefinite direct object: specifier positions are typically occupied by constituents that fulfill a particular function with respect to the relevant maximal projection. By associating these nominal quantifiers with SpecNumP, semantics and syntax meet.

Further evidence suggesting nominal quantifiers are maximal projections like specifiers rather than heads comes from the fact that they can be modified, as in (31), which is crucially not synonymous with (32). In (31), the intensifier *bien* modifies *beaucoup*; in (32), it is emphatic. (See also chapter 1, example (20).)

(31) Jean a   acheté [bien beaucoup] de livres.
     J.   has bought well *beaucoup* of books
     'J. bought a hell of a lot of books.'

(32) Jean a   bien acheté beaucoup de livres.
     J.   has well bought *beaucoup* of books
     'J. has indeed bought lots of books.'

Concluding, then, I adopt this second analysis of nominal quantifiers. I assume that, in the nominal structure:

1.   Nominal quantifiers bear the categorial features of nouns, i.e., [-V, +N].

2.   They bear the functional syntacticosemantic feature [+QUANTIFICATION].

3.   They appear as the syntactic specifier of Num°; DP is not projected.

4.   They are compatible with QàD.

5.   They can function, independent of an indefinite nominal, as left-peripheral adverbs.

2.2.4 *Pas* as a nominal quantifier

In this section, I argue—following Battye (1995) himself—that *pas* belongs to Battye's class of nominal quantifier along with *beaucoup* and similar items and that, consequently, the syntax of *pas* should be modeled on the analysis proposed in the previous section.[29] In other words, we argue that, where *pas* ne-

---

29. Obenauer (1983, 1984) also ascribes *pas* to the same category as *beaucoup* and so on, but wrote prior to Battye's proposals. Obenauer (1984: 155) suggests that all these elements are adverbs but does not concern himself with a detailed analysis. In a somewhat similar vein, Battye (1995) includes *pas* in his inventory of nominal quantifiers in a footnote but goes no further.

Note the following comment by Schwegler (1988: 26), which supports Battye's analysis of *pas* as a noun:

(i)   Over the history of Romance, and . . . that of several other well-documented language families, the rise of new negation strategies has often involved the development of a *nominal* element that eventually evolves into the primary exponent of negation by way of semantic "bleaching" and a category shift from noun to adverb (or sentence qualifier). (Schwegler's italics)

gates a clause containing a transitive verb and a pseudopartitive direct object, the sequence [pas de N] is generated as a constituent in direct object position in the base. In this, I follow something of the intuition expressed in Yvon (1948: 19) on the basis of the literary example in (33):

(33) Quoiqu' ils   eussent
　　　However they have-IMP:SUBJ
　　　　　　une liberté   plus absolue et   plus dangereuse que P. et   V.,
　　　　　　a   freedom more absolute and more dangerous   than P. and V.
　　　　　　point de famille,
　　　　　　point of family
　　　　　　point de mères   vigilantes et   tendres pour les   former à   la   vertu,
　　　　　　point of mothers vigilant   and tender for   them train   to the virtue
　　　　　　point de serviteur dévoué pour les   chercher le   soir   et   les
　　　　　　point of servant   devoted for   them fetch   the evening and them
　　　　　　　　ramener au   bercail,
　　　　　　　　return   to-the cradle
　　　　　　pas même un chien pour les   avertir du   danger,
　　　　　　pas even   a   dog   for   them avert   of-the danger
　　　ils   ne firent aucun genre de chûte.
　　　they *ne* made no   kind   of fall

'Although they had a more absolute and dangerous freedom than P. and V., no family, no vigilant and tender mothers to guide them toward virtue, no devoted servants to collect them every evening and return them to the cradle, not even a dog to ward them from danger, they came to no harm.'

According to Yvon, for the average speaker of the modern language:

Point et *pas*, indépendamment de *ne*, expriment l'exclusion, l'absence, le manque: *point de famille, point de mères* . . . est synonyme de *manque to-tal de famille, de mères.*

(Independent of *ne*, *point* and *pas* express exclusion, absence, lack: *point de famille, point de mères* . . . is synonymous with *manque total de famille, de mères.*)

In other words, as Yvon (1948: 21) puts it:

Il ne serait pas déraisonnable de considérer comme complément d'objet les groupes *point de famille*, etc., dans lesquels *point* ayant valeur de nom

---

What Battye suggests is that *pas* retains its nominal properties, even in the modern language.

　　　Winters (1987), within a cognitive account of the development of negation in French, suggests that the pseudopartitive structures, that is, [Ø de N], discussed in section 2.2.3, and licensed by negative markers such as *pas* (and the older *point* and *goutte*) are themselves indication that the negative markers were (and continue to be) nouns. As Winters points out (1987: 36), noun-noun expressions have, from the earliest evidence to the present day, been constructed with *de* 'of'.

aurait pour complément *famille*, etc., et se rattacherait moins étroitement au verbe.

(It would not be unreasonable to treat the phrases *point de famille*, etc., as the objects, whereby the nominal *point* would take *famille*, etc., as its complement and would be less intimately associated with the verb.)

While I have decided to reject an account whereby nominal quantifiers are analyzed as the lexical head of the construction, I argue later that the negative markers, such as *pas*, are generated within the nominal expression (NumP) in direct object position. First, I note the syntactic similarities between *pas* and the other nominal quantifiers (section 2.2.4.1); then I show that extraction facts suggest a derivational account of *pas* (section 2.2.4.2).

2.2.4.1 *Evidence:* pas *behaves like* beaucoup, *etc.*

First, like *beaucoup* and other quantifiers and as predicted by Battye (1995) and discussed in section 2.2.2, *pas* can be used, not only in association with indefinite direct objects, but also independently, as an adverb, in clauses that do not contain indefinite direct objects. As the data in (34) and (35) show, *pas* not only fills the same slot, in linear terms, at least, as *beaucoup*; it also fulfills the same adverbial function.

(34) a. Pierrette   voyage   en France.
     b. Pierrette   voyage beaucoup en France.
     c. Pierrette (ne) voyage pas   en France.
         P.   *ne* travels Ø/lots/*pas* in France
         'P. travels/travels a lot/doesn't travel in France.'

(35) a. Pierrette   a   voyagé en France.
     b. Pierrette   a   beaucoup voyagé en France.
     c. Pierrette (n') a   pas   voyagé en France.
         P.   *ne* has Ø/lots/*pas* traveled in France
         'P. has traveled/has traveled a lot/hasn't traveled in France.'

Second, in the same way that the distribution of *beaucoup* and the other terms in QàD structures is restricted, so the distribution of *pas* seems to be subject to a similar restriction. To be precise, among the class of transitive verbs in French, Obenauer distinguishes between those that are compatible with QàD and those that are not. The first group is illustrated in (36) (Obenauer's 1983: 68 (6)), the second in (37) (Obenauer's 1983: 70 (12)):

(36) a. Antoine a   trop   lu   de romans policiers.
         A.   has too-much read of novels detective
         '≈ A. has done too much detective novel reading.'

b. Max a   (très) peu composé de sonates.
    M.   has very little composed of sonatas
    '≈ M. has done (very) little sonata composing.'

(37) a. ★Le critique a   peu apprécié   de films.
         the critic   has little appreciated of films

b. ★Son regard a   beaucoup impressionné de minettes.
    his look has lots   impressed   of young-girls

c. ★La réorganisation a   beaucoup accéléré   de procédures.
    the reorganization has lots   speeded-up of procedures

d. ★La nouvelle a   beaucoup inquiété d' experts.
    the news   has lots   worried of experts

e. ★Loin de   la ville, il a   beaucoup regretté d' amis.
    far   from the town he has lots   missed of friends

Note that the unacceptability of the strings in (37) is not of the same nature as the unacceptability of (22). In (22), the problem is the quantifier, which is incompatible with both QàD and non-QàD. In (37), the problem is the fact that the verbs are incompatible with QàD. The non-QàD equivalents are perfectly fine, as in (38):

(38) a. Le critique a apprécié peu de films.
     b. Son regard a impressionné beaucoup de minettes.
     c. La réorganisation a accéléré beaucoup de procédures.
     d. La nouvelle a inquiété beaucoup d'experts.
     e. Loin de la ville, il a regretté beaucoup d'amis.
         (≈ (37))

Obenauer accounts for the distinction between the verbs in the examples in (36) and those in the strings in (37) and (38) in terms of types of what he calls "VP-quantification". What Obenauer means by this is simply that, in QàD structures, where *beaucoup* and other quantifiers are separated from the nominal they quantify over and appear in some left-peripheral position, that is, where they are extracted from SpecNumP in the direct object, as illustrated in (30), the quantification relationship is upheld by virtue of *beaucoup* or the other term quantifying *in a certain way* over the entire predicate and, hence, the direct object. The "in a certain way" is important here because Obenauer uses this condition to explain the contrast between (36) and (37). Consider the two examples in (39).

(39) a. Jean aimait beaucoup sa femme.   (intensity)
         J.   loved lots   his wife
         'J. used to love his wife a lot.'

b. Jean faisait beaucoup l' amour à sa femme.   (frequency)
    J.   made   lots   the love to his wife
    'J. used to make love to his wife often.'

In these two examples, the predicates are quantified by *beaucoup*. However, the nature of the quantification relationship is different in the two cases. In (39a), *beaucoup* indicates the intensity of the sentiment expressed by the predicate *aimer* 'to love' and is synonymous with *intensément*. In (39b), in contrast, *beaucoup* indicates the frequency of the activity expressed by the predicate *faire l'amour* 'to make love' and is synonymous with *souvent*. Importantly, the interpretation of *beaucoup* is determined by the predicate. Obenauer observes that the (un)availability of QàD in (36) and (37) depends crucially on the reading of the quantifier. Where the quantifier has a frequency reading, QàD is fine; where the quantifier has an intensity reading, QàD is impossible. Obenauer goes on to suggest that this is a consequence of the underlying quantificational relationship with the direct object. The logic goes something like this: in order to maintain the quantificational force over the direct object in a QàD structure, the predicate must be quantified with a frequency reading, since it is only by having multiple or frequent occurrences of the activity expressed by the predicate that it is possible to have multiple, or quantified, occurrences of the direct object. The problem with the examples in (36), then, is that two incompatible requirements are placed on the moved quantifier. The predicate wants the quantifier to take an intensity reading, while its binding relationship with its trace can be maintained only with a frequency reading. The clash cannot be resolved; the result is ungrammaticality.

Working on the assumption that the (underlying) quantification relationship with the direct object can be maintained only if, in the QàD structure, the quantifier is interpreted as a frequency rather than an intensity adverb, the ungrammaticality of the strings in (37) can be explained. The verbs in the strings in (37) are incompatible with QàD because the nominal quantifiers are interpreted as intensity adverbs rather than frequency adverbs, as in the grammatical strings in (40), in which all the direct objects are definite. Hence, in (37), the quantifier relationship with the direct object cannot be maintained.

(40) a. Le critique a   peu apprécié   ce film.
         the critic   has little appreciated this film
         'The critic appreciated this film little.'

    b. Son regard a   beaucoup impressionné cette minette.
        his look   has lots   impressed   this young-girl
        'His look impressed this young girl a lot.'

    c. La réorganisation a   beaucoup accéléré   cette procédure.
        the reorganization has lots   speeded-up this procedure
        'The reorganization speeded up this procedure immensely.'

    d. La nouvelle a   beaucoup inquiété cet expert.
        the news   has lots   worried this expert
        'The news worried this expert a lot.'

e. Loin de   la   ville, il a   beaucoup regretté cet ami.
    far   from the town he has lots   missed this friend
    'Once settled far from town, he missed this friend a lot.'

What is important for our purposes is not the explanation for the contrast between (36) and (37) per se but the fact that, where the nominal quantifiers in
(36) and (37) are replaced by *pas* similar effects are produced:

(41) a. Antoine n' a   pas lu   de romans policiers.
         A.   *ne* has *pas* read of novels detective
         'A. hasn't read any detective novels.'

    b. Max n' a   pas composé de sonates.
        M. *ne* has *pas* composed of sonatas
        'M. hasn't written any sonatas.'

(42) a. ??Le critique n' a   pas apprécié   de films.
         the critic   *ne* has *pas* appreciated of films
         'The critic didn't appreciate any films.'

    b. ??Son regard n' a   pas impressionné de minettes.
        his look   *ne* has *pas* impressed   of young-girls
        'His look didn't impress any young girls.'

    c. ★La réorganisation n' a   pas accéléré   de procédures.
        the reorganization *ne* has *pas* speeded-up of procedures
        'The reorganization didn't speed up any procedures.'

    d. ★La nouvelle n' a   pas inquiété d' experts.
        the news   *ne* has *pas* worried of experts
        'The news didn't worry any experts.'

    e. ★Loin de   la   ville, il n' a   pas regretté d' amis.
        far   from the town he *ne* has *pas* missed of friends
        'Once settled far from town, he didn't miss any friends.'

The native speakers I have consulted do not, in general, find the examples in
(42) as unacceptable as the strings in (37), but rather see them as somewhat odd,
especially examples (42c–e).[30] One might reason that, although (the necessary)
frequency adverbs are in theory incompatible with these verbs, where that frequency is reduced to zero, that is, with negative *pas*, the incompatibility is not
so marked.[31] The fact that the strings in (42) are not considered totally

30. I have no explanation for why (42a, b) are judged more acceptable than (42c–e).
31. Hugues Péters (personal communication) has drawn attention to the contrast between the
ungrammatical text examples and these grammatical ones:
(i) Le critique n' a   apprécié   aucun film.
     the critic *ne* has appreciated no   film
     'The critic didn't appreciate a single film.'

unacceptable like those in (37) deserves closer scrutiny. Nevertheless, the contrast between (41) and (42) is significant in that it is parallel to the contrast between (36) and (37). I therefore conclude that *pas* belongs to the same class of quantifier as *beaucoup*.

I now consider what Obenauer (1984) refers to as pseudo-opacity effects, which, once again, suggest that *pas* should be treated on a par with Battye's other nominal quantifiers, such as *beaucoup*. Obenauer notes the impossibility of associating one quantifier with a pseudopartitive direct object when another quantifier intervenes. Consider (43), in which *beaucoup* is interpreted as an intensity adverb (and therefore cannot be associated with the direct object by QàD):

(43) a.   ★Combien a-t- il beaucoup aimé de films?
           how-many has-he lots   liked of films

Rather, in (43a), it is *combien* that is associated with the direct object by QàD. I assume that the ungrammatical (43a) is derived from the grammatical (43b):

(43) b.   Il a   beaucoup aimé combien   de films?
          he has lots   liked how-many of films
          'How many films did he like a lot?'

Given the acceptability of (43b), I would argue that the problem with (43a) cannot be semantic in nature and must therefore be syntactic. Given, further, that (43a) is derived from (43b) and that, therefore, the structure of (43a) can be represented as in (43a′), I appeal to Relativized Minimality to account for its ungrammaticality.[32]

(43) a′. ★Combien$_i$ a-t-il beaucoup aimé [t_i de films] ?
          (= (43a))

In (43a′), *combien* has been extracted from the direct object; let us assume that it has been moved to SpecCP and that the attested inversion takes place at the CP level and is triggered by the *wh*-criterion–see section 1.4. To avoid an ECP violation, the trace of *combien* needs to be antecedent-governed by its A′-ante-

(ii)   Il n' a   regretté aucun ami.
      he *ne* has missed no   friend
      'He didn't miss a single friend.'
He notes further that the text examples can be rescued with a suitable continuation:
(iii) Il n'a pas regretté d'amis parce qu'il n'en avait aucun.
    32. That Relativized Minimality is at stake here is supported by the acceptability of (i):
(i)   [Combien de films]$_i$ a-t- il beaucoup aimé t_i
      how-many of films has he lots   liked
      'How many films did he like a lot?'
In (i), the θ-marked internal argument of *aimer* 'to like' has been moved to SpecCP. The result is grammatical despite the intervening *beaucoup*. This is arguably attributable to the fact that, as an argument trace, t_i does not need to be antecedent-governed in order to be properly governed. Rather, proper government can be achieved on the basis of θ-government by the verb.

cedent, a relationship arguably interrupted by the A'-element *beaucoup*, which counts as an intervening potential antecedent-governor.

Now consider (44):

(44) *Combien$_i$ n' a-t- il pas aimé [t_i de films]?
     how-many *ne* has he *pas* liked   of films

Here, *beaucoup* is replaced by *pas* and the same pseudo-opacity effect is created, suggesting that *pas* should be analyzed syntactically in parallel fashion to *beaucoup*.[33] So, in this section, I have demonstrated that *pas* parallels *beaucoup* and the other quantifiers in a number of interesting ways that suggest that one should analyze *pas* syntactically in essentially the same way as the other nominal quantifiers.

Before concluding this section, I address the important issue of the difference between *pas* and the other nominal quantifiers, which is a consequence of the former's [+NEG] specification and its (not surprising) use as a marker of sentential negation. For, while nonnegative nominal quantifiers can remain adjoined to VP at S-structure, the need to endow a functional head with the feature [+NEG], I have been assuming, obliges *pas* to raise to SpecNegP. Furthermore, the conclusions drawn in section 1.2.7.3 about the movement patterns of lexical infinitives back up this assumption. In section 1.2.7.3, I concluded that lexical infinitives can raise up to Mood° or T° but not to AgrS°. Assuming a CP-AgrSP-NegP-TP-MoodP-VP clausal hierarchy, I predict that the order LI-*beaucoup* is grammatical (where LI stands for lexical infinitive and *beaucoup* represents all nonnegative nominal quantifiers), while the order LI-*pas* is not. This is so since the only way for a lexical infinitive to precede *pas* (in SpecNegP) would be for it to raise into AgrS°, which it cannot do. In contrast, a lexical infinitive can precede *beaucoup* (VP-adjoined) simply by raising to Mood° or T°, which it can do. As the following examples illustrate, these predications are borne out by the data:

---

33. It should be stressed that the ungrammaticality of (43a) and (44) is due to their A'-binding configurations; it is not a consequence of any semantic incompatibility between the quantifiers in the examples. Sentence (43b) shows that *combien* and *beaucoup* can co-occur while (the admittedly rather archaic) exclamation in (i) shows that *pas* and *combien* are compatible:

(i) Combien il n' a   pas$_j$ voulu avoir [t_j d' enfants]!
     how-much he *ne* has *pas* wanted have   of children
     'How he didn't want children!'

In (i), *pas* has been extracted from the pseudopartitive. If the exclamative quantifier *combien* is generated AgrSP-adjoined or in SpecCP, the lack of Relativized Minimality effects and grammatical status of (i) are predicted: no potential antecedent-governor interrupts an A'-binding relationship. For discussion of exclamatives in French, see Radford (1989).

An analysis of (43b) involving LF raising of the direct object, that is, QR, is not a problem. Assuming that the entire direct object would undergo QR (rather than just *combien*) as in the example of overt movement in (i) in footnote 32, the absence of Relativized Minimality effects can be attributed to the fact that, as a θ-marked complement, the ECP is satisfied by virtue of the direct object being head and θ-governed by the verb.

(45) a. ★Il est inutile de ne parler pas.   (★LI-*pas*)
It is useless of *ne* speak *pas*
'It's pointless not talking.'

b. Il est inutile de parler beaucoup.   (LI-*beaucoup* = OK)
It is useless of speak *beaucoup*
'It's pointless talking a lot.'

I therefore conclude that *pas* raises to a position higher than *beaucoup*, namely
SpecNegP, and motivate this movement on the basis of the need to mark sentential negation, as discussed in section 1.3.5. More generally, though, I have
shown that the distribution of *beaucoup* and *pas* show similarities that lend
themselves to a parallel analysis of all these items. In the next section, I demonstrate that extraction facts also support a derivational analysis of *pas*.

2.2.4.2 Evidence: extraction facts

Support for a derivational analysis of *pas* comes from extraction facts. Following work on "islands" in the tradition of Ross (1967), there is a body of literature suggesting that PPs are islands in French but not in English. According to
Pollock (1991: 87–88), for example, "le français est, lui, rebelle à toute extraction à partir d'un PP" (French does not allow any extraction from a PP-embedded position). This constraint has been used to account for the fact that
preposition-stranding is, under certain conditions, possible in English but not in
French,[34] as illustrated in (46):

(46) a. There's [the guy]$_i$ Op$_i$ John used to go out with t_i.

b. ★Voilà [le type]$_i$ Op$_i$ que Jean sortait   avec t_i.
there the guy   that J.   went-out with
(= (46a))

Assuming that the contrast illustrated by the data in (46) can indeed be accounted for in terms of the respective island status of PPs in English and
French, and given that the analysis of *pas* proposed in this chapter is based on
movement, I predict that *pas* raising is impossible from an extraction site within
a PP to a landing site outside PP. I can use this prediction to evaluate my proposed syntactic analysis of *pas*: to do so, I need structures in which–according
to my analysis–*pas* is base-generated within a PP while the nearest SpecNegP
(to which *pas* must raise in order to mark sentential negation) is outside PP.

---

34. The reader is referred to Pollock (1991) for a recent discussion and account of PP-islands.
Pollock compares and contrasts French, English, and the Scandinavian languages. A precise
explanation of PP-islandhood is not central to my discussion here. The judgment for (46b) applies to
metropolitan French; Posner (1996: 342) gives Prince Edward Island French as an exception to the
general pattern. Uriagereka (1995) also addresses this contrast between English and the Romance
languages.

Assuming, further, that *pas* is one of Battye's nominal quantifiers and is therefore generated either within an indefinite NumP or as a VP-adverb, the relevant structures contain either a PP-embedded indefinite NumP (containing *pas*) or a PP-embedded verbal predicate (to which *pas* is adjoined). However, given the status of the null pronominal anaphor PRO–the assumed subject of embedded infinitives–and the proliferation of functional heads currently being proposed in the literature (e.g., AgrSP, AgrOP, TP, AspP, NegP), it is debatable whether a bare VP could be generated within a PP without being dominated by one or more functional projections including, where relevant, NegP. It is therefore unclear whether *pas* adjoined to a VP and embedded in a PP ever *needs* to cross the PP node to reach the nearest SpecNegP to mark sentential negation. For this reason, I restrict my attention to PP-embedded indefinite NumPs containing *pas* in SpecNumP.

Thus, I can test the prediction with respect to clauses containing a PP whose head P° takes an indefinite NumP as its complement. For, although my model allows the nominal quantifier *pas* to be generated in SpecNumP, the island status of the dominating PP does not allow *pas* to be extracted for promotion to SpecNegP to mark sentential negation. Consider (47):

(47) a.   J'aime tartiner mon pain [$_{PP}$ avec [Ø du   beurre]].
          I like spread my bread with   of-the butter
          'I like to spread butter on my bread.'

   b.   ⋆J'aime pas$_i$ tartiner mon pain [$_{PP}$ avec [t_i de beurre]].
          I like *pas* spread my bread with   of butter
          'I don't like to spread butter on my bread.'

   c.   J'aime pas tartiner mon pain avec du beurre.
        (= (47b))

The string in (47a) contains a PP whose head P° *avec* 'with' takes an indefinite nominal complement. As in (13), the non-overt noun Ø subcategorizes for a PP headed by *de* 'of'. This *partitive* structure, discussed in section 2.2.1 and illustrated in (48), is licensed in my model.

(48)

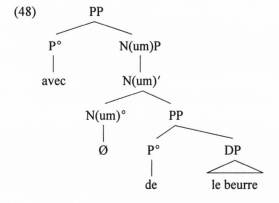

A similar structure, in which *pas* is generated in SpecNumP, is also licensed in my model. (See (30).) In this case, given that *pas* will absorb the oblique Case assigned by the preposition to its complement, the NP will be Case-marked by the prepositional Case-marker *de*, forming the basis of a *pseudopartitive* structure. If movement of *pas* from within the indefinite NumP to SpecNegP were then possible, that is, if the intervening PP node were not an island, one would expect the negative of (47a) to be (47b), with just such a pseudopartitive structure. Yet, the string in (47b) is not the negative of the one in (47a) and is, in fact, ungrammatical. Instead, the negative of (47a) is (47c), in which the indefinite nominal retains its *partitive* structure, as in (48). A consequence of this analysis is that, in (47c), *pas* cannot be generated within the PP-embedded indefinite. Rather, *pas* must be VP-adjoined. Thus, one can contrast (47b) with (47c). In the ungrammatical (47b), an attempt is made to move *pas* across a PP node, as illustrated schematically in (49), which is impossible given the island status of the PP; hence, the ungrammaticality of (47b).

(49) $\star$. . . pas$_i$ . . . [$_{PP}$ . . . [$_{NumP}$ . . . t_i . . .]]
      |_____ ✕ _____|

In (47c), in contrast, where *pas* originates from a position adjoined to the matrix predicate headed by *aimer* 'to like' rather than a position within the PP, promotion to SpecNegP is unproblematic, as in (50), since no island node is crossed.

(50) . . . pas$_i$ . . . [$_{VP}$ t_i [$_{VP}$ . . . [$_{PP}$ . . .]]]
      |_____|

Of course, this account of the ungrammaticality of (47b) hinges crucially on a derivational approach to the syntax of *pas*, as proposed in this chapter.

The data in (51) point to the same conclusion:

(51) a.   Le premier ($\star$n')est venu [$_{PP}$ avec [$_{NP}$ pas d' idées du   tout]].
          the first   *ne* is come   with   *pas* of ideas of-the all
          'The first one came without a single idea.'

     b. $\star$Le premier n' est pas$_i$ venu [$_{PP}$ avec [$_{NP}$ t_i d' idées du   tout]].
          the first   *ne* is *pas* come   with   of ideas of-the all
          (= (51a))

Although (51a) would probably be frowned upon by prescriptive grammarians and is certainly not standard written French, it is judged by many native speakers to be an acceptable utterance.[35] It would seem that, in (51a), *pas* appears in

---

35. Consider also the following examples from Gaatone (1971: 111), cited in H&L (1992/93: 45):
(i)   Aux cérémonies du   mois prochain, aucune délégation étrangère n' a été invitée.
      to-the ceremonies of-the month next   no   delegation foreign *ne* has been invited
           Non seulement PAS D' AMÉRICAINS, bien sûr . . .
           not only   *pas* of Americans   well sure
      'To next month's ceremonies, no foreign delegation has been invited. Not just no Americans, of course, . . . '

its base position, that is, within the complement of the preposition *avec* 'with'. Clearly, this is not a canonical instance of sentential negation: first, *ne* is excluded;[36] second, *pas* has not raised to SpecNegP, which, given the other examples we have reviewed, seems to be a property of sentential negation in French.[37] Indeed, given the (S-structure) island status of PP in French, I predict that it would be impossible for *pas* to be promoted to SpecNegP at that level. This prediction is borne out by the ungrammaticality of (51b), in which an attempt has been made to move *pas* from within the PP headed by *avec* 'with' to SpecNegP, outside PP. The judgment is perfectly straightforward and indeed expected, given the island status of PP in French and, more important for my purposes, the movement approach to the syntax of *pas* proposed in this chapter.

The final empirical argument I invoke here and that hinges on the island status of PP in French and a derivational analysis of *pas* is illustrated by the paradigm in (52). The relevant issue here is the reading of *pas un(e) seul(e) N* 'not a single N'. More specifically, the issue is whether this sequence can be interpreted idiomatically as 'no N at all' (cf. Vikner 1978: 88) or, rather, is to be interpreted as 'not just one N, but (possibly) more Ns'. The data suggest that the idiomatic reading is restricted to certain syntactic configurations, namely those in which the sequence can be generated as a single constituent.

(ii) Entre   nous, je préférerais une femme qui me fasse   souffrir à PAS DE FEMME
      between us   I prefer-COND a   woman who me make-SUBJ suffer   to *pas* of woman
            du   tout.
            of-the all
      'Between you and me, I'd rather have a wife who made me suffer than no wife at all.'
      36. This is the view of Muller (1991: 151) with respect to these examples:
(i)   Elle (⋆ne) s'   habille [PP pour pas cher].
      she   *ne* REFL dresses   for *pas* expensive
      'She wears inexpensive clothes.'
(ii) Il (⋆n')arrivera [PP dans pas longtemps].
      he   *ne* arrive-FUT in   *pas* long
      'He'll be here soon.'
(iii) Il (⋆ne) sort [PP avec pas un sou   en poche].
      he   *ne* goes-out with *pas* a   penny in pocket
      'He goes out without a penny on him.'
Muller's judgments in (i)–(iii) suggest that the marker of the scope of sentential negation, *ne*, must be licensed in some strictly syntactic way, such as by virtue of a spec-head configuration with an operator in SpecNegP, as argued in section 1.3.5. To that extent, the data in (i)–(iii) provide additional support for the approach adopted. The idea pursued here is that the necessary spec-head configuration can be created only by movement. See also Moritz and Valois (1993: 319), who say "sentential negation is best accounted for in terms of licensing of the head of a Neg(ation) Phrase. This licensing results from movement of a negative XP into the specifier of a NegP." I assume that *pas* in these examples is a constituent negator. Muller's judgments then follow H&L (1992/93: 38–39) who show that *ne* is incompatible with constituent negation.
      37. The failure of *pas* to raise, for example, to SpecNegP, at S-structure in the text examples is not necessarily problematic. The issue was addressed at the end of the discussion of true negative imperatives in section 2.1.1.3. It might be possible to invoke Rizzi's (1996) functional definition of operators. This would allow one to claim that, at S-structure, *pas* fails to take sentential scope and, hence, fails to count as an operator at that level. What seems clear about the examples in (51a) and footnote 36, examples (i)–(iii), is that the negative takes strictly local, that is, nonsentential, scope.

(52) a.   Avec pas une seule idée, il est allé voir son professeur.
          with *pas* a   single idea he is gone see his teacher
          'He went to see his teacher without a single idea.'

     b.   Marie n' a   pas reçu   une seule lettre depuis des   mois.
          M.   *ne* has *pas* received a   single letter since of-the months
          'M. hasn't received a single letter in months.'

     c.   Il est venu me voir [_{PP} avec pas une seule idée en tête].
          he is come me see   with *pas* a   single idea in head
          'He came to see me without a single idea in mind.'
          (= idiomatic reading)

     d.   Il n'est PAS venu [_{PP} avec UNE SEULE IDÉE en tête] . . .

In (52a), where *pas un(e) seul(e) N* appears as a single constituent in the absolute construction, the idiomatic reading is available. In (52b), where *pas* is separated from *un(e) seul(e) N* and, presumably, occupies SpecNegP (marking sentential negation), the idiomatic reading is also still available. I attribute this
availability to the fact that *pas un(e) seul(e) N* is generated as a single constituent and that *pas* is subsequently separated from *un(e) seul(e) N* as a consequence of raising to SpecNegP.[38] In (52c), *pas un(e) seul(e) N* appears in a PP-
embedded position, and the idiomatic reading is still available, as indicated by
the translation and due, once again, to the fact that the string is generated as a
single constituent. In (52d), in contrast, the idiomatic reading is unavailable.
What is crucially different about (52d) is the presence of the PP node between
pas and *un(e) seul(e) N*. The presence of this node, I argue, prevents *pas* from
raising out of the PP. The fact, therefore, that *pas* appears outside the PP in
(52d) indicates that *pas* was never inside the PP (given that the string is grammatical). This, in turn, means that *pas un(e) seul(e) N* could not have been generated as a constituent; hence, the lexicalized idiomatic reading is unavailable.
The only reading available for (52d), 'not just one N, but more Ns', should be
clear from (52d'):

(52) d'. Il n' est pas venu avec une seule idée, mais plusieurs!
          he *ne* is *pas* come with a   single idea but several
          'He didn't come with just one idea, but several!'

---

38. Note that, even in the idiomatic expression, for *pas* to license *ne*, it must raise to SpecNegP.
The example in (i), in which *pas* has failed to raise to the left of the past participle, is ungrammatical,
contra DeGraff (1993b: 74fn20).
(i)   ⋆Je n' ai   vu   pas une seule femme.
       I *ne* have seen *pas* a   single woman
       'I didn't see a single woman.'
The example in (i) becomes marginally possible if *ne* is omitted and the sequence *pas une seule femme*
is emphasized.

In conclusion, then, PP-extraction facts suggest that a movement analysis of the syntax of sentential negation involving *pas* such as the one advanced in this chapter is along the right lines.

2.2.5 Hirschbühler and Labelle (1992/93)

An early version of the analysis assimilating *pas* to *beaucoup* and other quantifiers is discussed by H&L[39] (pp. 41–53, section 2) and has been taken up by numerous members of audiences to whom this work has been presented. After presenting the analysis in Rowlett (1992b) (a preliminary version of Rowlett 1993a and of the modified analysis presented earlier), H&L (pp. 44–45) suggest—uncontroversially enough—that the following are desirable if the relationship between *pas* and pseudopartitive direct objects is to be maintained in terms of movement of the former out of the latter:

1. QàD should always be analyzed in terms of movement.

2. The restrictions on QàD (with and without *pas*) should be similar and analyzable in terms of base-generation of the quantifier within the direct object.

3. There should be no pseudopartitive structures that cannot be analyzed in terms of extraction of an (overt?[40]) quantifier.

H&L suggest (p. 46) that there are cases of pseudopartitive direct objects out of which it would not be plausible to suggest that an overt quantifier has been extracted, and that the parallels suggested here between QàD and negation are not as neat as the proposed parallel analysis would lead one to expect. In each of the cases discussed here, I suggest that the distinction to be drawn between *pas* and other nominal quantifiers is semantic in nature rather than syntactic and, therefore, that these cases do not present a problem for the parallel syntactic analysis proposed here.

First, H&L suggest that, while QàD involving *beaucoup* and other quantifiers is sensitive to subjacency, QàD involving *pas* is not, as illustrated in (53)–(55), H&L's (p. 46, (29)–(31)):

(53) a. Je n' ai   pas l' intention d' acheter de livres.
      I *ne* have *pas* the intention of buy   of books
      'I don't intend to buy any books.'

---

39. Unless otherwise explicitly specified, references in this section to work by these authors are to H&L (1992/93).

40. It is unclear to me why it should be necessary for the extracted quantifier to be overt. Note that, in the present analysis, the extracted quantifier can be Op.

    b. ⋆J'ai   beaucoup l'   intention d' acheter de livres.
           I have lots   the intention of buy   of books

(54) a. Je ne crois pas qu' il ait   acheté de livres.
        I *ne* think *pas* that he have-SUBJ bought of books
        'I don't think he has bought any books.'

    b. ⋆J'ai   beaucoup cru   qu' il a   acheté de livres.
           I have lots   thought that he has bought of books

(55) a. Je n' ai   pas vu Pierre acheter de livres.
        I *ne* have *pas* seen P.   buy   of books
        'I didn't see P. buy any books.'

    b. ⋆J'ai   beaucoup vu Pierre acheter de livres.
           I have lots   seen P.   buy   of books

Within the terms of the analysis proposed earlier, in each of the (a) examples, *pas* is assumed to have been generated within the pseudopartitive in the embedded clause. It is then assumed to have been extracted, ultimately raising to the matrix SpecNegP. This produces perfectly grammatical sentences, as indicated. In each of the (b) examples, in which *beaucoup* has apparently undergone the same movement, the strings are ungrammatical. H&L suggest the ungrammaticality of these (b) examples is due to a subjacency violation. This result is, of course, a problem if *pas* and *beaucoup* are analyzed in identical fashion, since subjacency should apply equally to both *pas* and *beaucoup*.

In response to H&L's discussion of the data, I suggest that the distinction between the (a) and (b) examples in (53)–(55) can be accounted for independent of the QàD issue (and subjacency) with reference to the ungrammaticality of (53c), (54c), and (55c):

(53) c. ⋆J'ai   beaucoup l'   intention d' acheter CES   livres.
        I have lots   the intention of buy   these books

(54) c. ⋆J'ai   beaucoup cru   qu' il a   acheté CES   livres.
        I have lots   thought that he has bought these books

(55) c. ⋆J'ai   beaucoup vu Pierre acheter CES   livres.
        I have lots   seen P.   buy   these books

The examples in (53c), (54c), and (55c) are identical to those in (53b), (54b), and (55b) but for the fact that the direct objects are definite rather than indefinite. Accordingly, I do not suggest that the quantifier *beaucoup* has been raised out of the direct object. Rather, I suggest that the quantifier is a regular adverb and generated adjoined to a VP. Nevertheless, the examples are ungrammatical. Given that no movement is posited in these examples, their ungrammaticality cannot be attributed to subjacency effects. Rather, the ungrammaticality of (53c), (54c), and (55c) is more likely to be due to some semantic incompatibility between *beaucoup* as an adverb and the verbal predicate. This being so, it is quite plausible that the ungrammaticality of (53b), (54b), and (55b) is not due to

subjacency effects, either. Recall the observation by Battye (1995) that the possibility of nominal quantification is dependent upon the possibility of VP-
adjunction. Since, in (53c), (54c), and (55c), such adjunction is impossible, I
predict that QàD will be impossible in (53b), (54b), and (55b), *without recourse
to subjacency*. If this line of reasoning is justified, the syntactic distinction H&L
draw between *beaucoup* and *pas* is unfounded. Rather, I suggest, the problem
with the (b) and (c) examples is a semantic incompatibility between *beaucoup*
on the one hand and *avoir l'intention de Vinf, croire*, and *voir Vinf* on the
other.[41] That the (a) examples are grammatical comes as no surprise, since the
following (d) sentences are also fine:

(53) d.   Je n' ai   pas l'   intention d' acheter CES   livres.
          I *ne* have *pas* the intention of buy   these books
          'I don't intend to buy these books.'

(54) d.   Je ne crois pas qu' il ait   acheté CES   livres.
          I *ne* think *pas* that he have-SUBJ bought these books
          'I don't think he has bought these books.'

(55) d.   Je n' ai   pas vu   Pierre acheter CES   livres.
          I *ne* have *pas* seen P.   buy   these books
          'I didn't see P. buy these books.'

Second, H&L suggest that the contrast between (56a) (H&L, p. 56fn13 (i))
and (56b) (H&L, p. 46, (32b)) undermines the parallel analysis I have given to
pas on the one hand and nominal quantifiers such as *beaucoup* on the other.

(56) a.   un sujet   sur lequel ne sont pas parus   de livres intéressants
          a subject on which *ne* are *pas* appeared of books interesting
          'a subject on which no interesting books have appeared'

     b.   ⋆un sujet   sur lequel sont beaucoup parus   de livres intéressants.
          a subject on which are lots   appeared of books interesting

Here again, though, the ungrammaticality of the example with the nominal
quantifier, (56b), can be attributed to a (semantic) incompatibility between the
quantifier and the particular predicate, rather than to any syntactic difference
between the nominal quantifier and *pas*. Consider (57):

(57) ⋆Ces   livres intéressants sont beaucoup parus.
      these books interesting   are lots   appeared

Here, there are no indefinite arguments, and no movement operations would be
posited to account for the surface position of *beaucoup*. Nevertheless, the string
is ungrammatical, presumably due to some semantic incompatibility between the
quantifier *beaucoup* and the predicate *paraître* 'to appear'. If this is true, it

41. Similar facts apply to *avoir envie de Vinf* 'to want to V'. Thanks to Odile Cyrille for pointing
this out.

would also account for the ungrammaticality of (56b), without the need to conclude any syntactic difference between *pas* and the nominal quantifiers.

Third, H&L (pp. 49–50, section 2.2.2.2) suggest that *pas* does not give rise to Relativized Minimality effects while other nominal quantifiers do. Consider (58) (H&L, p. 50, (43)), both of which are grammatical:

(58) a. Gérard ne mange pas souvent de dessert.
         G.   *ne* eats   *pas* often   of dessert
         'G. doesn't often eat dessert.'

     b. Gérard ne mange souvent pas de dessert.
         G.   *ne* eats   often   *pas* of dessert
         'Often, G. doesn't eat dessert.'

H&L note the scope difference between (58a) and (58b). In (58a), *pas* has scope over *souvent* 'often'; in (58b), the reverse is true. Scope properties are therefore reflected in or determined by superficial order. Given the (pseudopartitive) form of the direct object, I suggest, in both cases, that *pas* (or some larger constituent containing *pas*) has raised out of the direct object. In (58a), one might expect this to give rise to Relativized Minimality effects, since *souvent* intervenes between *pas* and its trace, as in (58a'). However, such effects are not produced; (58a) is perfectly grammatical.

(58) a'. Gérard ne mange pas$_i$ SOUVENT t_i de dessert.
          (= (58a))

H&L suggest that the ungrammaticality of (59) (in contrast with the grammaticality of (58a)) is a problem if *pas* is analyzed along the same lines as *beaucoup*.

(59) *Luc a   beaucoup souvent eu   de chance.   (H&L, p. 50, (45b))
      L.   has lots   often   had of luck

In (59), the ungrammaticality is attributed to the fact that *beaucoup* has been raised above *souvent* and that this movement violates Relativized Minimality, as expected:

(59') *Luc a beaucoup$_i$ SOUVENT eu t_i de chance.
       (= (59))

I deal with these data by suggesting that H&L's interpretation of the movement involved in (58a) is incorrect. Consider (60):

(60) A: Est-ce que tu vas au   cinéma?
        is it that you go to-the cinema
        'Do you go to the cinema?'

     B: Non, pas souvent.
        no *pas* often
        'No, not often.'

In the reply to the question in (60), *pas* modifies/qualifies *souvent* 'often' and is, therefore, presumably adjoined to *souvent*, forming a constituent: [$_\alpha$ pas [$_\alpha$ souvent]].[42] Now, assume that, in (58a), *pas* is also adjoined to *souvent* and that the entire constituent is generated in SpecNumP. I assume that, in order to take sentential scope, the negative feature of *pas* percolates up to the mother node of the entire constituent and that, consequently, the entire constituent will have to raise to SpecNegP to license *ne*. In this way, given that this constituent is raised as a unit, no potential intervening antecedent-governors are crossed, and no Relativized Minimality effects are expected. In (58a), *pas souvent* occupies SpecNegP as a single constituent, rather than *pas* occupying this position alone having raised over *souvent*. The grammaticality of (58a) is thus unproblematic. Turning now to (59), the question arises as to why a similar approach is not possible. The answer, it seems to me, lies in the fact that *beaucoup* and *souvent* cannot be generated together as a constituent: ⋆[beaucoup souvent]. Consequently, the only way to generate (59) is, as H&L suggest, for *beaucoup* to appear within the direct object at D-structure and for *souvent* to be MoodP-adjoined, as in (59'). The examples in (61) show that these are (separately, at least) perfectly possible:

(61) a. Luc a beaucoup eu de chance.   (H&L, p. 50, (45a, f))
        L. has lots   had of luck
        'L. has had lots of luck.'

     b. Luc a souvent eu de la chance.
        L. has often   had of the luck
        'L. has often had (good) luck.'

The ungrammaticality produced in (59), where *beaucoup* and *souvent* co-occur and where *beaucoup* raises over *souvent*, can then rightly be attributed to Relativized Minimality, as illustrated in (59'). Notice that, where these two elements co-occur but where *beaucoup* fails to raise over *souvent*, there are no problems:

(62) a. Luc a SOUVENT *beaucoup$_i$* eu t_i de chance.   (H&L, p. 50, (45d))
        L. has often   lots   had of chance
        'L. has often had lots of luck.'

     b. Luc a SOUVENT eu *beaucoup* de chance.
        L. has often   had lots   of chance
        (= (62a))

---

42. Alternatively, *pas* could be the specifier of *souvent*. The two elements would still form a constituent: [$_{\beta P}$ [$_\alpha$ pas] [$_{\beta'}$ souvent]]. Recall that Sportiche's (1988: 429) Adjunct Projection Principle and Chomsky's (1986b: 16) general theory of adjunction, together, oblige "modifiers" to appear adjacent to their nonargument XP "modifiee" or the head of their "modifiee". See also Kampers-Manhe (1992).

Once again, then, the contrast between *pas* and *beaucoup* can be accounted for on independent semantic grounds and does not undermine the syntactic parallels posited here.

Before leaving H&L's criticism of the approach to the syntax of *pas* adopted here, I discuss the data in (63) and (64), brought to my attention by an anonymous *Journal of French Language Studies* reviewer of Rowlett (1993a) as a difference between *pas* and the nonnegative nominal quantifiers. It seems to me that these data are in fact as unproblematic for my analysis as those presented by H&L.

(63) a.   Pierre (n')a   pas   voulu de cadeau(x).
     b.   ⋆Pierre   a   beaucoup voulu   de cadeaux.
          P.   *ne* has   wanted of present(s)
          'P. didn't want any presents' / 'P. wanted lots of presents.'

(64) a.   Pierre (n')a   pas   eu de peine.
     b.   ⋆Pierre   a   beaucoup eu   de peine.
          P.   *ne* has   had of pain
          'P. didn't have any trouble' / 'P. had lots of trouble.'

I mentioned these data in a footnote in Rowlett (1993a: 58fn5), suggesting that it might be possible to resolve the apparent problem with reference to Pollock's (1989: 389–91) observation that the past participles of French modals and *être/avoir* behave differently from lexical past participles. On reflection, it seems more likely that the ungrammaticality of the two (b) examples, the ones with *beaucoup*, should be handled in the same way as (65):

(65) a.   ⋆Pierre a   beaucoup voulu   ce   cadeau.
          P.   has lots   wanted this present

     b.   ⋆Pierre a   beaucoup eu   de la peine à finir   son repas.
          P.   has lots   had of the pain to finish his meal

In these examples, (65a) shows that the adverbial use of *beaucoup* is incompatible with *vouloir* 'to want'; (65b) shows that *beaucoup* is incompatible with *avoir de la peine à Vinf* 'to have difficulty doing something'. The distinction between the (a) and (b) examples in (63) and (64) is therefore independent of the syntax of *pas/beaucoup* and does not undermine the analysis proposed here.

In conclusion, then, it appears that the "problems" presented by H&L and the anonymous *JFLS* reviewer are not in fact problematic at all. Consequently, I shall continue to assume that the syntactic proposals presented here for *pas* are by and large correct.

2.3   Summary

In this chapter, I addressed issues surrounding the syntax of *pas*, the principal marker of sentential negation in Modern French. Following Pollock (1989), I assumed that, in the unmarked case, *pas* marks sentential negation and licenses *ne* by occupying SpecNegP at S-structure. Indeed, this assumption was, in part, the basis of my conclusions in chapter 1 about the extent of the movement of different types of infinitives in the language. However, unlike Pollock (1989), I argued that, rather than being the base position of *pas*, SpecNegP is, instead, its derived position. *Pas* was argued to be generated in a lower position and to raise, in the syntax, to SpecNegP. To be precise, I argued that, typically, *pas* is base-generated in a left-VP-adjoined position that reflects the nature of the relationship between the negation and the predicate. Alternatively, *pas* can be generated within an indefinite nominal expression. In either case, raising to SpecNegP was motivated in order to mark sentential negation and license *ne* at S-structure.

3

Jespersen's Generalization

In this chapter, I move away from predominantly French considerations and adopt a more cross-linguistic perspective. I consider the nature of the relationship between the way a given language marks sentential negation and the (un)-availability of a phenomenon known as negative concord (henceforth, NC), in which, roughly speaking, multiple negative items can co-occur without negation being canceled out. (See section 3.2 for illustration.) NC has provoked considerable interest among linguists over the years (e.g., in recent work by Newson 1994 and Déprez 1995, forthcoming) but has so far failed to be given anything like a generally accepted explanation. Indeed, in her recent (1995) study of the syntax of negation, Haegeman acknowledges (p. 304fn2) that it is not clear what the distinctive property of NC languages is and decides (p. 166) to leave the precise characterization of NC on the research agenda.

Haegeman does, however, make reference to early discussion of the topic by Jespersen, and it is with him that I start. Jespersen (1924: 333) observes that languages "in which the ordinary negative element is comparatively small in phonetic bulk" are characterized by NC, while languages that use "fuller negatives" fail to allow NC. (For a structural approach to the distinction between these two types of negative marker, see section 3.1.2.)

Jespersen notes further that the way languages mark pure sentential negation is subject to a cyclic development diachronically: languages fluctuate, over time, between marking pure sentential negation with negative markers that are "comparatively small in phonetic bulk" and using "fuller negatives". This diachronic pattern is referred to as the Negative Cycle. The (im)possibility of NC is thus determined by where a language stands in the Negative Cycle. The rather sturdy generalization that can be captured will be referred to as Jespersen's Generalization. The aim of this chapter is to account for Jespersen's Generalization.

The relevance of Jespersen's Generalization to the syntax of sentential negation in Modern French is as follows: if we know where Modern French stands in the Negative Cycle, Jespersen's Generalization allows us to predict whether or not Modern French is an NC language. As I demonstrate in subsequent sections and chapters, this makes crucial predictions about the properties of a certain class of "negative" element that, like *pas*, can appear in association with *ne* in contexts of sentential negation. These elements, and the import of Jespersen's Generalization are discussed in section 3.5.2 and especially in chapters 4 and 5.

The present chapter is organized in the following way. Section 3.1 discusses the Negative Cycle; more generally, it introduces Jespersen's (1924) typology of systems of sentential negation. In particular, section 3.1.2 shows how the Negative Cycle can be viewed within the template of NegP, introduced in section 1.2.1 and exploited in the discussion of *pas* in chapter 2. Within the NegP hypothesis, the locus of clausal polarity features is an autonomous syntactic projection. The typological difference between the two types of negative marker distinguished by Jespersen is viewed in structural terms: negative markers "comparatively small in phonetic bulk" are analyzed as head elements generated under Neg°; "fuller negatives" are phrasal elements associated with SpecNegP.

Section 3.2 presents the NC phenomenon, whereby (the negative feature of) multiple negative items appearing in the same domain fail to cancel each other out, contrary to what one might expect if the behavior of negation in natural language could be assimilated in straightforward fashion to the behavior of the Boolean logical negative operator ¬. In Boolean logic, the intrinsic properties of negation are such that, where one occurrence of ¬ has scope over another, the former cancels out the latter. In NC languages, multiple negatives do not cancel each other out; if anything, they reinforce each other.[1] NC is a common—but not universal—feature of natural language. Thus, in the Standard English (henceforth, SE) example in (1a), the two negative constituents cancel each other out, leading to logical Double Negation (henceforth, DN). In contrast, in the Italian example in (1b), the two negative constituents do not cancel each other out; rather, they reinforce each other. Italian is an NC language, while SE is not.

(1) a. No-one did nothing.   (SE: DN)
         (i.e., everyone did something)

     b. Nessuno ha   fatto niente.   (Italian: NC)
         no-one   has done nothing
         'No-one did *any*thing.'

From section 3.2 on, I deal with Jespersen's observation that whether or not a language is an NC language depends on where it stands in the Negative Cycle, that is, on the nature of its regular negative marker. In other words, whether or not a language is an NC language depends on whether its regular negative marker is generated under Neg° or associated with SpecNegP. Jespersen's observation is formulated as the generalization in (2):

(2) Jespersen's Generalization:
     A language is an NC language iff the regular marker of pure sentential negation is not associated with SpecNegP.

---

1. The distinction between the behavior of co-occurring negatives in NC and non-NC languages resembles the distinction between mathematical addition and multiplication of negatives. Where two negatives are added, the result is an even greater negative (cf. NC); where two negatives are multiplied, the result is positive (cf. non-NC). The apparent "disobedience" of NC probably explains why it is often vociferously condemned by prescriptivists, for example, in the anglophone world.

Section 3.2 is devoted to showing that (2) is a sturdy generalization.

Clearly, (2) is nothing more than a descriptive generalization that needs to be accounted for on the basis of fundamental principles. Before turning to such an account, I reconsider, in section 3.3, the spec-head agreement mechanism in Haegeman and Zanuttini's (henceforth, H&Z's) (1991: 244) Neg Criterion, the wellformedness condition governing the distribution and interpretation of negative constituents with sentential scope that I characterized, in section 1.4, as a construction-specific version of the more general AFFECT criterion. According to the Neg Criterion, irrespective of where a given language stands in the Negative Cycle, that is, irrespective of whether the overt marker of sentential negation is a functional head or an XP operator, *both* a "negative" head *and* a "negative" XP are syntactically active and "agree" with each other in a spec-head configuration. In section 3.3.2, I suggest that spec-head "agreement" should be reinterpreted as "nonincompatibility" in the light of Rizzi's (1996) work on Dynamic Agreement (henceforth, DA). DA is crucially deemed to be unidirectional, transferring features from SpecXP to $X°$ but not from $X°$ to SpecXP. In a spec-head configuration, then, in which a feature such as [+NEG] is borne by SpecXP but not $X°$, DA will transfer the feature to $X°$ (as I showed, crucially, in my analysis of *ne* and *pas* in chapters 1 and 2); in contrast, if the feature is borne by $X°$ but not by SpecXP, DA will not transfer the feature to SpecXP.

Returning to the (Neg) Criterion, within the revised approach to spec-head "agreement" advocated here, the agreement requirement needs to be modified: provided SpecXP does not bear any feature that is incompatible with the one(s) borne by $X°$, the (Neg) Criterion may be met *even though* the feature borne by $X°$ has not been passed on to SpecXP. It is in this sense that spec-head agreement is seen as compatibility rather than feature identity.

This revised approach to spec-head agreement allows the locus of the *abstract* feature [+NEG] to be subject to cyclic fluctuation—not just underlyingly—in the same way as the *overt* realization of sentential negation. In turn, this amounts to the claim that there is an abstract semanticosyntactic Negative Cycle alongside Jespersen's overt morphophonological Negative Cycle. In the same way that sentential negation does not have to be *overtly* associated with both Neg° and SpecNegP, neither does the *abstract* feature [+NEG] have to appear on *both* Neg° *and* SpecNegP in order for the Neg Criterion to be satisfied. This weaker version of spec-head agreement is exploited in section 3.4.1.3 to account for Jespersen's Generalization.

In section 3.4, I turn to the descriptive Jespersen's Generalization in (2) and endeavor to offer an account in terms of underlying grammatical principles. That account centers on the licensing of negative quantifiers and NPIs and the relationship between these items and negative markers proper. Before offering my own analysis, I review approaches to negative polarity item (henceforth, NPI) licensing proposed by Zanuttini (1991), based on L-marking (section 3.4.1.1), and by Progovac (1994), based on A'-binding (section 3.4.1.2). I conclude that Zanuttini's L-marking approach does not achieve empirical adequacy. At the same time, Progovac's A'-binding proposal raises a number of theory-internal questions. More precisely, while Progovac identifies clear parallels between the distribution of pronominals and anaphors on the one hand and negative quantifiers and NPIs on the other, her (A'-binding) analysis of negative quantifier and NPI licensing has a number of undesirable dissimilarities with the traditional (A-binding) analysis of the distribution of anaphors and pronouns. In addition, Progovac's A'-binding model is incapable of dealing with the attested cross-linguistic and diachronic variation at the heart of the Negative Cycle. In short, Progovac's proposal cannot, as it stands, account for the distinction between NC and non-NC languages.

In section 3.4.1.3, I propose an analysis of Jespersen's Generalization, based on Progovac's account of NPI licensing that resolves the problems mentioned with respect to Progovac's original proposals. Specifically, the analysis exploits the flexibility of the "weak" version of the spec-head relationship argued for in section 3.3.2. Together with an A'-binding mechanism that is more strictly parallel to the A-binding mechanism invoked in anaphor/pronoun licensing, the approach can deal with the attested cross-linguistic and diachronic variation that Progovac's analysis fails to capture. The proposed analysis is applied to concrete examples in section 3.4.2.

Section 3.5 deals with two apparent problems for Jespersen's Generalization, namely West Flemish (section 3.5.1) and Modern French (section 3.5.2). As a prelude to the analysis of negative adverbs and arguments in chapters 4 and 5, it is argued that Modern French is not in fact even an apparent problem for Jespersen's Generalization since the relevant and apparently "concordant" items are not in fact underlyingly negative; as for West Flemish, it is argued that, while the data do indeed represent counterexamples to Jespersen's Generalization as formulated in (2), other factors about the grammar suggest that this language is not problematic for the underlying explanation of Jespersen's Generalization proposed in section 3.4. It is argued that the properties of sentential negation in West Flemish actually provide empirical support for the approach proposed in section 3.4.1.3. In section 3.6.1, I speculate about another area of recent theoretical debate, namely the *pro*-drop or null subject parameter, which could possibly be illuminated by the suggestions made here. My conclusions are summarized in section 3.6.2.

3.1 The Negative Cycle

3.1.1 The data: Jespersen

Jespersen (1924) observes a cyclic pattern in the diachronic development of the overt marking of sentential negation. This cyclic pattern is known as the Negative Cycle and is illustrated in Germanic and Romance in (3) and (4) respectively, after Jespersen (1924: 335–36). The dates for the respective stages of the development in (3) are from Bennis et al. (1995b, 1997: 1010 (9)).

(3) *English*:[2]
    a. he ne secgeþ.   ("classical" Old English)
    b. he ne seiþ not.   (Middle English)
    c. he says not.   (late Middle English → late 17th century)
    d. he not says.   (early 15th century → second half 18th century)
    e. he does not say.   (15th century → present)
    f. he doesn't say.   (±1600 → present)

(4) *French*:[3]
    a. jeo ne di.   (→ 1600)
    b. je ne dis (pas).   (1600 → 1700)
    c. je ne dis pas.   (Standard written French)
    d. je (ne) dis pas.   (Standard spoken French)
    e. je   dis pas.   (Colloquial French)
        'I don't say.'

The sequences in (3) and (4) reflect the diachronic development in the respective languages;[4] however, contemporary languages are known to exemplify the various stages in the sequences.[5] In the "first"[6] instance, for example, sentential negation is marked by a pre-verbal, syntactically dependent, element alone, as in (4a). This is where Italian and Spanish currently stand in the Negative Cycle:

(5) a. Gianni *non* telefona a sua madre.   (Italian, Haegeman
        G.   *non* telephones to his mother   1995: 195 (43a))
        'G. doesn't phone his mother.'

2. The stage represented here by (3d) was not included in Jespersen's paradigm. It has been included here to take into account the work of Beukema (1994) and Bennis et al. (1995a, b, 1997). Beukema and his colleagues argue that the pattern in (3d) was rare and essentially served as a bridge between (3c) and (3e).

3. For discussion of the Negative Cycle in French, see Hopper and Traugott (1993: 58), McMahon (1994: 161–66), Price (1984: 252–57), Schwegler (1988: 26, 45–46), and Winters (1987). See also sections 3.1.2 and 3.5.2, as well as section 4.3.2.

4. To the extent that the illustrations in the text show nothing more than how sentential negation is overtly marked, they are likely to be a simplification of the underlying facts. As has been argued earlier in this book (for example, section 1.2.4), and as I demonstrate later, the expression of sentential negation can involve non-overt operators. The importance of these elements, and of their changing nature, is, of course, masked in (3) and (4).

5. For cross-linguistic and typological work on negation, see Croft (1991), Dahl (1979), de Haan (1997), Payne (1985), Ramat et al. (1987), and the contributions to Kahrel and van den Berg (eds.) (1994).

6. The word "first" is in inverted commas since it would be wrong to give the impression that the relevant varieties have no history prior to the stages illustrated by (3a) and (4a). Posner (1985b: 265–67) suggests that the negative marker *non* was reanalyzed over time from being a sentence adverb in Latin to being a clitic-like element that forms part of the verbal complex, for example, *ne* in French in (4). (See also Posner 1996: 302–5.) According to Vennemann (1974: 366–68), this reanalysis was a natural consequence of the typological shift from XV to VX. (See Schwegler 1988: 37 for a useful illustration of how the reanalysis of an adverb in Latin as a functional head in French can be explained by the typological shift from OV to VO order.) Burridge (1993: chapter 5) critically discusses Vennemann's typological approach to the syntax of negation in the history of Dutch. See also footnote 71.

b. La niña *no* está hablando por teléfono. (Spanish, Haegeman
    the girl *no* is talking by telephone 1995: 227 (81a))
    'The girl isn't talking on the phone.'

The next stage in the overt Negative Cycle comes when the pre-verbal element is "reinforced" by a syntactically independent post-verbal constituent,[7]
first only optionally,[8] "with emphatic import",[9] as in (4b), then obligatorily, as in
(4c). Once the post-verbal element becomes compulsory, I assume it is inherently negative. It would seem that the position in the Negative Cycle occupied
by some dialects of Berber is the same as that occupied by French in (4b). In the
(null-subject) Taqbaylit dialect, sentential negation is marked by an (obligatory)
proclitic marker, *ur*, with optional emphatic reinforcement by an independent
post-verbal negative marker, *ara* (Jamal Ouhalla, personal communication).

(6) *Ur* zrigh   (*ara*) Idir.   (Taqbaylit dialect of Berber)
     ur saw-1SG *ara* I.
     'I didn't see I.'

Further, the following Burmese data attributed to Denise Bernot by Lazard
(1994) suggest that this language is at the same stage in the Negative Cycle as
the variety of Modern French exemplified in (4c). In Burmese, sentential negation is marked by both a pre-verbal negative marker, *mə*, and a post-verbal one,
Phù:[10]

(7) a. ʔloʔ θu mə caN   Phù.   (Lazard 1994: 26 (3))
         work him *mə* organize *Phù*
         'He doesn't organize his work.'

     b. ʔə̀co Ko mə cá   Phù.   (Lazard 1994: 26 (2))
         profit REL *mə* happen *Phù*
         'There is no profit.'

     c. mìN ùN   mə θa   Phù là.   (Bernot 1980: 98, cited by
         you stomach *mə* be-happy *Phù* Q   Lazard 1994: 115 (86))
         'Aren't you satisfied?'

In the next stage of the Negative Cycle, the independent post-verbal negative
marker suffices to mark sentential negation on its own, and the clitic marker

---

7. A number of researchers, including Schwegler (1988: 26), have pointed out that the post-verbal
"reinforcer" is often a nominal element denoting a small amount. See chapter 2, footnote 29.

8. According to Hirschbühler and Labelle (1993: 3), in French "*ne* can be the sole lexical negative
element in a clause, and it is used alone much more than in combination with *pas* or *point*" "until at
least the end of the sixteenth century".

9. This phraseology is taken from Posner (1985a: 184). Posner suggests that, prior to the late fourteenth century, French *pas* had "emphatic import".

10. In the bipartite system of sentential negation used in some clause types in Fɔn, the pre-verbal
marker, *má*, is associated with SpecNegP, while the post-verbal marker, *ǎ*, is associated with Neg° (da
Cruz 1992, reported in DeGraff 1993b: 87). See also Navajo (Speas 1991b: 394-95; and chapter 2,
footnote 6).

becomes first optional, as in (4d), then disappears altogether, as in (4e). The data in (8) suggest that spoken Breton is at the same stage in the Negative Cycle as the variety of Modern French exemplified in (4d). In spoken Breton, sentential negation is marked by obligatory post-verbal *ket* and, optionally, by pre-verbal *ne*:[11]

(8) a. *Ne* ziskenn *ket* ar vugale betek an hent.   (Standard Breton,
         ne go-down *ket* the children to   the road   Stephens 1993: 397)
         'The children are not going down to the road.'

     b. 'ziskenn *ket* ar vugale betek an hent.   (Spoken Breton, Stephens
         (= (8a))   1993: 398)

In the "final" stage, the independent post-verbal negative marker weakens and is susceptible to reanalysis, or grammaticalization, in the sense of Hopper and Traugott (1993). The Negative Cycle is discussed further in section 3.1.2, where I suggest a structural template with which to view the developments.

3.1.2 The analysis: NegP

Pollock's NegP hypothesis, discussed and exploited in section 1.2.1 and chapter 2, that is, the idea that the locus of polarity features is an independent functional projection, provides Jespersen's Negative Cycle with a structural template within which to operate. NegP provides two positions, SpecNegP and Neg°, a phrasal position and a head position. This is particularly convenient for an account of Jespersen's typology of sentential negation and the Negative Cycle. Negative markers "comparatively small in phonetic bulk" identified by Jespersen can quite naturally be analysed as Neg°, while "fuller negatives" can be associated with SpecNegP. The relevant configuration is exemplified for Modern French in (9).

(9)

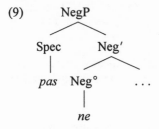

So, and simplifying grossly (see footnote 4), the (overt) Negative Cycle can be claimed to amount to cyclic to-ing and fro-ing of the overt realization of sentential negation between these two positions.

11. See also section 3.5.1 for discussion of West Flemish, which also seems to be at this stage in the Negative Cycle.

The stage reached by English and illustrated in (3f), in which the independent XP negative marker cliticizes onto the verb, can be analyzed in interesting ways within the NegP hypothesis. In SE, the relationship between *not* and the verb in (3f) is likely to be purely phonological in nature. In other words, the negative marker is syntactically associated with SpecNegP, but subsequently cliticizes onto the auxiliary verb in AgrS°.[12] In a number of nonstandard varieties of English, in contrast, it seems more likely that the negative marker is associated with a head position in underlying syntax. This distinction between SE and nonstandard varieties is exploited further in sections 3.2.1.2 and 3.2.2.1. (See Zanuttini 1991 and Pollock 1997b.)

Reanalysis of the SpecNegP-associated negative marker (*pas*) as a Neg°-associated element does not appear to have happened (yet) in metropolitan French, even in the most informal spoken registers. However, some researchers (e.g., Moritz and Valois 1994: 679fn12) have suggested that *pas* has been at least partially reanalyzed as a head in Québécois. Thus, in parallel to *not* in SE (see footnote 34), in Québécois, *pas* may have the dual status of head and maximal projection. Moritz and Valois venture that the status of *pas* in Québécois as a Neg°-associated element rather than a SpecNegP-associated element might form the basis of a principled explanation of the contrast between (10a) and (10b):

(10) a. J'ai   pas vu   personne.   (Standard Modern French)
         I have *pas* seen *personne*
         'I haven't seen no-one.'
         (= 'I have seen someone.')

     b. J'ai   pas vu   personne.   (Québécois)
         I have *pas* seen *personne*
         'I haven't seen anyone.'
         (= the opposite of (10a))

Thus, and without going into unnecessary detail at this point, the (apparent) NC interpretation of (10b) in Québécois is deemed to be possible because *pas* is generated as Neg°. The same interpretation is unavailable in Standard Modern French because *pas* is associated with SpecNegP. While Moritz and Valois's approach ties in well with Jespersen's Generalization in that it links the availability of NC with the syntactic nature of the negative marker, I reject the proposal that *pas* has grammaticalized as Neg° in the relevant varieties. The fact that *pas* and quantifiers like *personne* could co-occur in earlier stages in the development of the language (when Neg° was occupied by *ne*) and be interpreted as in the Québécois example in (10b) casts some doubt on the assumption that the interpretation of (10b) depends on the position of *pas* being Neg°. Quite apart from the implausible idea that Neg° could be occupied by both *ne* and *pas*

---

12. See Haegeman (1995: 189–90, section 1.4.4), Zwicky and Pullum (1983), and footnote 34 for discussion of *n't*.

in older varieties of French, one would also have to conclude that *pas*, associated with Neg° in the classical language, had degrammaticalized and been analyzed as an XP in the modern standard language, only to regrammaticalize as a head in Québécois. This strikes me as a highly implausible way to account for the data. (See Hopper and Traugott 1993.) Furthermore, the element *pas* in Québécois behaves in identical fashion to *pas* in Standard French, casting doubt on any claim that one is a syntactic head while the other is a syntactic specifier. For example, *pas* in Québécois can be modified, for example, by *même* 'even', just like *pas* in Standard French. More important, *pas* in Québécois fails to interfere with Verb Movement, just like *pas* in Standard French (Déprez forthcoming). Finally, there has been no typological shift to motivate reanalysis of *pas* as a syntactic head. (See also section 4.4.2.1.) I therefore reject an account of interpretations such as (10b) that are based on the conclusion that, in Québécois, *pas* occupies Neg°. I return to the distinction between the standard language and varieties that behave like Québécois in section 4.5.2, where I offer an alternative proposal.

With regard to the idea of the grammaticalization of *pas* as a negative head, similar—and more plausible—claims have been made for the negative marker *pa* found in *some* French-based creoles.[13] In all French-based creoles (apart from Réunionnais, according to Corne and Moorghen 1978, cited by Posner 1985a: 182, and according to Battye and Hintze 1992: 325; see also Louisiana French Creole), *pa* is pre-verbal (along with tense-mood-aspect markers), rather than post-verbal as in both metropolitan French and Québécois (Posner 1985a: 171, 180), suggesting perhaps that *pa* is a head rather than an XP.

(11) a. Li *pa* t   av   ap   vīnī.   (Haitian, D'Ans 1968,
         he NEG PST FUT PROG come   cited by Posner 1985a: 180)
         'He wouldn't be coming.'

     b. Nu *pa* ti   pu   rãtre.   (Mauritian, Green 1988: 450)
         we NEG PST PROS go-back
         'We wouldn't have gone back.'

As Chris Lyons has pointed out (personal communication), the issue arises as to whether its pre-verbal position is enough for one to conclude that creole *pa* is a head. An alternative would be to suggest that creole *pa*, like French *pas*, occupies the SpecNegP position and that the verb fails to raise to the left of it, as witnessed, for example, by infinitives in French (see sections 1.1.7.2–1.1.7.4). This theoretical possibility is supported by the fact that, in most creoles, *pa* comes directly between the subject and the tense-mood-aspect markers, as in (11). Indeed, Posner (1985a: 181–82 (18i) and (21ii)) cites just two examples of French-based creoles in which *pa* intervenes between a tense-mood-aspect mar-

---

13. See the comments by Posner (1985a: 172, 180–83). Note also that Bickerton (1981) claims that NC is a characteristic of all creoles.

ker and the verb, as in (12a), or between two tense-mood-aspect markers, as in (12b):

(12) a. Mo te *pa* konẽ.   (Louisiana [Saint Martin][14],
         I   PST NEG know   Morgan 1959, 1976)
         'I didn't know.'

    b.   Mwe te *pa* apre mãze.   (Réunionnais,
         I   PST NEG PROG eat   Corne and Moorghen 1978)
         'I wasn't eating.'

Nevertheless, in the more familiar Romance varieties, reflexes of the Latin adverb *non* usually intervene between the subject pronoun and any other pronouns present. They do not intervene between object pronouns and the verb.[15] As far as I know, no-one has used this fact to cast doubt on analyses of such elements as realizations of Neg°, that is, as heads. The particular matter of the syntactic status of Haitian Creole *pa* is taken up by DeGraff (1993b), who concludes that this element is the overt realization of Neg°.

Returning now to the Negative Cycle, once the negative marker is a syntactically dependent element again, the development has, in some sense, turned full circle. Numerous suggestions have been made to explain the Negative Cycle, that is, why, in the specific case of French, pre-verbal *ne* came first to be supported by a post-verbal element and subsequently to disappear. Most explanations have been phonological in approach, for example, those of Ewert (1943: 260) and Posner (1996: 303). Posner (1985a) examines the factors that might have conditioned the change in French from pre-verbal to post-verbal negation by comparing French and a number of other cognate languages (which have post-verbal negation) on the one hand with the majority group of Romance languages (which have pre-verbal negation) on the other. She suggests (pp. 171, 177) that changes in stress patterns, namely the transition, possibly in the fourteenth century, from word stress to breath group stress, favored a shift in

---

14. Of relevance in (mesolectal) Louisiana Creole is the fact that, where Verb Movement can be motivated on the basis of (a) its morphological makeup and (b) its position with respect to VP-adverbs, the verb *precedes* negative *pa*. Where no Verb Movement can be motivated, the verb follows negative *pa* (Rottet 1992: 268 (16)). Under the null hypothesis that the position of *pa* is the same in both cases, these facts mitigate strongly against analyzing *pa* as a functional head such as Neg°, since such an analysis would entail at least one instance of long head movement of the verb on its way from V° to whatever functional head it occupies in its pre-*pa* position (T° in Rottet's 1992: 278 (46) analysis). In addition, the fact that Verb Movement in mesolectal Louisiana Creole is incompatible with overt tense-mood-aspect markers but not with negative *pa* (Rottet 1992: 277) suggests that *pa* should not be treated in the same way as the overt tense-mood-aspect markers (functional heads). (DeGraff 1992, 1993b actually analyzes the tense-mood-aspect markers of Haitian Creole as verbs.) Rottet (1992: 285) therefore concludes that *pa* in mesolectal Louisiana Creole is associated with SpecNegP, rather than being generated in Neg°. This is arguably due to decreolization under strong influence from the acrolectal Cajun French dialect. A similar analysis is plausible of the Réunionnais data, given the extent of decreolization there, too. (Thanks to John Green for discussing the creole data with me.) See also DeGraff (1997).

15. Zanuttini (1997a: 217) gives the northern Italian dialect of Cairese as an exception.

emphatic stress toward the end of the breath group. Consequently, pre-verbal unstressed elements—including *ne*—were slurred, while post-verbal elements like *pas* often received emphatic stress.

It is also possible that more strictly syntactic issues are involved. Harris (1978: 118) suggests that the fate of *ne* could have been sealed by the fact that its position between subject clitics and object clitics hindered incorporation of the former with the latter (and the verb). Parry (1996) also links the loss of the pre-verbal negative marker with the accumulation of argument clitics in pre-verbal position. (Note, though, that this factor is likely to be sensitive to the null subject parameter.) Finally, as was noted in footnote 6, an underlying typological shift from XV to VX might explain the reanalysis of the pre-verbal negative marker in Romance from an XP adverbial element to a functional head. (See also Posner 1996: 304.)

Whatever the ultimate cause(s) of the (transitions between the different phases of the) Negative Cycle, the label "cycle" is clearly not a misnomer: once the syntactically independent negative marker has been grammaticalized as a functional head, the language is back where it started, and the cycle can be repeated.[16] Jespersen's overt Negative Cycle can therefore be reduced to fluctuation between marking sentential negation as a syntactically dependent constituent and as a syntactically *in*dependent constituent, with one intermediate stage in which sentential negation is bipartite and another in which the negative marker has an ambivalent status:

(13) *The Negative Cycle*:
    a. $\text{Neg}°$
    b. $\text{Neg}°$ (+ XP)
    c. $\text{Neg}°$ + XP
    d. $(\text{Neg}°)$ + XP
    e.   XP
    f. $[_{\text{Neg}°} \text{ XP }]$

3.1.3   Extensions: a prelude to an abstract Negative Cycle?

Given the availability within NegP of two positions of clearly different syntactic types, one head and one specifier, and mechanisms such as H&Z's (1991) Neg Criterion (section 1.3) and DA (section 1.2.4) to regulate the behavior of affective features such as [+NEG], there are, in principle at least, two potential posi-

---

16. Meillet (1912b: 140), cited in McMahon (1994: 165), comments as follows: "Les langues suivent ainsi une sorte de développement en spirale: elles ajoutent des mots accessoires pour obtenir une expression intense; ces mots s'affaiblissent, se dégradent et tombent au niveau de simples outils grammaticaux; on ajoute de nouveaux mots ou des mots différents en vue de l'expression; l'affablissement recommence, et ainsi sans fin." (So languages follow a kind of spiral development: extra words are added to heighten expressive power; these words then weaken, are eroded, and reduced to mere grammatical devices; new or different words are added for the sake of expressivity; the weakening begins again, and so on, and so on.)

tions within NegP with which [+NEG] can be associated (underlyingly, at least), as well as the possibility that [+NEG] is associated with both positions underlyingly. The empirical basis of Jespersen's Negative Cycle certainly suggests that the overt *morphophonological* locus of sentential negation can shift cyclically between SpecNegP and Neg°, with intermediate stages at which both positions are associated with phonological material or the overt negative marker has an ambivalent status. Under the assumption that sentential negation is always marked by an abstract *syntacticosemantic* feature [+NEG], there is, I suggest, no a priori reason to assume that the underlying locus of this abstract feature cannot fluctuate cyclically in (something like) the same way as the overt marker. This possibility has been implicitly recognized in the earlier discussion of non-overt negative operators. It is pursued and elaborated upon in section 3.3 and proves to be central to the proposed account of NC, to which I now turn.

3.2   NC and Jespersen's Generalization

Languages vary with respect to whether they allow multiple apparently inherently negative constituents to appear, say, within the same clause, without canceling each other out. Van der Wouden (1994: 95) distinguishes between two phenomena that he labels "negative spread" and "negative doubling".[17] Negative doubling is illustrated in (14a) and (15a) in the NC languages Spanish and Italian respectively.[18] Here, a negative XP, *nadie/nessuno* 'no-one', appears

---

17. The term "negative doubling" is also used in this way by Rizzi (e.g., 1982: 121). In early work, Labov (1972b) analyzes NC in nonstandard varieties of English as a process whereby the feature [NEG] is copied from the verb onto an indefinite.

18. It is only partially the case that Italian and Spanish show negative doubling. This is only generally so in the absence of pre-verbal negative XPs, as in text examples (14a) and (15a). In contrast, with a negative (subject) XP in pre-verbal position, negative doubling is excluded:

(i) a.   Nessuno (*non) ha telefonato.   (Italian)
          no-one   *non* has phoned
          'No-one phoned.'
     b.   Nadie (*no) hará   eso.   (Spanish, Suñer 1993: 3)
          no-one   *no* do-FUT that
          'No-one will do that.'

This contrasts with, for example, Serbian/Croatian, text example (23b), and a number of other Romance varieties, including Romanian and Ladin (a Rhaeto-Romansch variety spoken in Engadine, Switzerland):

(ii) Nimeni *nu* îmi   spune niciodată nimic.   (Romanian, Baciu 1978: 74,
      no-one *nu* to-me says   never   nothing   cited in Muller 1991: 305fn2)
      'No-one ever tells me anything.'

(iii) Alura üngün *nu* so   nouvas d' ünguotta.   (Ladin, Scheitlin 1962/72: 74, 97,
      so   no-one *nu* knows news   of no-one   cited in Muller 1991: 301)
      'So, no-one has any news about anyone.'

In the case of Ladin, Posner (1984: 13) tentatively attributes co-occurrence of the pre-verbal negative XP and the negative marker to Slavonic influence.

Where a *nonsubject* appears pre-verbally in Italian, the possibility of negative doubling appears to be subject to speaker and register variation (Acquaviva 1994; Haegeman 1995: 196):

together with—"doubled" by—the regular pre-verbal negative marker, namely *no/ non*. Examples (14b) and (15b) illustrate negative spread, whereby multiple negative XPs co-occur. Examples (14c) and (15c) show negative spread and negative doubling occurring simultaneously.

(14) a.   *No* conozco a *nadie*.   (Spanish)
      no know-1SG no-one
      'I don't know anyone.'

    b.   *Nadie* me ha dado *nada*.
      no-one me has given nothing
      'No-one has given me anything.'

    c.   *No* doy   *nada*   a *nadie*.
      no give-1SG nothing to no-one
      'I'm not giving anything to anyone.'

(15) a.   Mario *non* ha visto *nessuno*.   (Italian)
      M.   *non* has seen no-one
      'M. hasn't seen anyone.'

    b.   *Nessuno* ha fatto *niente*.
      no-one   has done nothing
      'No-one did anything.'

    c.   Gianni *non* dice *niente* a *nessuno*.
      G.   *non* says nothing to no-one
      'G. doesn't say anything to anyone.'

The crucial property of all the examples in (14) and (15) is that, although all the italicized constituents (the regular negative marker and the negative XPs) are arguably morphologically negative,[19] each sentence is interpreted as a single instance of sentential negation. They are not interpreted as containing multiple instances of logical negation. Spanish and Italian are NC languages.

    Languages that do not allow *multiple* occurrences of negative constituents to be interpreted as a *single* instance of sentential negation are termed non-NC lan-

---

(iv) A nessuno Gianni (*??*non*) telefona.   (Haegeman 1995: 196 (43c))
    to no-one G.   *non* telephones
    'G. doesn't call anyone.'
In similar configurations in Spanish, negative doubling is not attested:
(v)   A ninguna de ellos (*no) llamaría yo.   (Suñer 1993: 3)
    to none of them *no* call-COND I
    'I wouldn't call any of them.'
For cross-Romance discussion of NC, see Posner (1996: 148–49, 302–5).
    19. Etymologically, Spanish n-words are not negative (Laka 1993a). For contemporary speakers, however, one could plausibly assume that these elements are analyzed as being inherently (morphologically) negative. The situation in Italian is different; for Acquaviva (1995: 14fn3), *nessuno*, for example, is derived from the Vulgar Latin *ne-ipsu-unu* 'not-even-one', in other words etymologically negative.

guages. In these languages, where two negatives co-occur, the first negation takes scope over, and cancels, the second. Examples are SE and German:

(16) a. I've (*not*) seen *no-one*.   (SE)
    b. I've %(*not*) given *nothing* to *no-one*.

(17) a. Hans sieht *niemanden* (*nicht*).   (German)
       H.   sees no-one   not
       'H. can't see anyone.'

    b. Ich bin mit *niemandem nirgendwohin* %(*nicht*) gefahren.
       I   am with no-one   nowhere   not   travelled
       'I didn't drive anywhere with anyone.'

The SE examples in (16) show that one or more negative XPs cannot co-occur with the verbal marker of negation *not* (and receive the relevant NC interpretation). SE does not, therefore, demonstrate negative doubling. With respect to negative spread, the issue of whether *multiple* negative XPs can co-occur is unclear. Some speakers as well as prescriptivists reject (16b) without *not*; others do not. Dialectal variation seems to be at play. Clearly, though, negative spread needs to be distinguished from negative doubling. The judgments in (17) suggest that German patterns essentially with SE in this respect.

Ascertaining whether the Negative Cycle is relevant to NC amounts to establishing whether there is a correlation between (a) whether a language is an NC language and (b) where it stands in the Negative Cycle. Such a correlation would suggest that one was determined by the other. Given considerations of learnability, this would presumably mean that where a language stands in the Negative Cycle determines whether or not it is an NC language. Jespersen (1924: 333) suggests that there is such a correlation:

> There is one very important observation to be made, without which I do not think that we shall be able to understand the matter, namely that repeated negation [i.e., NC] becomes an habitual phenomenon in those languages only in which the ordinary negative element is comparatively small in phonetic bulk. . . . If this repetition is rarer in modern English and German than it was formerly, one of the reasons probably is that the fuller negative *not* and *nicht* have taken the place of the smaller *ne* and *en*.

Following my analysis of the Negative Cycle within the framework of the NegP hypothesis in section 3.1.2, I shall assume that Jespersen's observation amounts to what I referred to as Jespersen's Generalization in (2),[20] repeated here for convenience:

---

20. Note the following observation made by Acquaviva (1993: 60–61): "We can now formally characterize the difference between the English and the Romance (and nonstandard English) operators: only [in] the latter are specifiers of heads endowed with the morphological negative feature."

My analysis of Jespersen's Generalization differs in crucial ways from Acquaviva's; this is discussed in section 3.4.

(18) Jespersen's Generalization:
A language is an NC language iff the regular marker of pure sentential negation is not associated with SpecNegP.[21]

3.2.1 NC and nonnegative SpecNegP

In this section, I provide cross-linguistic data to show that NC is a characteristic of languages for which there is no reason to believe that SpecNegP bears the feature [+NEG],[22] that is, languages in which sentential negation is marked essentially in association with a syntactic head. The languages that follow this pattern include Serbian/Croatian, certain nonstandard varieties of English, and, as indicated in the previous section, Italian and Spanish. In addition to those languages already discussed here, Zanuttini (1991: 149, 161) gives data that show that Middle High German, Middle Dutch, Portuguese, and Catalan all fit into this category; Jamal Ouhalla informs me that Berber and Turkish belong here, too. Parry (1996) says that all modern dialects of Italy whose negative marker would be analyzed as a realization of Neg° are NC languages. DeGraff (1993b) argues that Haitian Creole, in which the negative marker *pa* is analyzed as Neg°, is also an NC language and, therefore, belongs in this group.

3.2.1.1 Serbian/Croatian

In Serbian/Croatian (henceforth, SC), pure sentential negation is realized as a negative particle, *ne* (Neg°), proclitic on the first finite verb form (Progovac 1994: 34–35):

---

21. Note that my interpretation of Jespersen's observation is slightly different from the one tentatively proposed by Haegeman (1995: 165). In the context of Jespersen's observation, Haegeman suggests that NC may be determined by the availability of an overt negative head. See also Haegeman (1991: 16):

> We might propose that in languages with NC readings the head of NegP is "strong": it is autonomously licensed: it has its NEG feature in the base. The Neg Criterion is met by a "strong" static agreement configuration. In non-NC languages, on the other hand, Neg is "weak" and would be assigned the NEG feature by its specifier by virtue of spec-head agreement. . . . What is crucial for NC . . . is that the NEG feature on Neg° is independently licensed, i.e., that Neg° is a strong head. In languages where the NEG feature on Neg° can only be achieved via dynamic agreement the negative head is not strong and NC is not possible.

For me, in contrast, NC correlates with the *absence* of a negative operator in SpecNegP. Assuming that the characterization of the data in sections 3.1 and 3.1.2 is correct and that languages can indeed mark sentential negation by overt material associated with both SpecNegP and Neg°, the difference between Haegeman's and my own (re-)interpretation of Jespersen's observation is not a trivial one. Note also that Haegeman's approach predicts that Modern French is a non-NC language. See section 3.5.2.

22. The consequences of the spec-head agreement mechanism inherent in the Neg Criterion notwithstanding, which is, in any case, discussed in section 3.3.2.

(19) Milan poznaje Marij-u.   (SC)
    Mi.   knows Ma.- ACC
    'Mi. knows Ma.'

(20) Milan *ne* poznaje Marij-u.
    'Mi. doesn't know Ma.'

(21) ⋆Milan poznaje *ne* Marij-u.

No other overt negative marker is required; *ne* cannot be omitted from negative clauses (Progovac 1994: 36); *ne* forms a syntactic unit with the finite verb. I conclude, therefore, that Neg° bears the feature [+NEG] underlyingly, rather than SpecNegP. If the generalization in (2) is correct, I predict that SC is an NC language.

SC has two series of what Progovac (1994) terms NPIs, labeled *i*-NPIs and *ni*-NPIs to reflect the fact that members of one set begin with the prefix *i*- while members of the second begin with the prefix *ni*-. Progovac glosses the *i*-NPIs and *ni*-NPIs as *anyone, anything*, and so on, and *no-one, nothing*, and so on, respectively, but stresses (Progovac 1994: 40, 42) that the distribution of these elements is by no means identical to that of the two series of indefinites in SE. A couple of comments are in order at this point. First, the fact that the distribution of the *i*- and *ni*-NPIs in SC is different from the distribution of the *any*- and *no*-XPs respectively in SE does not *necessarily* mean that the *i*-NPIs differ from the *any*-XPs or that the *ni*-NPIs differ from the *no*-XPs in respect of any nontrivial properties. It is entirely possible that the corresponding XPs in the two languages are essentially identical and that their divergent distributions are the result of differences elsewhere in the grammars of their respective languages. Indeed, this is what I conclude later in this chapter.[23]

Second, a word is perhaps in order on the issue of Progovac's use of the term NPI for the *ni*-prefixed series of XPs in SC. One might wonder whether the *ni*-XPs of SC (or, indeed, the *no*-XPs of SE or the n-words of various Romance varieties) are NPIs at all. These elements are more usually labeled negative indefinite universal quantifiers (with no particular licensing conditions) rather than polarity items (with specific—albeit complex—licensing conditions). However, there is some reason to suspect that even negative quantifiers (with

---

23. My view here contrasts sharply with that expressed in Acquaviva (1995) and Déprez (forthcoming), who seem to follow Progovac's line. In his account of NC, Acquaviva concludes that the relevant distinction between NC languages and non-NC languages concerns the properties of negative quantifiers. Thus, for Acquaviva, the fact that Italian is NC while SE is not is a consequence of the difference between, say, *nessuno* and *no-one*. My feeling is that this approach is counterintuitive for a number of reasons. First, it ignores Jespersen's Generalization entirely. Second, it leads to the conclusion that, for example, *nothing, no-one*, and so on, are fundamentally different in (non-NC) SE, on the one hand, and (NC) nonstandard and older varieties of English, on the other. For Déprez (forthcoming), too, the key to the NC/non-NC distinction is to be found in "the diverging structure and semantic nature of the N-words" (1995b: 4). Déprez (1992) and DeGraff (1993b: 75–76, section 6.2) disagree along these lines about how best to account for the differences between NC in Haitian Creole and Standard French. See footnote 30.

sentential scope) have licensing conditions and that, consequently, the term NPI may not be misplaced. As Haegeman (1996b: 1) puts it, these elements "carry the semantic-syntactic feature NEG and . . . this feature is subject to a specific syntactic licensing condition". (See also Rizzi 1982: 121–27, section 2, for relevant discussion.) There is, for example, evidence that the presence of negative quantifiers has necessary consequences–albeit sometimes non-overt–elsewhere in their clauses. In SC, for example, *ni*-NPIs necessarily co-occur with the preverbal negative marker *ne*. The presence of *ne* clearly satisfies some licensing condition of the *ni*-NPIs in much the same way that c-commanding negation is one way of licensing *any*-XPs in SE which are labeled NPIs without hesitation. Similar conditions can be argued to apply to negative quantifiers in other languages. Even in a language like SE, the presence of a negative quantifier can affect clausal polarity, even though this has no overt impact on verb morphology. For example, when familiar tests are performed on (22a) to determine the polarity of the sentence, they show it to be potentially negative:[24]

(22) a. John's done nothing.
     b. John's done nothing and neither/?so has Mary.
     c. John's done nothing, has he/?hasn't he?

I therefore conclude that negative quantifiers (with sentential scope) such as *ni*-NPIs (SC), *no*-XPs (SE), and n-words (Romance) are indeed polarity items in the sense that their occurrence is subject to licensing conditions.[25] In this respect, I am therefore happy to retain the term *ni*-NPI used for SC by Progovac and to adopt the term *no*-NPI for SE for consistency.[26] I now return to the discussion of SC negation.

The most salient characteristic of the *ni*-NPIs in SC is that, irrespective of their position, they must, as already mentioned, be clause-mate with the preverbal negative marker *ne* (Progovac 1994: 37 (98)):[27]

(23) a. Mario ⋆(*ne*) vidi *ni(t)ko-ga*.   (SC)
     M.   *ne* sees no-one-ACC
     'M. can't see anyone.'

     b. *Ni(t)ko* ⋆(*ne*) poznaje Marij-u.
     no-one   *ne* knows M.- ACC
     'No-one knows M.'

---

24. I assume with Haegeman (1995) that, where the negative tag is licit in (22c), that is, where the antecedent is positive, the negative quantifier has local scope, does not count as an operator, and is not associated with a NegP. The wide scope reading of the negative is therefore dependent on clausal negation being marked on the verb; it is in this sense that the negative quantifier (on this reading) is licensed by the polarity of the clause. On tags, see Lakoff (1969) and section 1.3.

25. See Quer (1993) for review and discussion of approaches to the licensing of negative quantifiers.

26. Within the terms of his analysis, Acquaviva (1993: 24) suggests that those elements often referred to as negative quantifiers "are closer to polarity items than to *wh*-operators".

27. *Niko* is Serbian; *nitko* is Croatian. The judgments in the text examples apply to both Serbian and Croatian.

Furthermore, multiple *ni*-NPIs can co-occur in a given clause without leading to logical DN, provided, of course, that pre-verbal *ne* is also present in the same clause (Ljiljana Progovac, personal communication).

(24) Milan ⋆(*ne*) daje   *ni(t)kome ništa.*   (SC)
     M.   *ne* gives no-one   nothing
     'M. isn't giving anything to anyone.'

The examples in (23a, b) show negative doubling; the one in (24) shows both negative spread and negative doubling. SC is clearly an NC language, as predicted by the generalization in (2).

3.2.1.2 Nonstandard English

In this section, I use Cockney as a representative of a certain class of nonstandard varieties of English.[28] In Cockney, pure sentential negation is always realized as the contracted *n't* rather than *not*, even if the use of *not* allows contraction elsewhere:[29]

(25) a.   ('E) ai*n't* comin'.   (Cockney)
     b.   ⋆E's *not* comin'.

I take this contrast to be suggestive evidence that, in sentential negation in Cockney, the [+NEG] feature is associated with a head rather than SpecNegP. One might assume, for example, that the morpheme *n't* is generated as Neg° and that it raises to the finite verb in AgrS°. An alternative analysis would be to assume that the negative auxiliaries of Cockney, namely *ain't*, *can't*, *won't*, and *don't*, are drawn directly from the lexicon as inherently negative auxiliaries rather than as polarity-neutral auxiliaries, which are associated with a negative morpheme in the syntax. Such a view is supported by the fact that none of these negative auxiliaries shows overt person and number agreement (cf. SE *isn't* versus *aren't* and *doesn't* versus *don't*). The important point is that, in Cockney, the negative feature is associated underlyingly with a syntactic head; in SE, in contrast, it is associated with an XP specifier position.

If I am right in concluding that, in Cockney, the feature [+NEG] is borne by a syntactic head, Cockney matches SC. The generalization in (2) then predicts that Cockney is an NC language.[30] This prediction is borne out by the facts: Cockney

---

28. Thanks to Joe Cunningham for judgments on Cockney. See Labov (1972a, b) for discussion of other NSEs that demonstrate NC.

29. See Yaeger-Dror (1997) for pragmatic and sociolinguistic discussion of negative and auxiliary contraction.

30. Note that the approach adopted here to the distinction between the non-NC SE and nonstandard NC varieties such as Cockney and the variety of Belfast English described by Henry (1995) and referred to in footnote 31 assumes that the crucial difference lies at the level of the functional structure of the clause. This is in sharp contrast to the approach adopted by Acquaviva (1995) and Déprez (forthcoming), who assume that the crucial difference between NC and non-NC languages is to be found in the (operator-binding) properties of negative quantifiers. See footnote 23.

has negative doubling with *n't* (but not with *not*[31]), as in (26), as well as negative spread, as in (27):

(26) a.   I ai*n't* done *nothin'*.   (Cockney)
     b.   ⋆I've *not* done *nothin'*.

(27) *No-one* ai*n't* done *nothin'*.

It could be objected at this point that the data in (26) and (27) do not represent NC at all; rather, it could be concluded that, in varieties of NSE such as Cockney, *nothin'*, *no-one*, and so on, are negative polarity items *à la* SE *anything* or *anyone*, that is, not inherently negative. This is, however, unlikely. If NSE *no*-NPIs were equivalent to SE *any*-NPIs, one might expect the two series to have parallel distributions. However, the parallel between the behavior of NSE *no*-NPIs and SE *any*-NPIs is far from complete. Unlike the *any*-NPIs of SE, the concordant readings of *no*-NPIs in NSE are possible only in the presence of *sentential negation*, either in the same clause or in a higher clause.[32] *No*-NPIs cannot appear in *non*negative polarity contexts in Cockney/NSE, whereas SE *any*-NPIs can (Ladusaw 1992):[33]

(28) *NSE*:
     a.   If you see *anyone*/⋆*no-one*, let me know.   (Conditional)
     b.   I doubt *anyone*/⋆*no-one* will come.   (Adversative predicate)
     c.   Do you want *anythin'*/⋆*nothin'*?   (Interrogative)

In NSE, then, the behavior of *no*-NPIs is strikingly similar to that of *ni*-NPIs in SC, which are also ungrammatical in nonnegative polarity contexts (Progovac 1994) and clearly inherently negative. In conclusion, then, NSE *no*-NPIs are indeed inherently negative; hence, NSE demonstrates NC, as predicted by (2), given that SpecNegP does not bear the feature [+NEG].

3.2.1.3 Italian and Spanish

Data from Italian and Spanish to show that these languages fit the generalization in (2) have already been given. The data in (5) suggest that [+NEG] is borne by Neg° rather than SpecNegP. Pure sentential negation in Italian and Spanish is marked by the pre-verbal negative particles *non* and *no*, respectively, which, like

31. Henry (1995) describes another NSE, namely a variety of Belfast English, in which NC is possible with *n't* but not *not*. Compare (i) with (ii) (Henry's (35) and (36)):
(i)   We aren't going nowhere.
(ii)   ⋆We're not going nowhere.
     32. In this respect, Cockney differs from SC. In the former, the verbal negative marker is not obliged to appear in the same minimal clause as the *no*-NPIs. In the latter, it is. This may be related to the fact that, in Cockney, and in contrast to SC, for example, the verbal negative marker *n't* is compatible only with finite verb forms.
     33. Alison Henry (personal communication) informs me that the judgments in (28) also apply to the variety of Belfast English discussed in footnote 31.

SC *ne*, are proclitic on the first finite verb. Following the discussion in section 1.2.1, I assume these elements head NegP. More significant, these negative markers are sufficient to mark pure sentential negation. Furthermore, the data in (14) and (15) show that Italian and Spanish are both NC languages, as predicted.

3.2.2   DN and negative SpecNegP

In this section, I provide data from languages to show that NC is generally *impossible* if SpecNegP bears the feature [+NEG]. In such languages, such as Latin, SE, and Standard Modern German and Dutch, where inherently negative items co-occur, their negative features cancel each other out, as in logical DN. Comments by Muller (1991: 304) and Posner (1996: 303) suggest that Sursilvan, spoken in the Swiss canton of Graubünden/Grisons, belongs in this category, too. In Sursilvan, negative quantifiers cannot co-occur with the verbal negative marker without producing DN. This is predicted by Jespersen's Generalization, given that the Sursilvan negative marker, *buc* (< BUCCA), is aligned with SpecNegP, rather than with Neg°. (See also Occitan and a number of Northern Italian varieties.)

3.2.2.1   Standard English

In SE, sentential negation can be marked either by *not*[34] or *n't*:

(29) a.   I do *not* like Vodka.
      b.   I do*n't* like Vodka.

Most recent work on negation in SE, such as Haegeman (1995: 190), has concluded that *not* is generated in SpecNegP[35] while *n't* is generated as Neg°. (Like French *pas*, English *not* used to co-occur with a clitic *ne*—see (3b) and (18).) If this is true, it would be natural to claim that *n't* is the grammaticalized (i.e., reanalyzed) equivalent of *not*. (See footnote 12.) While I accept the "standard"

---

34. The syntactic status of *not* is not entirely clear. See the discussion of the Negative Cycle in English in section 3.1 and in footnote 12. I have assumed that SE *n't* is a phonologically cliticized form of *not*. It seems to be the case that *not* can sometimes cliticize without phonological reduction. Witness the grammaticality of (i), in part taken from Quirk et al. (1985: 809), cited by Haegeman (1995: 306fn17 (i)):
(i)   a.   Has not John been there too?
      b.   Is not history a social science?
      c.   Does not everything we see about us testify to the power of Divine Providence?
Here, *both* the auxiliary *and* the negation occupy a position to the left of the subject. Assuming an analysis in terms of AgrS°-to-C° movement to be along the right lines, the auxiliary and the negative must first have formed a complex head, implying in turn that *not* is itself part of AgrS°. See Williams (1994a, b) for a different view of the syntax of *not*.
35. I do not address the issue of whether *not* should be deemed to be generated in an adverbial position and subsequently raised into SpecNegP in parallel to my proposals for *pas* in chapter 2.

assumption that *not* is associated with SpecNegP at S-structure if not before, I doubt the validity of the claim that, in SE, *n't* is associated with Neg°. It seems more likely that *n't* is nothing more than a phonologically cliticized version of *not* and that, in all relevant respects, *n't* is associated with SpecNegP exactly like *not*. (See the suggestion by Jean-Yves Pollock reported by Zribi-Hertz 1994: 464fn17 that weakening of *not* to *n't* preceded reanalysis of the item as a head. See also the discussion in section 3.2.1.2.) I conclude, therefore, that, in SE, SpecNegP bears the feature [+NEG].[36] Jespersen's Generalization in (2) predicts that SE should not be an NC language.

With respect to NPIs in SE, the "equivalent"[37] of the SC *ni*-NPIs, that is, the *no*-NPIs, cannot co-occur with *not* or *n't* and receive an NC reading:

(30) a.   [*]Michael can *not* see *no-one*.   (DN)
     b.   [*]Michael ca*n't* see *nothing*.

Not surprisingly, multiple instances of *no*-NPIs together with *not/n't* are also illicit:

(31) a   ★I did *not* give *nothing* to *no-one*.
     b   ★I did*n't* give *nothing* to *no-one*.

In conclusion, in SE negative sentences, the feature [+NEG] is borne by Spec-NegP, and SE is clearly a non-NC language, as predicted by (2).

3.2.2.2 German

As shown by the examples in (17), repeated here for convenience, German is a non-NC language.

(32) a.   Hans sieht *niemanden* (★*nicht*).
          H.   sees no-one   not
          'H. can't see anyone.'

     b.   Ich bin mit *niemandem nirgendwohin* %(★*nicht*) gefahren.
          I   am with no-one   nowhere   not   traveled
          'I didn't drive anywhere with anyone.'

The same judgments apply to Standard Modern Dutch. Both results are predicted by the fact that the principal negative markers in these two languages, *nicht* and *niet*, respectively, are associated with SpecNegP rather than Neg°.

---

36. Zwicky and Pullum (1983) claim that *n't* is in fact a (morphological) inflectional affix, rather than a (syntactic) clitic.

37. With respect to the issue of whether *no*-NPIs in English and *ni*-NPIs in SC are equivalents, see Progovac (1994: 40, 42) and the discussion in section 3.2.1.1.

3.2.3   Conclusion

The comparison between the two types of language reviewed in the two preceding sections is illustrated in the table in (33):

(33)

Language	SpecNegP = [+NEG]?	NC?
Sursilvan, Modern German, SE, Modern Dutch, Latin, Occitan, Northern Italian varieties, etc.	Yes	No
SC, Cockney, Spanish, Italian, MH German, Middle Dutch, Portuguese, Romanian, Rhaeto-Romance, Catalan, Berber, Haitian Creole, etc.	No	Yes

On the basis of the languages reviewed here, it seems that the observation made by Jespersen (1924) and formalized as (2) is quite sturdy.[38] In the next sections, I provide an analysis of Jespersen's Generalization.

3.3   The Neg Criterion revisited

As discussed in section 1.3, H&Z (1991) have argued that the familiar similarities between the properties of interrogative and negative constructions warrant the Neg Criterion in (34), alongside the *wh*-criterion in (35), after May (1985: 17) and Rizzi (1996):

(34)   *The Neg Criterion*:
    a.   Each Neg $X°$ must be in a spec-head relationship with a Neg operator.
    b.   Each Neg operator must be in a spec-head relationship with a Neg $X°$.

(35)   *The* wh-*criterion*:
    a.   Each *wh*-$X°$ must be in a spec-head relationship with a *wh*-operator.
    b.   Each *wh*-operator must be in a spec-head relationship with a *wh*-$X°$.

Indeed, the two criteria in (34) and (35) are seen as instantiations of a more general wellformedness condition on the distribution and interpretation of affective elements (with sentential scope), namely the AFFECT criterion:[39]

---

38. See Déprez (forthcoming) for reservations about this conclusion.

39. Haegeman (1995: 94) suggests that the AFFECT criterion in its various manifestations can be subsumed under the more general Checking requirements of Chomsky's (1993, 1995a, b) Minimalist Program. See sections 1.1.1 and 1.1.5, for example, for a discussion of Verb Movement in terms of Checking. Under a Checking approach, affective items are deemed to have morphological features that need to be checked against the features of functional heads within a spec-head configuration. See chapter 2.

(36) *The AFFECT criterion:*
    a.   Each AFFECTIVE X° must be in a spec-head relationship with a AFFEC-
        TIVE operator.
    b.   Each AFFECTIVE operator must be in a spec-head relationship with an
        AFFECTIVE X°.

Each clause of these criteria arguably has two requirements:

(37) a.   The first obliges a head and an operator of a specific type to be in a
        spec-head configuration.
    b.   The second says that the head and operator must "agree" with each
        other with respect to the relevant AFFECTIVE features.

These two requirements are discussed in the following two sections.

3.3.1 The configuration

According to (37a), Jespersen's Negative Cycle is nothing more than a superficial epiphenomenon: assuming that sentential negation is marked within a functional projection in clause structure, the Neg Criterion forces us to postulate the
presence in negative clauses of a ([+NEG]) head *and* a ([+NEG]) operator (in abstract syntactic terms at least), irrespective of where the language stands in the
Negative Cycle, that is, how a language overtly marks negation.

In languages with bipartite pure sentential negation, that is, languages that
overtly realize both a negative head and a negative operator, such as Standard
French (4c), Taqbaylit (6), Burmese (7), and Standard Breton (8a), as well as
Fɔn and Navajo (see footnote 10 and chapter 2, footnote 6), the configuration
requirement in the Neg Criterion might be said to be trivially satisfied by the
two overt constituents.

Where a variety overtly marks negation with a head element alone (e.g., Italian $[_{Neg°}$ non]), the Neg Criterion obliges one to posit the presence of an abstract
negative operator that will appear in a spec-head configuration with that head
(or its trace). In support of such a requirement, Rizzi (1990) provides evidence
for postulating the presence of an operator in SpecNegP in Italian by showing
that negative sentences exhibit inner island effects.[40] Consider the minimally
contrasting pair in (38):

(38) a.   Perché$_{1/2}$ hai   detto $[t_1]$ che Gianni è partito $[t_2]$?   (Italian)
        why   have-2SG said   that G.   is left
        'Why did you say that G. left?'

    b.   Perché$_{1/*2}$ *non* hai   detto $[t_1]$ che Gianni è partito $[t_2]$?
        why   *non* have-2SG said   that G.   is left
        'Why didn't you say that G. left?'

---

40. See also the discussion of a non-overt negative operator in French in section 1.2.4.

In (38a), the adverb *perché* 'why' can be construed either with a trace adjoined to the matrix AgrSP, $[t_1]$, or with one adjoined to the embedded AgrSP, $[t_2]$: the string can be interpreted as a question about saying or a question about leaving. In (38b), which differs from (38a) only with respect to the presence of sentential negation in the matrix clause, realized overtly as $[_{Neg^\circ}$ non], the second of these readings disappears; (38b) can be a question about saying only. In Rizzi's analysis, the unavailability of the long-distance construal of *perché* is attributed to the presence of a non-overt operator in the matrix clause that counts as a potential A'-antecedent intervening between the surface position of *perché* and a trace adjoined to the embedded AgrSP. No such potential antecedent intervenes between *perché* and the higher trace $[t_1]$. Long construal of *perché* thus violates Relativized Minimality.[41] Unless one were to postulate the presence of an abstract operator in SpecNegP in the matrix clause in (38b), the unavailability of long construal of *perché* would remain unexplained.[42]

Conversely, where the overt negative marker is an XP (e.g., SE $[_{SpecNegP}$ not]), the Neg Criterion obliges that one posit the presence of an abstract negative head. The following contrast provides evidence for the presence of an abstract Neg° in SE:

(39) a.   John likes chocolate.
    b.   ∗John (not) likes (not) chocolate.

Within the Checking Theory approach to morphological features of Chomsky (1993) (see section 1.1), the finite verb in (39a) is inserted into the derivation under V° fully inflected. Its morphological features are checked by post-spell-out head-to-head movement to the highest inflectional head, AgrS°. This is not possible in (39b). If *not* is analyzed as the specifier of a syntactically inert head or as an adjunct, there is no immediate way of accounting for the fact that the verb cannot be tensed *and* co-occur with sentential negation. If, on the other hand, *not* is analyzed as an affective operator necessarily—given the Neg

---

41. The following definitions are based on Rizzi (1990: 6-7): Relativized Minimality:
    A antecedent-governs B only if there is no C such that:
(i)   C is a typical potential antecedent-governor for B.
(ii)   C c-commands B and does not c-command A.
    Antecedent-government: A antecedent-governs B iff:
(i)   A and B are co-indexed.
(ii)   A c-commands B.
(iii)   No barrier intervenes.
(iv)   Relativized Minimality is respected.
    42. Den Besten (1989), among others, notes another empirical phenomenon that lends itself to an explanation on the basis of the requirement, expressed in the AFFECT criterion, that affective heads be in a spec-head configuration with an operator. Den Besten notes that embedded V°-to-I°-to-C° movement creates islands for extraction in a way that embedded simple V°-to-I° movement does not. Under the assumptions (a) that extraction out of CP uses SpecCP as an intermediate landing site and (b) that I°-to-C° movement is triggered by the abstract properties of C°, that is, the fact that C° bears (affective) features, the island effects can be readily accounted for by assuming that the AFFECT criterion obliges C° to be in a spec-head configuration with an affective operator in SpecCP, preventing extraction from within CP from using SpecCP as an appropriate intermediate landing site.

Criterion–co-occurring with an abstract head, the ungrammaticality of (39b) can be accounted for by arguing that, in SE, the abstract Neg head has the property of blocking post-spell-out movement of the verb to check its inflectional features. As a last resort option, 'dummy *do*' is used.

In conclusion, then, irrespective of the typological nature of the overt negative marker(s), I posit that negative clauses are indeed characterized by the presence of a (negative) head and a (negative) operator, both of which are syntactically active. In short, I accept the configuration requirement in the Neg Criterion.

3.3.2   The agreement

Turning now to (37b), the spec-head configuration required by the Neg Criterion has generally been interpreted as entailing "agreement".[43] Following Chomsky (1986b: 24), it is often assumed that spec-head agreement amounts to the matching of relevant features. Where both specifier and head bear matching features by virtue of their lexical properties, spec-head agreement can be seen as a "static" checking mechanism. Where the relevant features are not shared by both specifier and head, spec-head agreement might be interpreted as a dynamic mechanism passing on the relevant feature to the head or the specifier as required. Thus, the spec-head agreement that guarantees that verbs agree with subjects has been assumed to amount to φ-feature sharing, whereby the relevant features of head and specifier are obliged to match. Within the context of negation in Standard French, following the discussion in chapters 1 and 2, I assume that *pas* bears the feature [+NEG] inherently and that this feature is transmitted to *ne*.[44]

If the spec-head relationship is seen as feature identity, then the type of "abstract" Negative Cycle discussed in section 3.1.2, whereby the locus of the abstract feature [+NEG] fluctuates between Neg° and SpecNegP in the same way as the overt marker of negation, becomes unacceptable. Under this strong interpretation, the Neg Criterion obliges *both* Neg° *and* SpecNegP to bear the same feature: [+NEG]. Irrespective of where the feature is located underlyingly, a dynamic agreement mechanism will make sure head and specifier match in time for the Neg Criterion to come along and check that all is in order by LF at the latest, that is, at the level at which scopal relations are relevant. Consequently, no cross-linguistic or diachronic variation will be possible, and it will not be possible to relate NC to the Negative Cycle.

43. DeGraff (1993b: 71) suggests that NC results from structural configurations involving agreement between a [+NEG] XP and a [+NEG] head, where necessary, with LF movement of the former into the specifier position of the latter.

44. Note, however, that Acquaviva (1993: 9–10) believes there is a "sharp difference" between the nature of spec-head agreement involved in sharing φ-features and the nature of spec-head agreement sharing operator features.

The strong interpretation of spec-head agreement in terms of feature identity is, however, not the only one available, and I now consider a weaker alternative that is attractive on both theory-internal and empirical grounds. Consider the possibility that spec-head agreement is in fact nothing more than spec-head *anti-dis*agreement, guaranteeing feature compatibility rather than identity. Consider also the possibility that the only dynamic agreement mechanism available is Rizzi's (1996: 76) DA, discussed in section 1.2.4, and schematized here for the specific affective context of interrogation but which might be generalized to other contexts.

(40) *Dynamic Agreement (DA)*:   (Rizzi 1996: 76)
    Op X ⇒ Op X
    WH   WH WH

An important feature of DA is its unidirectionality. DA passes features from specifier to head but not vice versa. So, where a relevant feature is borne by both X° and SpecXP, DA has no effect. Where it is borne by SpecXP but not X°, DA passes on the feature to X° (as in the discussion of *ne* in chapter 1). In contrast, where it is borne by X° *but not* by SpecXP, DA crucially does *not* pass it on to SpecXP. Consider what this means for negation in a language such as Italian. Here, *non* in Neg° is specified [+NEG] as a lexical feature, but DA does not transfer the feature [+NEG] to the non-overt operator in SpecNegP (whose presence there is guaranteed by (37a)), which is, consequently, what Haegeman (1995) terms an "expletive" operator. Under the strong interpretation of spec-head agreement, the Neg Criterion would not be satisfied, since there is no feature identity between Neg° and SpecNegP. In contrast, with the weaker version of spec-head agreement, based on nonincompatibility, the Neg Criterion would be satisfied. Under such a view, the expletive operator in SpecNegP is not incompatible with Neg° and the Neg Criterion is not violated.

By way of illustration, in a structure such as (41), if X° bears the set of affective features, α, while the operator in SpecXP bears the affective features, β, where β is a proper subset of α, the AFFECT Criterion will be satisfied, since SpecXP is not incompatible with X° even though there is not full agreement. In contrast, if α were a proper subset of β, DA would transmit the "extra" features from SpecXP to X°.

(41)

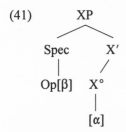

Note that this view of spec-head agreement is not at odds with Haegeman's (1995: 107) characterization of negative clauses as clauses in which the feature [+NEG] is borne by a functional head in the extended domain of V. For, irrespective of where the feature [+NEG] originates, under the model proposed here, [+NEG] will always ultimately appear on a functional head. Indeed, if Haegeman is right in her characterization of negative clauses, the conception of DA in (40) could be argued to follow from economy considerations. If all that is needed to mark sentential negation is the presence of the feature [+NEG] on a functional head, then transferring the feature to an operator in specifier position serves no purpose and should arguably not be allowed. Certainly, as an inter- pretable feature, the presence of [+NEG] on a functional head at LF should not in itself be problematic. Consequently, the presence of a suitable operator in Spec- NegP cannot be motivated for Checking reasons.

In contrast, transferring the feature from the operator to the head serves a clear purpose, since, in the absence of such a feature specification on the head, sentential negation will not be marked. Note also the motivation for *pas*-raising to SpecNegP given in chapters 1 and 2. Thus, there seem to be theory-internal reasons for adopting the concepts of spec-head agreement and DA proposed here.

On the empirical front, the "weak" conception of the spec-head relationship is strong enough to account for the ungrammaticality of the following strings from Italian discussed by Belletti (1990: 41 (29c, d)), arguably attributable to spec-head agreement:

(42) a.   *Maria *non* parlava *pur/ben* di lui.   (Italian)
          M.   *non* spoke   indeed   of him

     b.   *Maria *non* ha   *pur/ben* parlato di lui.
          M.   *non* has indeed   spoken of him

Belletti (1990: 39), following Lonzi (1991), describes adverbs such as *pur/ben* 'indeed' as having "the semantic function of reinforcing the assertive value of the sentence". She concludes that they are the positive counterpart of negative (sentential) adverbs and that, accordingly, they fill the specifier of a polarity phrase, SpecPolP or SpecΣP (see section 1.2.1). This analysis is supported by the fact that the distribution of *pur* and *ben* is identical to the negative adverbs *più* 'no more' and *mai* 'never', which are assumed by Belletti (1990) to occupy SpecNegP at S-structure (but see Zanuttini 1997a): in (42b), the positive ad- verbs intervene between the auxiliary and the past participle, just like negative adverbs do. As positive emphatic adverbs, these elements are likely to bear the feature [+POS], or at least [−NEG], and lead to ungrammaticality when they ap- pear in the specifier position of a PolP whose head is marked [+NEG], as in (42), since [+NEG] is incompatible with [−NEG]/[+POS]. Note, however, that a spec- head relationship based on compatibility is strong enough to rule out these structures; it is not necessary to posit agreement in terms of feature identity be- tween head and specifier.

Recent work by Lyons (1994b) suggests further that the "weak" version of spec-head agreement is in fact empirically better motivated than the "strong" one. Lyons discusses data from Spanish in which subjects appear to disagree with the verb. In (43), for example, the subject is third person plural while the verb is first person plural.

(43) a. Los estudiantes trabajamos mucho.   (Spanish)
        the students   work-1PL   much
        'We students work a lot.'

     b. Algunos estudiantes trabajamos mucho.
        some   students   work-1PL   much
        'Some students (including me) work a lot.'

The data in (43) are problematic if the spec-head relationship is formulated in terms of feature identity. If, rather, it is formulated in terms of compatibility, the problem does not arise. Assuming that third person is not a real person at all but is, rather, a default person, the data in (43) are straightforward.[45] In each sentence, the feature specification of the morphologically strong AgrS° is [1PL] (Spanish is a null-subject language). The subject in SpecAgrSP bears only number features, that is, [PL]. Given that [PL] is a subset of [1PL], SpecAgrSP is compatible with AgrS°. Of course, an analysis in terms of strict agreement or feature sharing would wrongly predict the ungrammaticality of the strings in (43). I conclude, therefore, that there are theoretical and empirical reasons for doubting that the spec-head relationship needs to be couched in terms of strict feature identity.[46] Most significant for my purposes, a weaker interpretation of the spec-head relationship in terms of compatibility rather than feature identity makes it possible to account for the link between the Negative Cycle and NC, and it is to this that I turn in the next section.

---

45. This analysis is also in line with proposals made by Hulk and van Kemenade (1995: 231), who suggest that third person and singular number are both default φ-features. It also ties in well with Benveniste's (1966: 225–36) claim that first and second person differ in important respects from third person with respect to morphological marking. Note that, in a number of languages, if not universally, negative quantifiers like *no-one*, which are semantically neither third person nor singular, are nevertheless syntactically third person singular. This also suggests that third person singular agreement morphology is a default setting. The agreement patterns in Spanish illustrated in (43) are also discussed in Torrego (1996: 114–16).

46. One of the anonymous reviewers of this book felt that the weaker version of the spec-head relationship proposed in the text effectively took the movement-inducing teeth out of, for example, the Neg Criterion. I feel that this concern is misplaced. Movement of a phrasal element into the relevant SpecXP is determined by the interplay of two factors, namely the feature marking on X° and the availability of a suitable null operator. With respect to the first factor, the absence or "weakness" of the feature specification on X° means that DA needs to transfer the feature from the specifier. This is possible only if the specifier is part of a chain/CHAIN containing a phrasal element bearing the required feature. If that element is lower than SpecXP, a CHAIN can be formed, providing that a suitable expletive element is available in SpecXP. If no such expletive element is available (as is the case of negation in French—see chapters 1 and 2), overt movement will be forced, forming a chain. The Neg Criterion therefore retains its movement-inducing power, *even if* spec-head agreement is reformulated as spec-head compatibility.

3.4   Jespersen's Generalization: analysis

An analysis of Jespersen's Generalization will depend on an analysis of how NPIs are licensed in negative contexts. Two proposals are evaluated in section 3.4.1, and a modified version of the latter is adopted. An analysis of Jespersen's Generalization itself is given in section 3.4.2.

3.4.1   NPI licensing in negative contexts

In this section, I consider NPI licensing in negative contexts with a view to laying the foundations for an account of Jespersen's Generalization. First, in section 3.4.1.1, I consider the approach adopted by Zanuttini (1991), which exploits Chomsky's (1986b) idea of L-marking. I show that this approach, while theoretically interesting, is empirically inadequate. In section 3.4.1.2, I consider the more promising approach adopted by Progovac (1994) based on A'-binding. In section 3.4.1.3, I suggest modifications to Progovac's A'-binding approach that, while exploiting her basic insight, have a number of empirical and theoretical advantages over her own execution of the idea: in the first instance, the revised analysis is truer to the nature of A-binding; second, it makes it possible to account for Jespersen's Generalization. The modifications are explored in section 3.4.2.

3.4.1.1   Zanuttini (1991): L-marking

Jespersen's Generalization is taken up by Zanuttini (1991: chapter 5) within the framework of her structural account of NC and NPI licensing in negative contexts. Zanuttini claims (1991: 151–52) that the co-occurrence of the pre-verbal negative marker (which she analyzes as the head of NegP-1, generated above TP[47]) with post-verbal negative quantifiers (n-words) is linked to the need for the latter to raise, at LF, to SpecNegP-1 to satisfy the Neg Criterion, crossing TP as they go, which, when indicative, is a barrier to LF movement (Zanuttini 1991: section 5.3). In this scenario, the function of an obligatorily overt pre-verbal negative marker is to L-mark—and hence to void the barrierhood of—the category it selects, TP, making LF movement of the negative quantifiers across TP into SpecNegP-1 licit, as illustrated in (44), adapted from Zanuttini (1991: 162). Negative quantifiers in pre-verbal position, such as negative subjects and topicalized negative constituents, do not co-occur with *non* because they do not need to cross TP and raise into SpecNegP at LF. In Zanuttini's analysis, *post*-verbal markers of negation such as French *pas* are associated with the specifier position of what she terms NegP-2, generated *below* TP, as in (45) (adapted

---

47. The reader is referred to Zanuttini's own work for discussion of the distinction between NegP-1 and NegP-2. In section 2.1.1.3, I ultimately reject NegP-2. In Zanuttini (1997a), four NegPs are proposed.

from Zanuttini 1991: 163), and do not therefore have the ability to L-mark TP, and NC is unavailable.

(44)

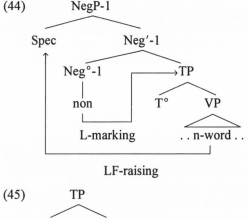

(45)

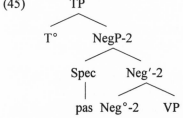

Thus, Zanuttini seems to have accounted for Jespersen's Generalization.

This analysis is problematic for a number of reasons. (See also Robbers 1992: 229 for objections to Zanuttini's analysis.) First, if, generally speaking, UG makes Zanuttini's NegP-2 available below TP, why can this projection not be generated in, say, Italian? If NegP-2 were available in Italian, post-verbal n-words could raise into SpecNegP-2 to satisfy the Neg Criterion without having to cross TP. Pre-verbal *non* would then not be needed to L-mark TP in order to void its LF barrierhood. The ungrammaticality of post-verbal n-words in Italian in the absence of pre-verbal *non* suggests that there is no SpecNegP-2 position available, casting doubt on Zanuttini's approach to NC, especially her NegP-2 hypothesis, and her approach to (45).[48]

Second, if the presence of *non* in Neg° is to L-mark TP to allow *LF* raising of n-words, why is *non* needed in the presence of *mai* 'never' and *più* 'no more', which, unlike argumental n-words, occupy SpecNegP-1 *at S-structure*? Given that any raising that takes place is in overt syntax, the LF-barrierhood of TP should be irrelevant. Recall from the discussion of the examples in (42) that the class of Italian emphatic positive adverbs including *ben/pur* 'indeed' has the same distribution in positive clauses as *mai* and *più* in negative clauses. Exploiting the parallel, Belletti (1990, 1992, 1994a, b) argues that these positive adverbs have a matching distribution because they occupy SpecΣP/SpecPolP,

---

48. See also section 2.1.1.3 for additional reasons for rejecting Zanuttini's NegP-2 hypothesis.

presumably to satisfy the AFFECT criterion.[49] If these elements can occupy this position without TP being L-marked, why is *non* required in the corresponding negative contexts?

Third, why, in SC (see (23) and (24)) and a number of Romance varieties like Romanian and Ladin (see the examples in (ii)–(iii) in footnote 18) but not Italian (but note the stylistic and dialectal variation referred to in footnote 18), is it the case that the need for the verb to appear with an overt negative marker is not sensitive to whether or not the verb is preceded by a negative quantifier? Why should this be the case if, as Zanuttini argues, the overt nature of the negative marker is to L-mark TP? If Zanuttini's analysis is along the right lines, SC, and so on would be expected to pattern with Italian, contrary to fact. The obverse of this objection to Zanuttini's analysis can be made with respect to West Flemish. West Flemish has an (optional) pre-verbal negative marker, *en*, but obligatory raising of negative quantifiers (with sentential scope) at S-Structure. Why should morphologically negative quantifiers in West Flemish not be able to remain in situ at S-structure, safe in the knowledge that *en* will L-mark TP and allow LF-raising to SpecNegP, thus guaranteeing a concordant reading? Zanuttini's analysis fails to answer these questions. (Negation in West Flemish is discussed in some detail in section 3.5.1.)

Finally, in a number of languages, for example Italian, an interesting scenario is provided by strings in which one negative quantifier appears pre-verbally while another appears post-verbally, as in (1b). In such a configuration, pre-verbal *non* does not appear. Under the assumption that the post-verbal negative quantifier has to raise at LF to SpecNegP to satisfy the Neg Criterion, one wonders why the presence of *non* is not necessary. It seems implausible to claim that the pre-verbal negative quantifier somehow manages to L-mark TP in the absence of an overt Neg° marker.

On the basis of these considerations, I reject Zanuttini's L-marking account of NC. An alternative analysis of the NPI licensing involved in NC has been proposed by Progovac (1994). This approach is evaluated in the next section.

3.4.1.2 Progovac (1994): A′-binding

On the basis of distributional parallels between anaphors and pronominals, on the one hand, and polarity items/negative quantifiers, on the other, Progovac (1994) suggests that (A′-)Binding Theory (henceforth, BT) should be called upon to account for NPI licensing. It is within this general framework that she analyzes the *ni*-NPIs of SC as A′-anaphors that, just like A-anaphors, need to be bound within a given domain (Principle A of BT). (See section 3.2.1.1.) In BT terms, the *ni*-NPIs need a local antecedent in the same way that (A-)anaphors

---

49. Recall that the Neg Criterion and *wh*-criterion are construction-specific instantiations of the AFFECT criterion in (36). Raising of Italian *ben/pur* into the equivalent of SpecNegP could be motivated by the AFFECT criterion if emphatic elements are deemed to bear affective features.

do. In (46), for example, Principle A is satisfied by virtue of the fact that the *ni*-NPI *ni(t)ko-ga* 'no-one' is A'-bound by the c-commanding [$_{Neg°}$ ne], a functional (A'-)head. The element *ne* functions as the A'-antecedent of the *ni*-NPI. This binding relationship is represented by co-indexation.

(46) Mario ⋆(*ne$_i$*) vidi *ni(t)ko-ga$_i$*.   (SC)
     M.   *ne* sees no-one-ACC
     'M. can't see anyone.'

This analysis is compatible with the standard assumption (e.g., in Haegeman 1995: 70–71 and references therein) that polarity items are licensed by a c-commanding negative or interrogative element. However, as Haegeman (1995: 294fn3) points out, this standard assumption says nothing in X'-theoretic terms about the nature of the c-commanding licenser of a polarity item: should it be a head or an XP? Haegeman herself (1995: 71) exploits both possibilities (arguably unnecessarily[50]). Progovac clearly takes the former option with respect to the A'-binding of *ni*-NPIs in SC, which, she argues, are bound by Neg°, that is, *ne*. Here, Progovac essentially follows the line of Aoun (1986: 136), who was writing prior to the NegP hypothesis and the proposal of the Neg Criterion and who suggests for negation in Italian that post-verbal negative quantifiers are A'-bound by pre-verbal *non*, their antecedent in his terms. Nevertheless, this move by Progovac is surprising, given her more general objective, namely to subsume NPI licensing under a version of BT generalised to the A'-system. While Progovac's claim that the distribution of *ni*-NPIs and *i*-NPIs in SC patterns surprisingly closely with anaphors and pronominals seems convincing enough, it is odd that Progovac chooses to have *ni*-NPIs (phrasal constituents) obligatorily A'-bound by the head *ne*. This is not the way A-binding is generally assumed to function. On the contrary, A-binding—in its most familiar form—involves one XP binding another XP, for example, an overt antecedent binding an overt A-anaphor, as in (47a), or an overt NP binding its non-Case-marked trace (also assumed to be an A-anaphor) following NP-movement, as in (47b).

(47) a. Susan$_i$ loves herself$_i$.
     b. John$_i$ was killed t_i.

---

50. For example, in (i) (Haegeman's 1995: 70 (1a)), Haegeman assumes that the interrogative feature on the inverted auxiliary, i.e., X°, licenses (by binding?) the NPI.
(i) Did you see anyone?
However, given that the *wh*-criterion obliges an operator to co-occur with a *wh*-head, Haegeman might alternatively have assumed that it is the operator that is responsible for licensing the NPI. NPI-licensing by heads would then no longer be needed at all, and the theory would be more constrained. (See also Haegeman 1995: 294fn3.) The AFFECT criterion, that is, the requirement that affective heads co-occur with an affective operator, could also be used to avoid the need for Laka (1990) and Progovac (1991) to claim that, in (ii), the NPI is licensed by the affective feature on the embedded C°. (See Haegeman 1995: 90 (56c).)
(ii) He denies/doubts that anything happened.
Instead, one could argue that the NPI is licensed by the null operator required to occupy SpecCP in order to satisfy the AFFECT criterion.

Progovac's claim that *ni*-NPIs are A'-bound by Neg° is even more surprising in view of her Relativized Principle A of BT, given in (48):

(48) *Relativized Principle A*:
A reflexive R must be bound in the domain D containing R and an *X-bar compatible* SUBJECT.
If R is an X° (morphologically simple) reflexive, then its SUBJECTs are X° categories only, i.e., Agr (as the only salient (c-commanding) head with pronominal features).
If R is an X^{max} (morphologically complex) reflexive, its SUBJECTs are X^{max} specifiers with pronominal features, thus SpecIP and SpecNP.
(Progovac 1994: 12 (60); my emphasis)

Within the terms of (48), it is only another XP that should be able to A'-bind the XP *ni*-NPIs of SC. So what could that XP be? Although negative, NegP itself will not count as a suitable A'-binder, given that it actually contains the NPIs: co-indexation would violate the *i*-within-*i* filter. However, given the Neg Criterion, a potential A'-antecedent would be the operator in SpecNegP. In the following section, I propose that Progovac's Relativized Principle A of BT should be respected and that one should assume that A'-anaphors that are maximal projections can be bound only by antecedents that are also maximal projections, for example, an operator in SpecNegP.

3.4.1.3 Modified version of NPI licensing in negative contexts by A'-binding

In this section, I propose an account of NPI licensing in negative contexts that exploits the basic insight behind Progovac's (1994) analysis, reviewed in the previous section. First, it exploits theoretical apparatus already available and well motivated, namely Generalized (A'-)BT. However, as is shown later, the A'-binding account put forward here is arguably more faithful to the principles of A-binding than Progovac's original analysis. Second, and more important, it opens the door to an account of Jespersen's Generalization. Third, it goes some way toward bringing natural language negation (back) into the sphere of the negation of (Boolean) logic. There is a tradition of observing that natural language negation (at least in NC languages) cannot be subsumed under logical negation; however, no convincing alternative has been proposed, suggesting that the realm of logic was where natural language negation belonged all along. Finally, it allows me to claim, *contra* Acquaviva (1995) and Déprez (forthcoming), that inherently negative NPIs, that is, negative quantifiers, are identical in the relevant syntactic respects cross-linguistically—despite their diverging distributions, which can be attributed to a difference elsewhere in the grammar of the respective languages, namely their position in the Negative Cycle. This is a welcome result, since it serves to reduce the range of variation attested cross-linguistically, a consequence that has clear benefits for the explanation of language acquisition.

In order to make the A'-binding of NPIs parallel to the A-binding of anaphors, I suggest that Progovac's Relativized Principle A of BT in (48) be respected. Consequently, if *ni*-NPIs in SC are indeed XP A'-anaphors (as Progovac argues and as I assume), then they will need to be locally A'-bound by an XP antecedent rather than by a head antecedent. So what XP could the A'-binder be? As suggested in the previous section, the answer to this question comes from the Neg Criterion. Under the assumption that the SC negative sentence in (46) contains a NegP with a head bearing the feature [+NEG] and realized phonetically as *ne*, the Neg Criterion obliges one to posit the presence of an affective operator, Op, in SpecNegP. I claim that it is this operator that A'-binds—and thus licenses—the *ni*-NPI in (46). In other words, the *ni*-NPI is A'-bound by the operator, Op, in SpecNegP, its antecedent, as in (46'):

(46') $[_{AgrSP}$ Mario $[_{AgrS'}$ *ne* vidi $[_{NegP}$ Op$_i$ $[_{Neg'}$ . . . $[_{VP}$ . . . *ni(t)ko-ga$_i$*]]]]]

Following Progovac (1994), I assume that the fact that *ni*-NPIs are not licensed by superordinate negation or in nonnegative polarity contexts is due to the fact that, in such contexts, *ni*-NPIs are not A'-bound in the domain, D, referred to in (48). Progovac takes this domain to be NegP with possible extension to IP (=AgrSP) as a consequence of head-to-head movement of Neg° to I° (=AgrS°). Crucially, the domain never extends as far as CP. Given that SpecCP is arguably the position occupied by the polarity operator, Op, in the nonnegative polarity context in (49a) or in the clause embedded under matrix negation in (49b), this assumption is necessary to account for the ungrammatical status of the examples.

(49) a. ⋆Sumnja-m $[_{CP}$ Op $[_{C'}$ da   Milan voli   *ni(t)ko-ga*]]
       doubt-1SG   that M.   loves no-one-ACC
       'I doubt M. loves anyone.'   (Progovac 1994: 64 (17))

    b. ⋆Milan *ne* tvrdi $[_{CP}$ Op $[_{C'}$ da   Marija poznaje *ni(t)ko-ga*]]
       Mi.   *ne* claims   that Ma.   knows   no-one-ACC
       'Mi. isn't claiming that Ma. knows anyone.'
                                        (Progovac 1994: 41 (111))

If the *ni*-NPIs are A'-bound at all in (49), they are A'-bound by Op in SpecCP. However, this binder is not close enough to satisfy (48).

The strings in (49) are grammatical if the *ni*-NPIs are replaced with *i*-NPIs. I follow Progovac in attributing this to the fact that, as "pronominals", *i*-NPIs obey BT Principle B and must therefore be A'-free in the domain D. Nevertheless, *i*-NPIs also need to obey a requirement that they be A'-bound somewhere in the sentence outside the domain D. Unlike Progovac, though, I assume that an *i*-NPI, as a morphologically complex element, is also bound by a maximal projection, such as Op in SpecCP in (49), rather than by a head such as C°.

3.4.2   Jespersen's Generalization

By adopting a "weak" interpretation of spec-head agreement in terms of compatibility and an A'-binding approach to NPI licensing in which XP NPIs can be bound only by XP antecedents and not by heads, I am now in a position to account for Jespersen's Generalization.

Assume that the negative quantifiers referred to in the context of NC, for example, *ni*-NPIs, *no*-NPIs, and n-words, are inherently negative, that is, they bear the feature [+NEG]. As polarity items (A'-anaphors), these will need to be licensed–by A'-binding, by hypothesis. Assume further that, in these languages, the feature [+NEG] is borne by the lexical item under Neg° as a lexical characteristic.

3.4.2.1   Why NC languages are NC languages . . .

In underlying representations, it was suggested earlier that, in NC languages, [+NEG] is to be seen as a feature of Neg° but not SpecNegP. Given such an underlying configuration, the Neg Criterion in (34) obliges one to posit the presence of a non-overt operator in SpecNegP. Given the unidirectionality of DA, it is impossible for the [+NEG] feature to be passed from Neg° to SpecNegP. Accordingly, I assume that the operator in SpecNegP is Haegeman's (1995: 192–93) "expletive" polarity operator (Op_{exp}). Further, the weak spec-head relationship based on compatibility rather than on feature identity means that the Neg Criterion is satisfied. I further assume that the operator is the element responsible for A'-binding and licensing the inherently negative polarity items: Op_{exp} in SpecNegP (unselectively) A'-binds the [+NEG] polarity item in situ, creating a representational CHAIN.[51]

This can be illustrated using the Italian example in (50). The relevant features of the representation of (50) are given in the tree in (51). Neg° bears the feature [+NEG] as a consequence of the lexical properties of *non*. In accordance with the Neg Criterion, SpecNegP must be filled by an operator, Op. Weak spec-head agreement checks that SpecNegP and Neg° are compatible, but DA does not transmit the [+NEG] feature from Neg° to SpecNegP. Op is therefore Op_{exp}. The inherently negative NPI *nessuno* 'no-one' is an A'-anaphor and needs to be A'-bound by forming a representational CHAIN with an antecedent in order to be licensed. The antecedent is Op_{exp}; hence the coindexing.

(50) Mario *non* ha visto *nessuno*.   (Italian)
     M.   *non* has seen no-one
     'M. hasn't seen anyone.'

---

51. See Acquaviva (1993), who also exploits unselective binding in the licensing of negative quantifiers but in a slightly different way. See also Ladusaw (1992).

(51)

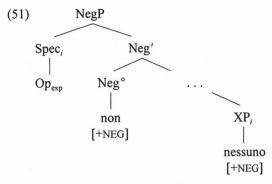

Crucially, this does not produce a configuration in which the two instances of [+NEG] interact syntactically. This is a welcome result, since it provides an explanation for why the two occurrences of [+NEG] in (51) do not interact with each other semantically, either, that is, do not cancel each other out. One of the [+NEG] elements is a syntactic head; the other is a maximal projection, and the two are independent of each other.[52] Note that this analysis brings natural language negation closer to logical negation. The interpretation of (50) is not one of DN since, in (51), no negative constituent takes scope over any other negative constituent.

Note that, if I had maintained the strong interpretation of spec-head agreement, I would have had to assume that the polarity operator in SpecNegP in (51), Op, was what Haegeman (1995: 192–93) terms a "contentive" operator, that is, positively specified for the feature [±NEG] (as a consequence of being in a spec-head configuration with a [+NEG] head). Consequently, the inherently negative NPI would be in the scope of a negative operator, and the explanation for NC within logical negation would have been lost. Further, if I had maintained the Aoun/Progovac analysis of A'-binding of NPIs by Neg°, the cross-linguistic explanation for the (un)availability of NC would have been lost, too, since the [+NEG] negative quantifier would have been bound by the [+NEG] negative marker in Neg°. I take these results to provide substantial support for the approach adopted here.

Before considering non-NC languages, I turn to the possibility, in NC languages, of multiple negative quantifiers co-occurring with a concordant reading, as in van der Wouden's (1994: 95) "negative spread". Here, I discuss two possible approaches to how it is that, in these languages, the [+NEG] features of multiple negative quantifiers do not cancel each other out in structures such as (24), repeated here for convenience:

(52) Milan *ne* daje   *ni(t)kome ništa*.   (SC)
     M.   *ne* gives no-one   nothing
     'M. isn't giving anything to anyone.'

---

52. The notion of heads and maximal projections not interfering with each other is, of course, not new. Within the context of movement, the two are usually regarded as separate and independent.

There are two issues to be resolved with respect to (52). First, given that the two *ni*-NPIs are XPs, how is it that one of them fails to take scope over and cancel out the negative feature of the other? I assume that the answer to this question needs to exploit the A/A'-distinction. Under the assumption that the mechanism by which a negative constituent takes scope over another is A'-binding, then the absence of such scope relations in (52) can be accounted for, since both negative quantifiers occupy A-positions.

The second issue to be addressed with respect to (52) concerns how multiple negative quantifiers are licensed in the first place. The first possibility is to assume that the structure of (52) is essentially identical to the one in (51), the only difference being that two *ni*-NPIs appear in the lower portion of the tree, unselectively bound by a unique Op_{exp} in SpecNegP. Within this approach, I assume a single operator can license a potentially unlimited number of *ni*-NPIs within the same clause. This is the approach adopted by Suñer (1993) and Acquaviva (1993): a single operator is associated with all post-verbal negative quantifiers by unselective binding. (See also Haegeman 1995: 202 for discussion.) As an alternative, I could assume that each negative quantifier is bound by its own Op_{exp}, as in (53).

(53) Milan $[_{AgrS'}$ *ne* daje $[_{NegP}$ Op_{expi} Op_{expj} ... *ni(t)kome$_i$ ništa$_j$* $]]$

An approach similar to this is adopted by Brody (1995) for the relationship between null *wh*-operators and multiple overt *wh*-phrases in situ. Haegeman applies the same approach, albeit tentatively, to negative structures (1995: 201–5), suggesting that it allows a more unified approach to the syntax of negation: given that, in languages with multiple overt movement of negative quantifiers, such as West Flemish (see section 3.5.1), multiple distinct chains are formed, it would be desirable for the same to be true of the representational CHAINs assumed in languages such as SC. This is possible only if the in situ negative quantifiers are bound by distinct expletive operators. However, given that absorption is ultimately assumed to take place in both cases, the creation of multiple representational CHAINs in the first place might be argued to be uneconomical and therefore ruled out by the grammar.

3.4.2.2   ... and why non-NC languages are not

In non-NC languages like SE in which the feature [+NEG] is borne by the operator in SpecNegP, the situation is necessarily different. Here, the co-occurrence of the marker of pure sentential negation with a negative quantifier leads to logical DN, as in (54):

(54) I've not seen nothing.   (DN)

Let us assume that *no*-NPIs in SE are to all intents and purposes identical to the *ni*-NPIs of SC. If this assumption is justified, *nothing* in (54) will be an anaphor and will have to be A'-bound within a local domain, presumably by an operator in SpecNegP, as was the case in SC. This configuration is illustrated in (55):

(55)

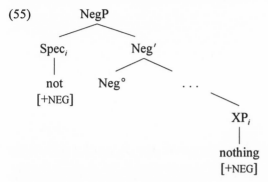

The structure in (55) contrasts with the scenario sketched in the previous section and with the structure in (51) in that it produces a configuration in which the two instances of [+NEG] interact with each other syntactically. The [+NEG] operator in SpecNegP (the antecedent) binds and therefore takes scope over the [+NEG] *no*-NPI (the anaphor). The fact that such structures are impossible (with the relevant NC interpretation) is predicted by the analysis proposed here and supports the claim that natural language negation is closer to logical negation than is sometimes assumed. As predicted by Boolean logic, where one [+NEG] element takes scope over another [+NEG] element (e.g., by A'-binding), as in (54) and (55), the two instances of negation cancel each other out, producing DN.

This result also allows me to conclude, *contra* Acquaviva (1995) and Déprez (forthcoming), that it was right to assume that there are no nontrivial differences between negative quantifiers cross-linguistically—a desirable result from the point of view of acquisition, as suggested earlier. SC *ni*-NPIs, English *no*-NPIs, and Romance n-words are all essentially identical. They are A'-anaphors and need to be A'-bound within a local domain. Their different distributions can be attributed, for the most part, to the fact that the languages in which they appear stand at different points in the Negative Cycle, that is, that these languages vary with respect to whether SpecNegP is marked [+NEG].

SE adopts one of two possible strategies to avoid DN in the context of indefinite quantifiers.[53] The first is to use NPIs that are not inherently negative and that do not, therefore, cancel out the negative force of the [+NEG] operator in SpecNegP when bound by it, namely the *any*-NPIs:

(56) I've not seen anything.

---

53. I assume that choosing the unmarked alternative between (56) and (59) is a language-specific issue. According to Ramat et al. (1987: 173), Icelandic adopts a strategy analogous to (59), while Danish prefers (56).

(57)

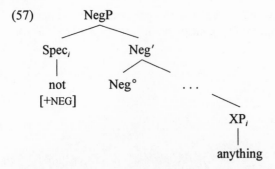

In (57), *anything* (A'-bound by the operator in SpecNegP) is not inherently negative. DN is thus avoided, since one negative element is not in the scope of another.[54]

So, what of multiple NPIs licensed by a single instance of sentential negation
in non-NC languages, as in (58)?

(58) I've not seen *any*thing *any*where.

In section 3.4.2.1, I discussed multiple negative quantifiers in NC languages.
There, two possible analyses were envisaged. The first possibility was for all
post-verbal negative quantifiers to be licensed by unselective A'-binding from a
single Op_{exp} in SpecNegP. The second possibility was for each post-verbal negative quantifier to be associated with its own Op_{exp} in SpecNegP. Similarly, there
are two possible approaches to the licensing of multiple NPIs by a single instance of sentential negation as in (58). Either I can assume that each and every
NPI is licensed by association (via unselective A'-binding) with a *single* contentive operator in SpecNegP, that is, *not*, or I can assume that each and every NPI
is licensed by association with its own Op_{cont}. Note that, in the case of SE, this
second model involves one *any*-NPI being bound by the overt operator *not*,
while all other *any*-NPIs would be bound by a non-overt Op_{cont}. This discrepancy is arguably a weakness of the second model. In the first model, all the *any*-
NPIs are licensed by *not*.

The second (and more marked) strategy adopted by SE to avoid DN in the
context of indefinite quantifiers is to avoid the negative operator,[55] as in (59):

(59) I have seen nothing.

Two possible analyses come to mind for (59). In the first and most natural instance, and in order for *nothing* to take sentential scope, *nothing* is assumed to
be bound by an expletive polarity operator in SpecNegP. This is the approach

---

54. Furthermore, I argue that the configuration in (57) is also the one found in Modern French.
Here, the [+NEG] operator is phonologically null and the *personne, rien, jamais*, and so on, series of
quantifiers are NPIs like the *any*-NPIs of English: they need to be A'-bound to be licensed but are not
themselves inherently negative. See section 3.5.2 and chapters 4 and 5 for detailed analysis.

55. See (22), as well as sections 1.2.1 and 1.3, for evidence suggesting that, in (59), the clause and,
presumably, therefore, the verb are negative in abstract terms.

adopted by Haegeman (1995: 185–86, section 1.4.2.2.3). This allows the Neg Criterion to be satisfied by virtue of the relationship between Neg° and the CHAIN containing the non-overt expletive operator and the negative quantifier. The negative head is then, by DA, endowed with the feature [+NEG] and the sentence is negative. Second, and less natural, the negative quantifier has local scope and an echoic reading. It does not then count as an operator and is not associated with a NegP. The sentence is then positive in all relevant senses.

Although such optionality is, in principle, undesirable, it is a possibility supported by the following observation. The two possibilities make predictions with respect to possible tag questions. In (60), the tag questions have to have the opposite polarity to the "antecedent":

(60) a. You like squid, don't you? / ⋆do you?
     b. You don't like squid, ⋆don't you? / do you?

Where the "antecedent" has a structure along the lines of (59), both polarities are (just about) possible in the tag:

(61) a. You've done nothing all day, have you?
     b. You've done nothing all day, haven't you?

How can this choice be accounted for? On the basis of the tags, it looks like the antecedent clause in (61) can be seen as *either* negative *or* positive. This could be taken to be the consequence of the two possible ways of licensing *nothing*. If *nothing* takes sentential scope by being bound by Op_{exp} in SpecNegP, the antecedent clause will end up being negative and the positive tag will be licensed: (61a). If, alternatively, the negative quantifier has local scope, there will be no binding and no NegP; the antecedent will be positive, and the negative tag will be licensed: (61b).

Before moving on to deal with two apparent counterexamples to Jespersen's Generalization, I return briefly to the contrast with respect to NC discussed in sections 3.2.2.1 and 3.2.1.2 between SE and closely related nonstandard varieties such as Cockney.

(62) a. I ain't done nothin'.   (Cockney: NC)
     b. I haven't done nothing.   (SE: DN)

In SE, NC is unavailable with *n't*; in Cockney, in contrast, it is available. As suggested throughout, this contrast will not be dealt with by assuming some abstract distinction between Cockney *nothin'* and SE *nothing*. Rather, I assume that the negative marker on the verb is significantly different in the two varieties. In Cockney, I assume that negative auxiliaries like *ain't* are drawn from the lexicon as such. Consequently, the [+NEG] feature is borne underlyingly by a head. The non-overt operator licensing *nothin'* in (62a) will therefore be Op_{exp}. To all intents and purposes, Cockney behaves like Italian. In (62b), *n't* is deemed to be no more than a phonologically cliticized version of *not* in SpecNegP. Thus, in (62b), *nothing* is bound by a contentive negative operator, hence DN.

3.5   Counterexamples to Jespersen's Generalization?

3.5.1   West Flemish

At first sight, the data presented here suggest that Jespersen's Generalization falls down in the case of West Flemish (henceforth, WF). In section 3.5.1.1, I present the data; in section 3.5.1.2, I suggest an analysis, following Haegeman (1995), that somewhat weakens the status of WF as a counterexample.[56]

3.5.1.1 The data

In some respects, sentential negation in WF and French are similar: like French *ne*, the optional pre-verbal *en* is insufficient to mark sentential negation on its own, as in (63), and must co-occur with a negative phrasal constituent, either the negative adverb *nie* 'not', equivalent to French *pas*, as in (64), or some other negative element, as in (65):[57]

(63) ⋆da   Valère dienen boek *en*-eet   (Zanuttini 1991: 170 (278))
      that V.   that   book *en*-has

(64) da   Valère dienen boek *nie* (*en*-)eet   (Zanuttini 1991: 171 (279a))
      that V.   that   book not *en*- has
      ' . . . that V. doesn't have that book'

(65) a.   da   Valère ier   *niemand* (*en*-)kent   (Haegeman 1995: 116 (5b))
           that V.   here no-one   *en*- knows
           ' . . . that V. doesn't know anyone here'

      b.   da   Valère dienen boek *nieverst* (*en*-)vindt   (Zanuttini 1991:
           that V.   that   book nowhere *en*- finds   171 (280b))
           ' . . . that V. doesn't find that book anywhere'

      c.   da   Valère *geen geld* (*en*-)eet   (Zanuttini 1991: 171 (281a))
           that V.   no   money *en*- has
           ' . . . that V. has no money'

On the basis of these data, and given the discussion of French in chapters 1 and 2, I want to conclude that, in WF, like SE (and, indeed, Standard Dutch and Modern German), the abstract feature [+NEG] is borne by SpecNegP underlyingly, and I expect WF to pattern with the languages discussed in section 3.2.2. That is to say, I do not expect WF to be a non-NC language.

However, in contrast to Standard Modern Dutch and German, negative quantifiers can co-occur in WF, without canceling each other out, as in (66), taken from Haegeman (1995: 132–33 (39)):

56. For detailed discussion and analysis of negation in WF, see Haegeman (1992b, 1995: chapter 3) and H&Z (1996).
57. The data from WF are given in the context of embedded clauses to compensate for V2 effects.

(66) a.   da   Valère [*an niemand*] [*niets*]   gezeid (*en-*)oat
        that V.   to no-one   nothing said   *en-* had
        ' . . . that V. hadn't said anything to anyone'

    b.   da   Valère [*nooit*] [*an geen mens*] [*niets*]   gezeid (*en-*)oat
        that V.   never to no   person nothing said   *en-* had
        ' . . . that V. had never said anything to anyone'

    c.   da   Valère [*nooit*] [*van niemand*] ketent   (*en-*)was
        that V.   never of no-one   contented *en-* was
        ' . . . that V. was never pleased with anyone'

The XPs co-occurring with each other and, optionally, with *en* in (66) are clearly inherently negative: they are inherently negative quantifiers, rather than *any*-type NPIs.

Furthermore, the negative adverb *nie* can co-occur with negative quantifiers, again without the negation being canceled, as in (67), taken from Haegeman (1995: 133 (40)):

(67) a.   da   Valère [*an niemand*] [*niets*]   [*nie*] gezeid (*en-*)oat
        that V.   to no-one   nothing not said   *en-* had
        (= (66a))

    b.   da   Valère [*nooit*] [*an geen mens*] [*niets*]   [*nie*] gezeid (*en-*)oat
        that V.   never to no   person nothing not said   *en-* had
        (= (66b))

    c.   da   Valère [*nooit*] [*van niemand*] [*nie*] ketent   (*en-*)was
        that V.   never of no-one   not contented *en-* was
        (= (66c))

So, WF appears to be a counterexample to Jespersen's Generalization. The crucial negative marker *nie* occupies SpecNegP and, although *en* exists in WF as a pre-verbal negative marker associated with Neg°, its status seems comparable to that of *ne* in French (see section 3.1 as well as chapter 1, footnote 3) or Breton (see (8)). In WF, the feature [+NEG] seems to be associated with SpecNegP. Nevertheless, the data in (66), and especially (67), suggest that WF is an NC language, *contra* (2).

3.5.1.2   The analysis: NC and scrambling

The data from WF in section 3.5.1.1 suggested this language might be a counterexample to Jespersen's Generalization.[58] On the basis of (63) and (64), I concluded that, in WF, the feature [+NEG] is borne by SpecNegP. Accordingly, WF is predicted to be a non-NC language. The data in (66) and (67) show that this is

---

58. I am grateful to Liliane Haegeman for helpful discussion of the analysis put forward in this section. However, she cannot be held responsible for the suggestions I make here.

not in fact the case. In (66) and (67), negative quantifiers, for example, *niemand* 'no-one', *niets* 'nothing', *nooit* 'never', and *nieverst* 'nowhere', co-occur with an NC reading, not only with each other but also with the negative adverb *nie* 'not'. Is it possible to square these data from WF with Jespersen's Generalization? In this section, I show that there are a number of restrictions on NC in WF that suggest that Jespersen's Generalization (or, rather, the underlying principled account of the superficial descriptive generalization) can in fact be salvaged. In particular, the restrictions on NC suggest that the analysis of Jespersen's Generalization in terms of A'-binding from SpecNegP proposed in section 3.4.2 is along the right lines.

For the concordant readings in (66) and (67) to be available, the negative quantifiers must scramble leftward out of their base position. Following Haegeman (1995), I analyze this leftward scrambling as raising to (or above) Spec-NegP and conclude that, for reasons independent of the Neg Criterion, for example, WF is able to exploit this mechanism in order to avoid DN. This overt operation on negative constituents produces "negative absorption" (along the lines of *wh*-absorption) and leads to the observed concordant readings. The negative constituents associated with SpecNegP at S-structure are thus treated, to all intents and purposes, as a single negative constituent.[59] Consequently, while, on the surface of it, WF is indeed an exception to the generalization, the analysis presented in section 3.4.2 holds for this language, too.

In Haegeman's account of negative absorption (1995: 117–20), she assumes that the WF negative adverb *nie* 'not' has a fixed (S-structure) position, namely SpecNegP (generated to the left of Neg'). It seems to me that this is a reasonable assumption to make, one that is supported both by Pollock's (1989) and my own chapter 2 analyses of (the derivation of) French *pas*. Irrespective of whether the traditional SOV West Germanic languages such as WF are analyzed as being head-final or head-initial,[60] the position of phrasal constituents within an embedded domain with respect to *nie* will provide a diagnostic for whether their structural position is above or below NegP. Material preceding *nie* is either in SpecNegP as well or above a minimal NegP; material following *nie* but preceding the finite verb in AgrS° is contained within Neg'.

Like Standard Dutch and German, WF is a scrambling language. Scrambling is optional or compulsory, depending on various factors that I do not need to go into here. The discussion here is limited to what is relevant for NC. The acceptability of both examples in (68) shows that scrambling of the PP complement of an adjective is optional. The PP can remain in situ in post-adjectival position, as

---

59. This could be seen as a consequence of the Neg Criterion and the bi-uniqueness Haegeman assumes (1995: 97) between heads and specifiers. In discussion, Liliane Haegeman has suggested to me that "negative absorption" should not require the concordant negative XPs to occupy SpecNegP as such. Rather, the phenomenon should be possible from "extended" specifier positions, in the sense of Grimshaw (1993). See also Kayne (1994).

60. See the version of the Universal Base Hypothesis proposed by Kayne (1994) and implemented for Standard Dutch by Zwart (1993).

in (68a) or, alternatively, may scramble out of the AP, as in (68b) (data from Haegeman 1995: 130 (33)):

(68) a.   da   Valère [$_{AP}$ ketent [$_{PP}$ me   zenen kado]] was
          that V.   contented with his   present was
          ' . . . that V. was satisfied with his present'

     b.   da   Valère [$_{PP}$ me   zenen kado] [$_{AP}$ ketent   *t*] was
          that V.   with his   present   contented   was
          (= (68a))

In contrast to the optional nature of scrambling in (68), where the PP contains a negative quantifier, scrambling is compulsory for the negative to take sentential scope. Failure to scramble means that the negative quantifier has narrow/local scope and the pre-verbal negative marker *en* is not licensed; hence the ungrammaticality of (69a) with the pre-verbal negative marker:[61]

(69) a.   da   Valère [$_{AP}$ ketent [$_{PP}$ me   niets]] (⋆en)-was
          that V.   contented with nothing   *en*- was
          ' . . . that V. was satisfied with nothing'

     b.   da   Valère [$_{PP}$ me   niets] [$_{AP}$ ketent   *t*] (en)-was
          that V.   with nothing   contented   *en*- was
          ' . . . that V. wasn't satisfied with anything'

Haegeman (1995: 135) explains the contrast between (69a) and (69b) in terms of the Neg Criterion. In order to be licensed, *en* requires a spec-head configuration with a negative operator (like French negative *ne*; see chapter 1), such as the negative PP. Raising of the PP to SpecNegP or above, for example, as I assume has happened in (69b), produces the necessary configuration, and *en* is licensed. The position of the PP in (69b) is therefore assumed to be (no lower than) SpecNegP.

In addition to licensing pre-verbal *en*, scrambling of negative quantifiers in WF is relevant to NC. Consider the interpretation of the strings in (70), taken from Haegeman (1995: 132 (38)):

(70) a.   da   Valère [$_{PP}$ van niemand] nie [$_{AP}$ ketent   *t*] en-was   NC
          that V.   of no-one   not   contented   *en*-was
          ' . . . that V. wasn't pleased with anyone'

---

61. If the pre-verbal negative marker *en* is omitted, (69a) is not, in fact, ungrammatical as such. Rather, the negative constituent fails to achieve sentential scope as a consequence of not having scrambled out of its containing AP and has narrow scope. Haegeman (1995: 136–37) suggests that (69a) would then be interpreted in one of two ways. Either the negative constituent is echoic or *Valère* is very easy to please, that is, 'he is happy (even) when he has very little (or even nothing at all)'. With pre-verbal *en* in place, (69a) is indeed ungrammatical, as indicated in the text, since failure of the negative constituent to raise (to SpecNegP) fails, in turn, to mark sentential negation and license *en*. See also the discussion of French *ne* and *pas* in chapters 1 and 2. Note that these facts are further evidence to suggest that WF *en* has parallel licensing conditions to French *ne*.

b.   da Valère nie [$_{AP}$ ketent [$_{PP}$ van niemand]] en-was   DN
c.   da Valère nie [$_{PP}$ van niemand] [$_{AP}$ ketent t] en-was   DN
      b and c: ' . . . that V. was not pleased with no-one'

Given the presence of *nie* in SpecNegP in the strings in (70), the clauses are interpreted as negative, and pre-verbal *en* is licensed throughout. There is, however, a crucial difference between (70a) and (70b, c). In (70a), in which the negative PP has scrambled to the left of *nie* in SpecNegP, the two occurrences of negative XPs (*niemand* and *nie*) contribute to a single instance of sentential negation; (70a) is an example of NC. This is not the case in (70b, c). In (70b), the negative PP remains in situ while, in (70c), the negative PP scrambles locally but is still to the right of *nie* in SpecNegP. In both cases, NC is unavailable; the two negative XPs cancel each other out, leading to DN. The contrast is clear from the translations.

The different interpretations witnessed in (70) show that WF is not an NC language *à l'italienne*. Rather, it seems that there are clear *configurational* constraints on NC in this language. Given the interpretation of (70b, c), that is, the unavailability of NC, Haegeman (1995) concludes that these configurational constraints amount to the need for negative XPs to be associated with SpecNegP for a concordant reading to be available. The string in (70a) respects this constraint if the surface position of the negative PP is "associated with SpecNegP", that is, if it occupies an (extended) SpecNegP position. Haegeman argues that this is indeed the case, suggesting that the scrambled negative constituent is adjoined either to NegP or to SpecNegP itself. In contrast, given that, in (70b, c), the negative PP has not raised to an (extended) SpecNegP position, the strings do not satisfy the configurational constraint on NC; hence the DN interpretations. (See also DeGraff 1993b: 73fn16.)

What, then, is one to make of WF? To what extent does it represent a problem for Jespersen's Generalization? I suggest that, while the data reviewed here clearly show that Jespersen's Generalization needs to be qualified, the configurational constraint on NC in WF in fact lends support to the analysis of NC proposed in section 3.4.2. A number of points need to be made. First, Jespersen's Generalization predicts that WF is not an NC language. Indeed, the data in (70b, c) show that, at the very least, WF is not a generalized NC language. Jespersen's Generalization does not therefore fail entirely in the case of WF.

Second, the nature of the configurational constraint on NC in WF suggests that, in order for NC to be available, negative XPs need to move to a position outside the scope of the negative marker *nie* in SpecNegP, whereby scope relations are determined, at least in part, by A'-binding, itself defined in terms of c-command. In (70a), the negative PP is higher than *nie* and escapes its scope. The fact that, in its surface position, the negative PP is itself then associated with the same SpecNegP and Neg° positions by negative absorption, it could be argued, prevents the PP from taking scope over (and canceling out) the negative marker *nie* in SpecNegP. In (70b, c), the negative PP fails to move to a position outside the c-command domain of *nie* and, hence, remains in its scope, leading to logical DN. All these facts are, arguably, predicted by the analysis of NC and DN proposed in section 3.4.2. To that extent, the facts from WF back up the account of Jespersen's Generalization suggested here.

Finally, given that Jespersen's Generalization is, after all, nothing more than a label for an observed set of empirical facts, it is, I suggest, more important that WF be compatible with the explanation of the facts than that it be in accord with the generalization based on the facts. In the next section, I turn to Modern French, which might also be regarded as problematic for Jespersen's Generalization.[62]

3.5.2 Modern French

Like Italian *non* and Spanish *no*, the French negative marker *ne* is proclitic on the first finite verb in a clause. In contrast to the Italian and Spanish markers, though, Modern French *ne* is generally neither sufficient nor necessary to mark sentential negation, although it was at earlier stages in the development of the language.[63] In this respect, Modern French *ne* is like WF *en*, discussed in the previous section. As was seen in section 3.1, proclitic *ne* came to be reinforced by syntactically independent constituents, the most sturdy of which proved to be the element *pas*.

(71) Je (*ne*) vois ⋆(*pas*) ta   mère.   (Modern French)
     I *ne* see   *pas* your mother
     'I can't see your mother.'

In view (a) of the obligatory presence of *pas*, and the only optional presence of *ne*, to mark pure sentential negation in the modern language and (b) of the fact that *ne* can appear without contributing a negative feature to the clause, I conclude that, underlyingly at least, it is SpecNegP (rather than Neg°) that bears the feature [+NEG].[64]

Given this conclusion, the generalization in (2) predicts that Modern French is a non-NC language. Evaluating this prediction, that is, determining whether negative concord exists in Modern French as in SC, Cockney, Italian, or

---

62. There is an NC-like phenomenon in Afrikaans, another language related to Dutch, which deserves brief mention. NC appears to be possible with a sentence-final particle, *nie*. Given that the primary negative marker in Afrikaans, (also) *nie*, is associated with SpecNegP, Jespersen's Generalization predicts that Afrikaans is a non-NC language. However, if Robbers (1992) is right in analyzing the sentence-final *nie* as the realization of Neg°, then the nature of the NC is no longer problematic. That sentence-final *nie* is Neg° is supported by its incompatibility with true imperatives and nonsentential negation. Of course, grammaticalization of a SpecNegP-associated element as a Neg°-associated element is perfectly in keeping with the Negative Cycle, as discussed in section 3.1.

63. See (4a, b) and the discussion in section 1.2.4.

64. See section 1.3.4 for arguments that *ne* is not inherently negative, in examples such as (i):

(i) Jeanine craint que Pierrette ne soit   en retard.
     J.   fears that P.   *ne* be-SUBJ in lateness
     'J. fears P. might be late.'
     ≠ 'J. fears P. might *not* be late.'

Spanish, is not a straightforward issue, since, with the exception of the determiner *nul*, no French "negative" can convincingly be argued to be morphologically negative (on a par with the *ni*-NPIs of SC or the *no*-NPIs of SE).[65] A set of morphologically negative indefinite quantifiers did not develop in French.[66] Consequently, it is unclear whether the "negatives" that do exist in the language, such as *rien* 'nothing/anything', *personne* 'no-one/anyone', and *jamais* 'never/ever', are inherently negative, that is, whether they are equivalent to the *no-/ni*-NPIs or the *any-/i*-NPIs of SE and SC, respectively.

On the basis of the generalization in (2), one would, of course, predict that these French "negatives" are equivalent to the *any-/i*-NPIs. The generalization in (2) predicts that Modern French is a non-NC language; if these "negatives" were in fact inherently negative, Modern French would be an NC language, contrary to prediction. Nevertheless, arguments have been advanced to support both analyses in the literature. For example, while Laka (1990) and Déprez (forthcoming) treat them as polarity items in the traditional sense of the term, that is, not as inherently negative, Zanuttini (1991) argues that they are negative quantifiers, that is, that they *are* inherently negative.

I do not review the arguments presented for and against the two positions here; instead, I refer the reader to the literature. (See also Quer 1993 for discussion.) However, given the otherwise robust nature of the generalization in (2), I adopt the analysis of these "negatives" as being equivalent to the *any-/i*-NPIs and conclude that Modern French is a non-NC language. This is, however, not merely a convenient move, given the general argument put forward in this chapter. Support for the conclusion can be drawn from a comparison of Modern French with earlier forms of the language. NC of a fashion was possible in seventeenth-century French (henceforth, C17Fr). Examples are given in (72), taken from Haase (1969: 256 §102A):

(72) a. Encore qu' ils *n'* aient   *pas* la mesure d' *aucune* sorte de
         yet   that they *ne* have-SUBJ *pas* the measure of *aucune* kind of
         vers.
         verse
         'Even though they don't sound like verse of any kind.'

---

65. But see Haase (1969: 110 §52B), who claims that even the negative value of *nul* has been progressively lost. Posner (1985a: 170) also suggests that the few Latin negatives other than *non* that survived, such as *nullus*, from which French *nul* is derived, "were treated more as negative polarity items than as inherently semantically negative". Posner (1996: 302) comments on the considerable number of "negative items" within the Romance languages–and French in particular–that are derived from etymologically positive ones. For discussion of the etymology of Romance n-words, see Laka (1993a).

66. This is a fact that itself deserves investigation. The same can be said for Catalan. What is perhaps significant in this respect about these two varieties is the fact that they have phrasal negative markers, namely *pas* in both cases.

b. *Ne* faites *pas* semblant   de *rien*.
    ne do-IMP *pas* semblance of *rien*
    'Don't pretend anything.'

c. Ce *n'* est *pas* que je pense à *personne* d'   ici.
    it *ne* is *pas* that I think of *personne* from here
    'It's not that I'm thinking of anyone here.'

d. On *ne* veut *pas rien* faire   ici   qui   vous déplaise.
    we *ne* want *pas rien* do-INF here which you displease-SUBJ
    'We don't want to do anything that might upset you.'

In these examples, post-verbal *pas* co-occurs with the "negatives" *aucun, rien*, and *personne* (as well as with *ne*). While the "negatives" can, with some exceptions,[67] co-occur with each other in the modern language, they cannot co-occur with *pas* (in all clause-mate and most multiclausal contexts—see section 5.5.2) with a concordant interpretation in the way that they do in (72). Where they do co-occur, the interpretation is of logical DN.

The crucial difference between C17Fr as described by Haase (1969) and the modern language is that the former was still at the stage in the Negative Cycle illustrated by (4b), whereas the latter is at the stage in the Negative Cycle illustrated by (4c–e) (depending on the variety of Modern French under consideration). That is to say, in C17Fr, the pre-verbal negative marker *ne* was necessary and sufficient to mark sentential negation. While *ne* was compulsory, the appearance of post-verbal *pas* for reinforcement was optional. At this point, pre-verbal *ne* was clearly still inherently negative (like *no/non* in Modern Spanish/Italian). This is illustrated in (73), taken from Haase (1969: 251 §100B).[68] In Modern French, in contrast, the appearance of post-verbal *pas* is an obligatory marker of pure sentential negation, as shown in (71).

(73) a. Il *ne* meurt de cette peine.
         he *ne* dies   of this pain
         'This pain isn't killing him.'

     b. Je *ne* veux du tout vous voir.
         I *ne* want at all you see
         'I don't want to see you at all.'

     c. Aussi pour *ne* vous ennuyer, je vous les   dirai.
         also for *ne* you annoy   I you them say-FUT
         'Therefore, in order not to annoy you, I will tell you them.'

---

67. See Muller (1991: 269) for details of possible combinations.

68. In fact, it was during the seventeenth century that the appearance of a post-verbal marker of pure negation began to be obligatory. The examples given in the text are still typical during the early part of the century but are rarer by the turn of the eighteenth century. Posner (1985a: 171) claims that, certainly by the seventeenth century, *pas, point, mie, rien*, and so on, had become "virtually obligatory disjunctive appendages of pre-verbal *ne*".

C17Fr thus belongs with those languages reviewed in section 3.2.1. According-ly, the generalization in (2) predicts that C17Fr should be an NC language. In-deed, it seems clear that this is the case.

The question to be addressed, though, is this: in (72), which negative ele-ments enter into NC with each other? I suggest that it is pre-verbal *ne* that enters into NC with the post-verbal *pas*:[69] both pre-verbal *ne* and post-verbal *pas* are inherently negative, yet are interpreted together as a single instance of sentential negation, that is, in an NC reading. I assume this to be attributable to a structure like the one in (51). The inherently negative *ne* occupies Neg°. SpecNegP is occupied by Haegeman's (1995) non-overt expletive operator: Op_{exp}. Op_{exp} binds *pas*, which, consequently, does not have to raise into SpecNegP.[70] In turn, nega-tive *pas*, adjoined to VP, takes scope over the elements *aucun(e)*, *rien*, and *per-sonne*, which I assume are non-inherently negative NPIs like the *any*-NPIs of SE. (See Kayne 1984: 39fn4 for correspondences between French *personne* and SE *anyone*.)

What, then, of the difference between Modern French and, say, C17Fr? The generalization in (2) predicts that Modern French is a non-NC language. What has changed? I argue that the change underlying the shift from NC to non-NC status centers on the pre-verbal marker *ne*. Up to C17Fr, *ne* (= Neg°) was inher-ently negative; it bore the abstract feature [+NEG] underlyingly and could serve as the unique marker of sentential negation. Subsequently, and for reasons dis-cussed in section 3.1.2, *ne* lost this property. Given that one of the two original elements entering into NC is then no longer negative, the issue of NC is no lon-ger relevant. On such a view, Modern French is a non-NC language.[71]

The issue that remains to be addressed, however, is why the NPIs (e.g., *rien*, *personne*, *jamais*), while compatible with each other, are no longer compatible with *pas*. This issue is addressed in section 4.4.2.[72]

---

69. This interpretation of the data is also suggested by Hirschbühler and Labelle (1993: 18).

70. This was the conclusion drawn in section 2.1.2 on the basis of the relative position of *pas* and lexical infinitives.

71. With respect to the pre-French period, Vennemann (1974: 366–68) suggests that the Latin negative marker *non* is an adverb (like *pas* in Modern French). In a verb-final language like Latin, *non* is therefore expected to be pre-verbal. One would therefore want to associate *non* with SpecNegP rather than Neg°. Consequently, Jespersen's Generalization predicts, correctly (Posner 1984: 1, Winters 1987: 28, 30), that Latin is a non-NC language: "With minor exceptions, if one of the negative words in view occurs in a negative clause as just defined, the effect is for the two negative features to cancel each other out and result in a non-negative, i.e., affirmative, predication" (Agard 1984: vol. 2, p. 151). The claim that Latin *non*, adopted in Old French, is a phrasal constituent rather than a head is supported by the fact that sentence-initial *non*, when used emphatically in sentence-initial position in Old French, triggered inversion, as in (i). (See Posner 1985a and references there.)

(i)   Non fera   il.   (Old French, Posner 1985a: 179 (12))
       non do-FUT he-EMPH
       'He certainly won't do so.'

It seems plausible that, like Latin *non*, tonic *non*, which survives in Modern French, is also an XP (adverbial) element.

72. DeGraff (1993b: 73fn15) suggests that the incompatibility between *pas* and the other "negat-ives"—the unavailability of negative absorption, in his analysis—is that, while the other "negatives" are quantifiers, *pas* is not. Given that the analysis proposed for the other "negatives" in chapters 4 and 5

3.6   Discussion and summary

3.6.1   Discussion

The analysis of Jespersen's Generalization proposed in this chapter has relied crucially on what I have termed a "weak" interpretation of the relationship between a head and its specifier in terms of compatibility rather than strict agreement. According to this interpretation, where a head bears relevant (agreement, affective) features underlyingly, its specifier is prevented from bearing incompatible features, but does not have to bear identical features. In other words, Rizzi's DA is unidirectional, from specifier to head, but not from head to specifier. Such a modification to the spec-head relationship was arguably derived from considerations of economy and made it possible to account for Jespersen's Generalization on the basis of cyclic fluctuation in the underlying position of the abstract feature [+NEG].

Of course, given that natural languages can be distinguished in terms of other cyclic parameters, too, the question arises as to whether the approach adopted here, if justified, can be used to explain distinctions between natural languages other than the "NC-versus-non-NC" distinction. One parameter that has received considerable attention over the last decade and a half is the *pro*-drop or null subject parameter.[73]

Pro-drop is traditionally viewed as parametric variation in the (morphological) "strength" of AgrS°. Languages in which AgrS° is morphologically strong are *pro*-drop; languages in which AgrS° is morphologically weak are not. In the original terms of Rizzi (1982: 42), strong AgrS° and, hence, (referential) *pro*-drop amounted to [+PERSON] specification.[74] One conclusion that it might be possible to draw is that the "strong-versus-weak-AgrS°" distinction and, hence, the *pro*-drop parameter could be due to (cyclic) fluctuation of the underlying position of some abstract agreement feature, which one might label [AGR]. Thus, in *pro*-drop languages, it could be argued that AgrS° bears the feature [AGR] as an inherent or underlying property.[75] This would correspond to "strong AgrS°". Significantly, in such a language, AgrS° is not reliant upon its specifier for the

does not take recourse to negative absorption, such an approach will not work. It would also be difficult to square such an idea with the facts from Québécois, in which *pas* is perfectly compatible with the other "negatives" apart from *plus*. (See (10) and section 4.4.2.1 and section 5.5.2 for discussion of Québécois.) Note, though, that Haegeman (1996b) uses a similar approach to distinguish between two sets of negative elements in WF that cannot enter into NC with each other.

73. See the studies in Jaeggli and Safir (eds.) (1989).

74. See also Pollock (1997a: chapter 13, section 2.1). Dupuis et al. (1992) suggest the relevant feature is [+NUMBER]. See footnote 75.

75. Rizzi (1982: 131) calls this feature [+PRONOUN] and suggests that it is optionally borne by INFL (my AgrS°) in a *pro*-drop language such as Italian. As an alternative, however, Rizzi (1982: 176fn16) envisages the possibility that such a primitive feature may not be necessary and that, rather, the properties attributed to it could be a consequence of feature specifications as person and number, that is, [AGR].

[AGR] feature; hence the null-subject nature of the language.[76] In contrast, in non-*pro*-drop languages, [AGR] would *not* be borne by AgrS° underlyingly. In this second scenario, AgrS° could be assigned the feature only by association with an overt specifier, by DA, which is perfectly in keeping with my "weak" version of the spec-head relation based on compatibility. This would correspond to "weak AgrS°". Consequently, subjects cannot be non-overt; overt subjects have to raise from SpecVP to SpecAgrSP; the language is non-*pro*-drop. Cyclic diachronic fluctuation between *pro*-drop and non-*pro*-drop could then be argued to be the result of an (abstract) "Agreement Cycle" running alongside the familiar Negative Cycle. It seems to me that this is a potentially fruitful line of inquiry that deserves attention. (See the comments in Déprez forthcoming.)

3.6.2 Summary

In the course of the preceding sections it was suggested that the pattern observed by Jespersen and referred to as the Negative Cycle amounts to cyclic toing and fro-ing of the *overt* realization of sentential negation between the head and specifier of NegP. It was further suggested that the *abstract* realization of sentential negation, that is, the locus of the feature [+NEG], could also fluctuate in a similar, if not the same, cyclic fashion.

This conclusion led me to reconsider the nature of the spec-head relationship. Instead of assuming an obligatory two-way dynamic process guaranteeing that the relevant features borne by specifier and head are identical, it was suggested that spec-head "agreement" should be interpreted as nothing more than a process that makes sure that feature incompatibility is excluded. While this interpretation of spec-head agreement did not exclude the possibility, within NegP, of both SpecNegP and Neg° being positively specified for the feature [±NEG], it did make it possible to satisfy the Neg Criterion without specifier and head *necessarily* both bearing the feature [+NEG]. The importance of this move for my purposes was that it allowed the Neg Criterion to be satisfied without SpecNegP bearing the feature [+NEG].

The cross-linguistic variation that this allowed for paved the way to an account of the (im)possibility of NC. In some languages, SpecNegP is specified [+NEG]; in others, it is not. The empirical observation to be accounted for is that NC is unavailable in the first group of languages, yet available in the second. The account provided for this generalization was a modified version of Progovac's (1994) analysis of NPI licensing, itself based on A'-binding. In the implementation proposed, inherently negative polarity items are seen as A'-anaphors that need, following Principle A of BT, to be bound within a given domain. It is assumed, with Progovac, that the relevant domain is NegP, with possible exten-

---

76. Plausibly, the fact that *pro*-drop languages tend to allow free inversion (analyzed as subjects in situ in SpecVP) could also be attributed to the fact that a strong AgrS° would not need an overt specifier to raise from SpecVP to SpecAgrSP in order for AgrS° to be associated with [AGR] features.

possible extension to AgrSP. Capitalizing on Progovac's Generalized Principle A of BT, which guarantees that binders are X'-compatible with bindees, it is concluded that the A'-binder of inherently negative NPIs is the polarity operator in SpecNegP, whose position there is guaranteed by the Neg Criterion. In non-NC languages, that is, languages in which SpecNegP is specified [+NEG], co-occurrence of a negative marker and a negative NPI leads to DN because the former has scope over the latter.

4

Other Negative Adverbs

Having dealt with *ne* (chapter 1) and the core negative marker *pas* (chapter 2) and having concluded that Modern French is a non-NC language (chapter 3), I turn, in chapters 4 and 5, to what might be termed the periphery, or the "negative" elements other than *pas*, which Muller (1991) labels *semi-négations*. After establishing an inventory of the relevant lexical items, I subdivide the group into two, considering here just the *adverbs* (*plus* 'no/any more/longer', *jamais* '(n)ever', and *guère* 'hardly (ever)'), leaving the *arguments* for chapter 5 (*rien* 'anything/nothing' and *personne* 'anyone/no-one').

In section 4.1, I distinguish between negative adverbs and arguments. After initial discussion of the distribution and interpretation of the adverbs, one feature of the data becomes clear, namely the far-reaching parallels between the distribution of these elements and that of *pas*. With this observation in mind, I consider some possible conclusions about the syntactic properties of negative adverbs, drawing heavily on those made in chapter 2 for *pas*. In particular, given that I analyzed $[_{XP}$ pas $]$ in terms of Move-α, I assume, a priori, that it is probably best to approach the syntax of the negative adverbs in terms of XP movement as well. In section 4.2, I reconsider the data. Although it seemed, at first glance, warranted to throw negative adverbs into the same bag as *pas*, it becomes apparent that the distributional parallels are not total. First, the negative adverbs differ from *pas* in terms of their co-occurrence possibilities (section 4.2.1); negative adverbs can readily co-occur with each other but not—in the standard language, at least—with *pas* (with the relevant NC reading). Second, they differ in terms of the positions they can occupy with respect to infinitives (section 4.2.2); negative adverbs have a freer distribution than *pas*. These differences are taken into account when I come to my conclusions in section 4.3. These exploit the discussion in chapter 3, especially section 3.5.1.1, and the idea that Modern French is a non-NC language. I interpret this as indicating that the negative adverbs (and, as I shall show, the negative arguments, discussed in chapter 5) are not in fact themselves inherently negative. Rather, it is suggested that they appear canonically in the scope of the non-overt operator, Op, which, as has been discussed in earlier chapters, *is* inherently negative. It will be argued that an analysis of the negative adverbs in terms of Op allows a principled account of the differences between the negative adverbs and *pas*, as well as allowing one to maintain the conclusion that Modern French is a non-NC language.

Section 4.4 shows how the analysis proposed accounts for the data. My conclusions are summarized in section 4.5.

4.1 Inventory: negative adverbs and arguments

The elements that will be considered in this chapter are *plus* 'no/any more/longer', *jamais* '(n)ever', and *guère* 'hardly (ever)'. I assume, on the basis of their distributions, illustrated in (1c–e), that these elements, like *pas*, are all adverbial in nature.[1]

(1) a. Paul sera   riche.
          P.   be-FUT rich
          'P. will be rich.'

     b. Paul ne sera   PAS riche.
          P.   *ne* be-FUT *pas* rich
          'P. won't be rich.'

     c. Paul ne sera   PLUS riche.
          P.   *ne* be-FUT *plus* rich
          'P. will no longer be rich.'

     d. Paul ne sera   JAMAIS riche.
          P.   *ne* be-FUT *jamais* rich
          'P. won't ever be rich.'

     e. Paul ne sera   GUÈRE riche.
          P.   *ne* be-FUT *guère* rich
          'P. will hardly be rich.'

In association, optionally, with *ne*, these elements modify a positive utterance, for example (1a), just like *pas* in (1b). One might assume, therefore, that the negative adverbs share the properties attributed to *pas* in chapter 2, namely that they are [+NEG] XPs, base-generated in a relatively low position reflecting their scope over the predicate and subsequently raised into SpecNegP to mark sentential negation (and thereby license *ne*). These assumptions are explored in more detail and partially revised in sections 4.2 and 4.3. The data presented here further illustrate the parallel between these adverbs and *pas*.

(2) a. Marie ne va   PAS   être   en retard.
     b. Marie ne va   JAMAIS   être   en retard.
          M.   *ne* goes *pas/jamais* be-INF in lateness
          'M. won't (ever) be late.'

1. As discussed in section 1.2.4, pre-verbal *ne* is optionally dropped in most varieties of spoken French. See chapter 1, footnote 3, for references.

(3) a. J-P n' a PAS   lu de romans depuis des années.
    b. J-P n' a PLUS lu de romans depuis des années.
        J-P *ne* has *pas/plus* read of novels since of-the years
        'J-P hasn't read any (more) novels for years.'

In (2), *pas/jamais* intervenes between *va* (the finite form of *aller* 'to go') and the infinitive *être* 'to be'. In (3), *pas/plus* intervenes between *a* (the finite form of *avoir* 'to have') and the past participle *lu* 'read'.[2] Note further that both *pas* and *plus* license the pseudopartitive [$_{NumP}$ Ø [de romans]] in (3). (See section 2.2.1 for discussion of pseudopartitives.)

In a purely intuitive sense, the parallel behavior noted between *pas* and the other adverbs may be attributable to the fact that all these items have a parallel function. Like *pas*, the negative adverbs are predicate-modifying functors. In terms of the distinction drawn by Di Sciullo and Williams (1986) between different types of modification, negative adverbs and *pas* modify the predicate by a mechanism of "function composition". Crucially, negative adverbs and *pas* do not affect the θ-structure of the verb or VP with which they are associated. This contrasts with the negatives in the strings in (4):

(4) a. Paul ne mange rien.
        P. *ne* eats *rien*
        'P. isn't eating anything.'

    b. Personne ne m' écrit plus.
        personne ne me writes *plus*
        'No-one writes to me any more.'

In (4), *rien* and *personne* absorb a θ-role assigned by the verb: the internal theme θ-role of *manger* 'to eat' in (4a), the external agent θ-role of *écrire* 'to write' in (4b). These elements, therefore, contribute to saturating the θ-grid of the verbal predicate and are argumental in that sense. They bear Di Sciullo and Williams's (1986) modification relation of "θ-role satisfaction". This, I assume, involves underlying association with an A-position. In contrast to the negative adverbs illustrated in (1c–e), *personne* and *rien* cannot therefore freely be

---

2. Gaatone (1971: 138) notes that, with compound tense forms, such as (3), the adverb *jamais* may exceptionally follow the past participle. He labels this "un effet de style recherché".
(i) Celle-ci n' avait ensuite conçu   JAMAIS qu' Albertine pût   me quitter
     She   *ne* had then   conceived *jamais* that A.   could-IMP:SUBJ me leave-INF
     d' elle-même . . .
     of her self
     'She had then never considered that A. might leave me on her own initiative . . . '
(ii) Si bas que l' eût   traîné JAMAIS l' ingénieux ennemi, tout lien n' était pas
     So low that him had-IMP:SUBJ dragged *jamais* the ingenious enemy all link *ne* was *pas*
     rompu ni tout écho du   dehors étouffé . . .
     broken nor all echo from-the outside deadened
     'As low as the ingenious enemy might ever have dragged him, no ties were ruptured and no sounds from outside blocked . . . '
I assume this is a relic from some earlier stage in the development of the language.

"added" to a clause to negate it. For this reason, I distinguish between the likes of adverbial (function compositional) *plus*, *jamais*, and so on and argumental (θ-role satisfying) *rien* and *personne*, dealing with the former here and postponing consideration of the latter until chapter 5.

The translations of the examples in (1) show a clear *interpretative* distinction between *pas* and the negative adverbs. Whereas *pas* corresponds to the Boolean negative connective ¬, the negative adverbs are interpreted as composite elements comprising ¬ *plus something else*. In other words, the negative adverbs are interpreted as containing *pas*. The negative adverb in (1c), *plus*, is interpreted as equivalent to an unmarked adverb of duration, *encore* 'still/yet', combined with *pas*. In (1d), *jamais* is a lexicalized version of something like *toujours* 'always' combined with *pas*. In (1e), *guère* is a lexicalized equivalent of an adverb of extent, intensity, or degree combined with *pas*.

This informal discussion suggests two things. First, given my characterization of the way *pas* is interpreted as ¬, it is not surprising that it plays a central role in negation in Modern French. In contrast to the negative adverbs, *pas* is atomic, an absolute negative. *Pas* is more central for the simple reason that it is more basic. This is relevant later. Second, one should not be surprised to note distributional similarities between the syntax of *pas* and the syntax of the negative adverbs, given that the latter are interpreted as if they contain the former. Recall that, in (1c–e), (2b), and (3b), the negative adverbs pattern with *pas* in (1b), (2a), and (3a), respectively. Tentatively, one might assume that the negative adverbs can be generated in either of the same two configurations discussed in chapter 2 in the context of *pas*, namely in an adjoined position or in Spec-NumP within a pseudopartitive. However, a strictly parallel analysis would lead one to predict that the distribution of *pas* is *identical* to the distribution of the negative adverbs. Yet, this prediction is not borne out by the data, as shown in section 4.2. It is therefore not possible to claim that the negative adverbs and *pas* are syntactically identical. A precise syntactic characterization of the negative adverbs in question is proposed in section 4.3, based on the insight that these negatives are semantically complex, comprising ¬ and another element. The syntactic analysis exploits this complexity and suggests that the two elements enjoy a certain degree of autonomy with respect to each other.

4.2   Distribution of negative adverbs

In addition to the semantic properties distinguishing *pas* from *plus*, *jamais*, and *guère* discussed in the previous section, there are a number of distributional differences that show that the parallel suggested by the data in (1b–e), (2), and (3) is not complete. In section 4.2.1, I show that co-occurrence patterns distinguish *pas* from negative adverbs (and arguments) (in the standard language); in section 4.2.2, I show that negative adverbs have a freer distribution than *pas* with respect to infinitives.

4.2.1   Co-occurrence restrictions

The first difference between *pas* and the negative adverbs that I consider relates to co-occurrence possibilities. As illustrated in (5a-c), the negative adverbs can —a certain number of lexical-item-specific restrictions notwithstanding (see (5d-f))—co-occur in the same clause, as well as with the negative arguments to be discussed in chapter 5 (see (6) and (7)), without leading to logical Double Negation (henceforth, DN).[3]

(5)   a.   Paul ne verra   plus jamais son père.
          P.   *ne* see-FUT *plus jamais* his father
          'P. won't ever see his father again.'

      b.   Paul ne verra   plus guère son père.
          P.   *ne* see-FUT *plus guère* his father
          'P. won't see much of his father any more.'

      c.   Paul ne verra   jamais plus son père.
          P.   *ne* see-FUT *jamais plus* his father
          'P. will never see his father again.'

      d.   ★Paul ne verra jamais guère son père.

      e.   ★Paul ne verra guère plus son père.

      f.   ★Paul ne verra guère jamais son père.

(6)   Paul ne verra   jamais personne.
     P.   *ne* see-FUT *jamais personne*
     'P. will never see anyone.'

(7)   a.   Paul ne verra   plus jamais rien.
          P.   *ne* see-FUT *plus jamais rien*
          'P. won't ever see anything again.'

---

3. The ungrammaticality of (5d) and (5f) indicates that *jamais* and *guère* are mutually incompatible. This could be due to the fact that both are adverbs of extent of one sort or another. (See Zanuttini 1997a and Cinque 1995, 1996, 1998 for an approach to adverbs as specifiers of functional projections. This approach accounts for ordering restrictions among adverbs and, under the assumption that *jamais* and *guère* occupy the specifier position of the same functional projection, may provide some insight into the fact that the two are mutually incompatible.) The ungrammaticality of (5e) does not indicate mutual incompatibility between *plus* and *guère*, since (5b) is acceptable. See Muller (1991: 269) for a tabular representation of the co-occurrence possibilities of pairs of negative adverbs/arguments. Note that Muller considers only *pairs* of negative elements. He does not consider n-tuples where n>2 such as my examples in (7).

     In (i), whose grammaticality represents an apparent counterexample to the pattern illustrated in (5e), only *guère* is interpreted in association with *ne*. The element *plus* is a positive element, common in comparatives. I am grateful to Bernadette Plunkett for providing the example.
(i)   Paul NE voit son père   GUÈRE PLUS qu' il   ne voit sa mère.
     P.   *ne* sees his father *guère plus* that he *ne* sees his mother
     'P. doesn't see his father much more than (he sees) his mother.'

  b. Paul ne verra   plus guère personne.
      P.   *ne* see-FUT *plus guère personne*
      'P. won't see much of anyone any more.'

  c. Paul ne verra   jamais plus rien.
      P.   *ne* see-FUT *jamais plus rien*
      'P. will never see anything again.'

In sharp contrast, the distribution of *pas* is more restricted in that it cannot (in standard metropolitan Modern French, at least) be a clause-mate with any of the negative adverbs with an NC reading.[4]

(8) a. ⋆Paul ne verra jamais pas son père.

     b. ⋆Paul ne verra pas plus son père.

(9) [*]Paul ne voit pas rien.[5]   (DN)

This state of affairs leaves one with something of a problem. Given the parallels between *pas* and the negative adverbs already discussed, one could conclude that, like *pas*, the elements *plus*, *jamais*, *guère*, and so on are also inherently negative. The grammatical strings in (5)–(7) would then represent examples of NC, familiar from chapter 3. However, given the syntactic nature of the principal negative marker in (standard and nonstandard varieties of)

---

4. Of course, *pas* can co-occur with "negatives" to produce logical DN, as in (9). The only exceptions to the generalization given in the text for standard metropolitan Modern French are strings of the basic pattern *Pas un(e) (seul(e)) N ne VP*, as in (i) and (ii), in which a negative adverb may be associated with the verb:

(i)   PAS une seule proposition n' a   JAMAIS été   acceptée.
      pas a   single suggestion *ne* has *jamais* been accepted
      'Not a single suggestion has ever been accepted.'

(ii) PAS un seul   étudiant ne désire PLUS venir   me voir.
      pas a   single student *ne* wants *plus* come-INF me see-INF
      'Not a single student wants to come and see me any more.'

Nominal expressions with the structure *pas un(e) N* cannot generally be treated in the same way as other uses of *pas*. Indeed, Vikner (1978: 88) lists *pas un(e)* as a negative item distinct from bare *pas*. Therefore, the acceptability of the examples in (i) and (ii) is not entirely unexpected. See also chapter 2, example (51).

As mentioned in footnote 3, the negative adverb *plus* has a homograph that is nonnegative. This element is commonly used in comparatives and can be negated using *pas*:

(iii) Il N' y   a   PAS PLUS d' une centaine de personnes à la fête.
      it *ne* there has *pas plus* of a   hundred of people   at the party
      'There aren't more than a hundred or so people at the party.'

5. [*] is the symbol used by Moritz and Valois (1994) to indicate that logical DN is the only possible interpretation.

This restriction did not apply in earlier stages of the language. Grevisse (1986: 1485 §979) points out that, "à l'époque classique" (roughly the seventeenth century), *pas* could co-occur with *personne* and *rien*, for example, without producing logical DN. See sections 3.1.1, 3.1.2, and 3.5.2, as well as section 4.3.2 for a discussion of the synchronic development of the system of sentential negation in French. See also chapter 3, footnote 3 for references.

Québécois does not show the restriction illustrated in text example (9). This is relevant to our discussion in section 4.4.2.1.

Modern French, that is, *pas*, which is associated with SpecNegP rather than being generated under Neg°, I concluded in the discussion of Jespersen's Generalization in chapter 3 that French is a non-NC language. As such, one expects
multiple occurrences of negative elements in the same minimal clause to lead to
logical DN. Yet, in the text examples given here, the interpretation is clearly not
DN. In order to maintain the conclusions from chapter 3 and my analysis of the
diachronic development of sentential negation in French, I must assume that the
negative adverbs discussed earlier (as well as the negative arguments to be discussed in chapter 5) are not in fact inherently negative. This conclusion is exploited in interesting ways in section 4.3.2.

   What can one conclude about the syntactic nature of negative adverbs on the
basis of their distributions? Exploiting the informal idea that the negative adverbs are interpreted "as if" they "contain" *pas*, it seems that, when used in isolation, a negative adverb is interpreted negatively, that is, as $\neg$ [α].[6] However,
when negative adverbs are combined, the negative, that is, polarity-reversing,
content ($\neg$) is not repeated. Thus, when two co-occur, as in (5a), the interpretation is something along the lines of:

(10) $\neg$ [α [β]]

When three co-occur, as in (7a), the interpretation is:

(11) $\neg$ [α [β [γ]]]

Crucially, the interpretation of (5a) is not:

(12) $\neg$ [α [$\neg$ [β]]]

since this would result in the unattested logical DN. Similarly, the interpretation
of (7a) would presumably not be:

(13) $\neg$ [α [$\neg$ [β [$\neg$ [γ]]]]]

   The fact, then, that these elements are semantically complex seems to be reflected in syntactic structure. Were this not the case, the interpretations discussed here could not be explained. If *plus* or *jamais* were syntactically atomic
negatives, one would expect their co-occurrence in a non-NC language like
French to result in polarity reversal, contrary to fact. The nonnegative semantic
content of the adverbs therefore enjoys limited independence, which allows it to
"combine" with another adverb. The single instance of negation then has scope
over all the lexical adverbs present. I explore a formal mechanism that can be
used to account for this in sections 4.3.3 and 4.3.4.

   Of course, what this does not explain is why the adverbs cannot co-occur
with the *overt* negative marker *pas* (with the relevant interpretation), as indicated by the ungrammaticality of (8). I address this restriction in section 4.4.2
and return to it in chapter 5. Before I develop in detail a syntactic analysis of

---

   6. In this paragraph, α, β, and γ represent the semantic content of each negative adverb minus the
negation itself.

negative adverbs, I consider a second distributional difference that distinguishes
negative adverbs from *pas*. That difference concerns linear order.

4.2.2 Linear order

In addition to the co-occurrence restrictions illustrated in the previous section,
which suggest that the distribution of *pas* is more restricted than that of the negative adverbs, there are differences in linear order that, once again, show the
distribution of *pas* to be less flexible than that of the negative adverbs. The differences discussed here are in relation to the possible positions that negative adverbs can occupy with respect to infinitives. The data support the informal conclusion reached in the previous section, namely that negative adverbs are both
semantically and syntactically complex and that the nonnegative content of
these items enjoys a limited independence from the negation itself.

Reinforcing the examples in (1)–(3), the data in (14)–(19) show that, where
a verb is finite, it must precede all negative adverbs, irrespective of the nature of
the adverb or the verb:

(14) Marc n' est PAS à la hauteur de la tâche.   (copular *être* + *pas*)
     M.   *ne* is *pas* at the height of the task
     'M. isn't up to the job.'

(15) Myriam ne serait   JAMAIS venue si . . .   (auxiliary *être* + *jamais*)
     M.   *ne* be-COND *jamais* come if
     'M. would never have come if . . . '

(16) Marie n' aura   PLUS vingt ans.   (possessive *avoir* + *plus*)
     M.   *ne* have-FUT *plus* twenty years
     'M. will no longer be twenty years old.'

(17) Alain n' a   GUÈRE eu de devoirs   à faire   depuis . . .
     A.   *ne* has *guère* had of homework to do-INF since
     'A. has hardly had any homework to do since . . . '
                                                   (auxiliary *avoir* + *guère*)

(18) Elise ne pouvait PLUS marcher.   (modal verb + *plus*)
     E.   *ne* could *plus* walk-INF
     'E. could no longer walk.'

(19) Jean ne passerait   JAMAIS pour un Français.   (lexical verb + *jamais*)
     J.   *ne* pass-COND *jamais* for a Frenchman
     'J. would never pass for a Frenchman.'

In my discussion of Verb Movement in section 1.1, I followed Pollock
(1989) and Belletti (1990) in assuming that finite verbs in French move in the
syntax from their base position to the highest functional head encoding verbal
inflectional morphology, which I identified as AgrS°. The data in (14)–(19)
show, therefore, that the canonical position(s) occupied by *pas* and the negative

adverbs is/are lower than AgrS°. In chapters 1 and 2, I followed Pollock (1989) in assuming that the S-structure position of *pas* is SpecNegP, which is indeed below AgrS°.

Turning to negative adverbs, my null hypothesis is, of course, that these elements also occupy SpecNegP. On the basis of the data with respect to finite verb paradigms reviewed so far, I have no reason to assume otherwise. However, if I consider infinitives (which, following the discussion in sections 1.1.7.2–1.1.7.4, I assume do not necessarily occupy AgrS°), I find evidence to suggest that the null hypothesis is in fact wrong. In other words, the evidence suggests that negative adverbs do not *necessarily* occupy SpecNegP at S-structure. The evidence comes in the form of possible orderings of infinitives with respect to negative adverbs and *pas*, and the picture is quite complex. Before reviewing the data, I revisit the conclusions I drew about infinitival Verb Movement in Modern French. These were summarized in section 1.1.7.5, and are repeated here for convenience:

(20) *Overt Verb Movement patterns in French*:
   a. All finite verbs move to AgrS°.
   b'. Infinitival auxiliaries (*être, avoir*) freely move to Mood°, T°, or AgrS°.
   b". Infinitival modal verbs (e.g., *pouvoir, devoir*) move to Mood° or T°, *and only exceptionally to AgrS°*.
   b‴. Infinitival lexical verbs move to Mood° or T°, but not as far as AgrS°.

Of relevance to my discussion are the movement patterns of infinitives in (20b')–(20b‴).

In the case of the infinitival auxiliaries, *être* and *avoir*, all negative adverbs (*pas* and the negative adverbs) can either precede or follow the verb, as in (21) and (22), after Pollock (1989: 373 (15)).

(21) a. Ne   PAS/PLUS ÊTRE heureux est une condition pour . . .
     b. N' ÊTRE PAS/PLUS   heureux est une condition pour . . .
         ne (be) *pas/plus* (be) happy   is a   condition for
         'Not/No longer being happy is a condition for . . . '

(22) a. Ne   PAS/GUÈRE AVOIR d' enfance   heureuse est une condition . .
     b. N' AVOIR PAS/GUÈRE   d' enfance   heureuse est une condition . .
         ne (have) *pas/guère* (have) of childhood happy   is a   condition
         'Not/Hardly having a happy childhood is a condition . . . '

According to Grevisse (1986: 1488 §980), in "la langue ordinaire", the norm is for the negative adverb to precede the infinitival auxiliary, as in (21a) and (22a), while, in "la langue soignée", the negative adverb may follow the infinitival auxiliary, as in (21b) and (22b). Given my conclusion that *pas* occupies SpecNegP in (21) and (22), and my assumption in (20b') about the movement of infinitival auxiliaries, it seems that there are stylistic implications associated with movement of an infinitival auxiliary from T° (over *pas*) into AgrS°.[7]

With regard to the issue at hand, namely the possible position(s) of negative adverbs such as *plus* and *guère* in (21) and (22), given the flexibility of the infinitival auxiliaries, that is, the fact that they can freely occupy Mood°, T°, or AgrS°, no firm conclusions can be drawn on the basis of these data.

In the case of infinitival *modals,* the situation is more complex. Where an infinitival modal is negated by *pas*, the preferred order is for the adverb to precede the verb, as in (23a)–(25a). However, the reverse order is not regarded as ungrammatical. Pollock (1989: 375, 1997b) judges examples (23b)–(25b) (based on Pollock's 1989: 375 (20)) to be "somewhat marginal" and "more exceptional", suggesting that they have "a very literary ring to them". (Grevisse 1986: 1487 §980 also mentions the possibility of *pas* following an infinitive when the infinitive is itself followed by another infinitive, for example, a modal.) Indeed, the pattern in (23)–(25) formed the basis of my conclusion, given in (20b''), that modal infinitives *only exceptionally* raise from T° (over *pas*) to AgrS°.

(23) a.   Je pensais ne   PAS POUVOIR dormir dans cette chambre.
     b.   ?Je pensais ne POUVOIR PAS   dormir dans cette chambre.
           I   thought *ne* (be-able) *pas* (be-able) sleep   in   this room
           'I thought I couldn't sleep in this bedroom.'

(24) a.   Il estimait ne   PAS DEVOIR donner suite   à ma
     b.   ?Il estimait ne DEVOIR PAS   donner suite   à ma
           he thought *ne* (must) *pas* (must) give   continuation to my
                demande.
                demande.
                request
           'He thought he wouldn't have to answer my request.'

(25) a.   Il avait dit ne   PAS VOULOIR donner suite   à ma
     b.   ?Il avait dit   ne VOULOIR PAS   donner suite   à ma
           he had   said *ne* (want) *pas* (want) give   continuation to my
                demande.
                demande.
                request
           'He had said he didn't want to answer my request.'

What is interesting and significant about negation and infinitival modals is that, if *pas* is removed from the (b) examples in (23)–(25) and replaced with a negative adverb, the judgments change. While the ordering *modal infinitive* + *pas* is

---

7. In a similar vein to Grevisse's comments, but in reference to infinitivals in general and not just infinitival auxiliaries, Gaatone (1971: 138) suggests that *jamais* usually precedes infinitivals and follows them only "dans le style littéraire"; he also claims (1971: 149) that post-infinitival *plus* is less common than pre-infinitival *plus*.

judged "somewhat marginal", "more exceptional", or "very literary", the ordering *modal infinitive + plus/guère/jamais* is not:

(26) a.   Je pensais ne PLUS POUVOIR dormir dans cette chambre.
     b.   Je pensais ne POUVOIR PLUS dormir dans cette chambre.
        'I thought I would no longer be able to sleep in this bedroom.'

(27) a.   Il estimait ne GUÈRE DEVOIR donner suite à ma demande.
     b.   Il estimait ne DEVOIR GUÈRE donner suite à ma demande.
        'He thought he would hardly have to answer my request.'

(28) a.   Il disait ne JAMAIS VOULOIR donner suite à ma demande.
     b.   Il disait ne VOULOIR JAMAIS donner suite à ma demande.
        'He said he never wanted to answer my request.'

The important contrast is shown in (29), in which *devoir* stands for modal infinitives in general and *plus* stands for negative adverbs in general:

(29) a.   ?ne devoir pas
     b.   ne devoir plus

In other words, a modal infinitive followed by *pas* is "somewhat marginal", is
"more exceptional", and has a "very literary ring" to it, as indicated by the question mark in (29a). The same is not true of sequences of a modal infinitive followed by a negative adverb. What is to be made of this contrast? In chapter 2, I
showed that *pas* obligatorily occupies SpecNegP where that position is available
and sentential negation is to be marked. This obligatory raising was accounted
for on the basis of Haegeman's (1995: 107) characterization of negative clauses
as clauses in which the feature [+NEG] is borne by a functional head. Failure of
pas to raise to SpecNegP means that the necessary feature specification cannot
be achieved and leads to fairly sharp ungrammaticality in the modern language.
Given that the strings in (23b)–(25b) are merely somewhat marginal and not
ungrammatical as such, I assume that, in these examples, *pas* occupies Spec-
NegP as required. The position of *pas* in the structure is not, therefore, the reason for the marginal status of these strings. Their marginality is then due to the
position of the infinitival verb to the left of *pas*, that is, in AgrS°, as concluded
in (20b").

As for (26b)–(28b), these examples are not marginal, despite the fact that the
infinitival modal precedes the negative adverb. Consequently, I assume that the
infinitival modal has not raised to AgrS°. Assume, for concreteness, that the
verb occupies the immediately lower inflectional head position, namely T°.
Where does this analysis leave one with respect to the negative adverbs? Clearly
these cannot occupy SpecNegP. If they did, they would precede the verb in T°,
which they do not. So where are they? There are two possibilities. First, they
could occupy a lower position in the same clause, as illustrated in (30)
(= (27b)), for example, a lower specifier position or an adjoined position. If this
analysis is along the right lines (as I ultimately conclude), this shows a major
difference between *pas* and the negative adverbs. While *pas* needs to occupy

SpecNegP at S-structure to mark sentential negation and license *ne*, negative adverbs do not.

(30) [$_{AgrSP}$ ne [$_{NegP}$ [$_{TP}$ [$_{T°}$ devoir] guère [$_{MoodP}$ *t* [$_{VP}$ *t* [$_{AgrSP}$ donner]]]]]]

(= (27b))

The second possible position for the negative adverbs in (26b)–(28b) to occupy (assuming a biclausal structure) is SpecNegP in the lower clause. This would entail positing a clause boundary between the infinitival modal and the negative adverb in (26b)–(28b), as illustrated in (31), but would allow one to maintain the generalization that negative adverbs and *pas* occupy SpecNegP.

(31) [$_{AgrSP-1}$ [$_{NegP}$ [$_{TP}$ devoir . . . [$_{AgrSP-2}$ . . . [$_{NegP}$ guère [$_{MoodP}$ donner VP]]]]]]

(= (27b))

An argument in support of this second scenario could be advanced if, in each pair of examples in (26)–(28), there were a difference in interpretation between the (a) string and the (b) string, that is, if the negative took scope over the infinitival modal verb in the (a) examples while taking scope over the (embedded) infinitival lexical verb *only* in the (b) examples (or were at least ambiguous with respect to scope). That is to say, for this second possibility to be taken seriously, it would have to be possible to interpret (26b)–(28b) (repeated here as (32a)–(34a) for convenience) as being synonymous with (32b)–(34b), in which the lower infinitival clause is negated:

(32) a. Je pensais NE POUVOIR PLUS DORMIR dans cette chambre.
     b. Je pensais POUVOIR NE PLUS DORMIR dans cette chambre.

(33) a. Il avait estimé NE DEVOIR GUÈRE DONNER suite à ma demande.
     b. Il avait estimé DEVOIR NE GUÈRE DONNER suite à ma demande.

(34) a. Il avait dit NE VOULOIR JAMAIS DONNER suite à ma demande.
     b. Il avait dit VOULOIR NE JAMAIS DONNER suite à ma demande.

However, the necessary interpretations are not available. The strings in (32a)–(34a) are not synonymous with those in (32b)–(34b), as illustrated, for example, by the glosses to (34a, b) given in (35a, b). This lack of synonymy is initial evidence undermining the plausibility of the second a priori possible scenario, illustrated in (31).

(35) a. He said he had never wanted to answer my request.
     b. He said he had wanted never to answer my request.

Further evidence to undermine the plausibility of the second analysis of the examples in (26b)–(28b) comes from sentences such as the one in (36). This sentence contains the infinitival modal *vouloir* 'to want' with a *finite* CP complement. Crucially, the negative adverb *jamais* intervenes between *vouloir* and the complementizer, *que* 'that', presumably heading CP. It is therefore implausible to claim that the adverb appears in the lower clause.[8]

(36) Il avait dit ne vouloir jamais qu' elle parte.
      he had   said *ne* want   *jamais* that she leave-SUBJ
      'He had said he never wanted her to leave.'

With respect to interpretation, the string in (36) is admittedly ambiguous. It can be interpreted synonymously with (37), as if NEG-raising had taken place, that is, as if the negative adverb had been base-generated in the lower clause and raised into the higher clause.[9]

(37) Il avait dit vouloir qu' elle ne parte   jamais.
      he had   said want   that she *ne* leave-SUBJ *jamais*
      'He had said that he didn't want her ever to leave.'

Alternatively, (36) can be interpreted as if NEG-raising had not taken place, that is, as if the negative adverb were base-generated in the higher clause. This ambiguity is not a problem; the important point for my purposes here is that, in (36), the negative adverb occupies a surface position in the higher clause that is crucially *not* SpecNegP, since it is to the right of the infinitival modal in T°. I am therefore obliged to accept the first of the two analyses given earlier, namely the one illustrated in (30), and to conclude that, unlike *pas*, negative adverbs do not have to occupy SpecNegP at S-structure to mark sentential negation and license *ne*.

Before moving on from infinitival modals and turning to lexical infinitives, there are two final reasons to reject the second analysis, namely that, in (26b)–(28b), the negative adverbs occupy SpecNegP in the embedded clause, as in (31). First, if the adverbs in (26b)–(28b) are in a lower SpecNegP, there is no reason to assume that such a position cannot also be occupied by *pas*. Yet the judgments in (23b)–(25b) show that this is not possible. Consequently, it is unlikely to be the case in (26b)–(28b).

Second, in section 1.2.5, I discussed the licensing conditions of pre-verbal *ne*. I concluded that "negative" *ne* can be licensed only by an S-structure spec-head configuration with a negative operator in SpecNegP. This too would undermine the plausibility of the type of structure in (31). If *plus/jamais/guère*

---

8. An alternative approach to the example in (36) would be to assume an analysis along the lines of the one sketched in section 1.2.2, for the *pour ne pas que* construction, namely in terms of a null light verb. In other words, one might conclude that the CP headed by *que* is not in fact the complement of *vouloir*. One might assume, instead, that the complement of *vouloir* is an infinitival clause headed by a null light verb, *v*, which is negated by *jamais* and which, in turn, takes the CP head by *que* as its complement. This approach is unlikely to be along the right lines since, in contrast to the contexts discussed in section 1.2.2, the pre-verbal marker *ne* cannot appear to the left of *jamais*, as shown in (i).
(i)   *Il avait dit vouloir ne jamais qu' elle parte.
      he had   said want   *ne jamais* that she leave-SUBJ

9. For discussion of NEG-raising, see de Cornulier (1973, 1974), Daoust-Blais and Kemp (1979), Fillmore (1963), Forest (1983), Horn (1978a, b, 1989), Iordanskaja (1986), Lakoff (1969), Prince (1976), and Shlonsky (1989).

could occupy an *embedded* SpecNegP position, one would not expect *ne* to be licensed in the *matrix* clause, since no negative operator would occupy the matrix SpecNegP in order to satisfy the licensing conditions of the Neg°.

I now turn to infinitival full lexical verbs. In such structures, *pas* must precede the verb, as in the grammatical examples (38a) and (39a), taken from Pollock (1989: 374 (16)), the reverse order in (38b) and (39b) being ungrammatical (outside literary language with a distinct archaic flavor to it; see Grevisse 1986: 1487 §980):

(38) a. Ne   PAS SEMBLER heureux est une condition pour . . .
     b. ★Ne SEMBLER PAS   heureux est une condition pour . . .
         ne (seem) *pas* (seem) happy is a   condition for
         'Not appearing happy is a condition for . . . '

(39) a. Ne   PAS POSSÉDER de voiture en banlieue rend   la vie
     b. ★Ne POSSÉDER PAS   de voiture en banlieue rend   la vie
         ne (possess) *pas* (possess) of car   in suburb   makes the life
           difficile.
           difficile.
           difficult
         'Not having a car (while living) in the suburbs makes life difficult.'

Maintaining my assumption that, in the grammatical (38a) and (39a), *pas* occupies SpecNegP, the lexical infinitive must occupy a lower functional head position in these examples, either Mood° or T°. The ungrammatical status of (38b) and (39b) could be explained in either of two ways. First, with the verb in T° or Mood°, it could be that *pas* has failed to raise to SpecNegP. Second, if *pas* is indeed in SpecNegP, the verb would need to have raised from T° to AgrS°, which I therefore assume to be impossible, as in (20b‴).

But what about contexts in which a negative adverb is used to negate the lexical infinitive, instead of *pas*? Here, the distribution is freer, and both relative orderings are acceptable, although the adverb more commonly precedes the infinitive.

(40) a. Ne   JAMAIS SEMBLER heureux est une condition pour . . .
     b. Ne SEMBLER JAMAIS   heureux est une condition pour . . .
         ne (seem) *jamais* (seem) happy is a   condition for
         'Never appearing happy is a condition for . . . '

(41) a. Ne   PLUS POSSÉDER de voiture en banlieue rend   la vie
     b. Ne POSSÉDER PLUS   de voiture en banlieue rend   la vie
         ne (possess) *plus* (possess) of car   in suburb   makes the life
           difficile.
           difficile.
           difficult
         'No longer having a car (while living) in the suburbs makes life difficult.'

In (40a) and (41a), I assume that the adverb occupies SpecNegP and that the verb occupies T°. Given my earlier conclusion that lexical infinitives cannot raise from T° to AgrS°, I further assume that, in (40b) and (41b), the verb occupies a position no higher than T°. This being the case, the post-verbal negative adverb cannot occupy SpecNegP in these sentences. Rather, it must occupy a lower position. This is further evidence to suggest that the syntax of negative adverbs is less strict than the syntax of *pas*. While the latter must appear in SpecNegP at S-structure for reasons that are by now familiar, the former are not obliged to do so.

4.3   The syntactic status of *jamais*, *plus*, *guère*

4.3.1   Preliminary remarks

In section 2.1, I concluded that, where the operator *pas* is used to negate a clause containing an intransitive verb, [$_{XP}$ pas] bears the feature [+NEG], is generated adjoined to VP, and then raises to SpecNegP in the syntax to mark sentential negation and license *ne*. Maintaining my assumption from section 1.2.4 that *ne* is not inherently negative, I assume that DA transmits the feature [+NEG] from the negative operator in SpecNegP to the Neg head, as illustrated in (42). This is in line with Haegeman's (1995: 107) minimal assumption that negative clauses are characterized by the presence of the feature [+NEG] on a functional head in the extended domain of V.

(42)

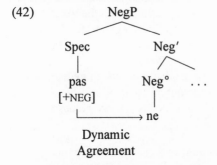

So what about the negative adverbs? In what way does (42) have to be modified in order to account for their syntax? Before considering this, it's necessary to decide what needs to remain constant. First, sentences containing a negative adverb can appear with *ne*, as I have already shown. Given that I have not had to posit more than one kind of *ne* so far, I shall assume that the *ne* that appears with negative adverbs is the same *ne* I considered in sections 1.2.2, 1.2.4, and 1.2.5, that is, the one that appears with *pas*. Recall that *ne* is not inherently negative. In the case of "expletive" *ne*, it is never associated with negative features and is licensed by indirect extended selection from above; in the case of the *ne* that co-occurs with *pas*, it is licensed and "acquires" its "negativity", via DA, in association with the inherently negative *pas* in SpecNegP at S-structure, as in

(42). The null hypothesis therefore must be that, in (1c-e), *ne* is also licensed via DA by a negative operator in SpecNegP.

Further, there is no reason to suppose that sentences containing negative adverbs are any less "negative" than sentences containing *pas*. Under the assumptions I have made so far (Haegeman 1995: 107), this means that, one way or another, a functional head within the extended domain of V will bear the feature [+NEG] at S-structure. I assume that it is in fact Neg° that bears this feature, that is, *ne* (with possible raising to AgrS°–see Acquaviva 1994). Since (a) *ne* is not itself negative, (b) SpecNegP is not occupied by *pas*, (c) as I showed in section 4.2.2, the negative adverbs are not obliged to raise into SpecNegP, and (d) I am assuming that *ne* needs to be licensed and sentential negation marked at S-structure in Modern French, I can conclude only that, in (26b)-(28b), (40b), and (41b), the non-overt operator, Op, occupies SpecNegP at S-structure and, given DA, transmits its [+NEG] feature to Neg°, thus ensuring that *ne* is licensed and that the sentence is interpreted as being negative. Finally, given the analysis of NPI licensing advocated in sections 3.4.2ff, Op unselectively A'-binds the negative adverb(s). In other words, I conclude that, in the examples in (40b) and (41b), sentential negation is marked in the same way as in (43) and (44), discussed in section 1.2.4:

(43) a.   Je n' osais venir.
          I *ne* dared come
          'I didn't dare come.'

     b.   [$_{AgrSP}$ Je n'osais [$_{NegP}$ Op [$_{Neg'}$ ... *t* ... venir]]]

(44) a.   Jean ne voit que Marie.
          J.   *ne* sees *que* M.
          'J. can only see M.'

     b.   [$_{AgrSP}$ Jean ne voit [$_{NegP}$ Op [$_{Neg'}$ ... *t* ... que Marie]]]

Before speculating further about possible syntactic characterisations of negative adverbs, it is insightful to consider how they relate to *ne* and *pas* diachronically.

4.3.2   The development of sentential negation in French

In order to understand the nature of the relationship among *ne*, *pas*, and the negative adverbs, one must appreciate something of the way the system of sentential negation in Modern French has evolved (see sections 3.1.1, 3.1.2, and especially 3.5.2). As discussed by Grevisse (1986: 1477 §973), Harris (1978: 23-29), Posner (1996: 302), Winters (1987: 28-30, 33-47), and, in more recent theoretical work, Pearce (1990, 1991, 1993), the canonically post-verbal markers of negation in the modern language, that is, the negative adverbs/arguments and *pas*, were not originally negative. Rather, they were nouns denoting small amounts that came to reinforce *non/ne*; they were essentially emphatic elements

(Posner 1985a: 184). This development took place during the Middle French period, from the twelfth century on (Harris 1978: 25).

The development has been accounted for on both phonological and syntactic grounds, and, in both accounts, the trigger can be seen as the initial grammatic-alization/weakening of *non/ne*, that is, its (re)analysis as Neg°. On a phonologi-cal level, it has been suggested that phonetic weakening of the pre-verbal mark-er left it incapable of marking sentential negation on its own. Since it had not been possible to use *non* with a finite lexical verb since the early Old French period (according to Grevisse 1986: 1477 §973), another strategy needed to be developed to mark/reinforce sentential negation. On a syntactic level, the immo-bility of the pre-verbal marker, the very fact that it was always pre-verbal, meant that it was interpretatively inflexible. Negation expressed by the pre-verbal mar-ker alone was always interpreted as an instance of absolute negation. In other words, the entire propositional content of the clause was being denied. It could not be used for local constituent negation (Grevisse 1986: 1482 §977), that is, to negate a subclausal unit, such as a purpose clause. Since the post-verbal markers of negation were distributionally more flexible, their position *could* indicate the part of the proposition being negated.

French thus followed Jespersen's Negative Cycle, with the erstwhile em-phatic post-verbal elements, and *pas* in particular, losing their original (positive) value. They then came to carry clausal negation alone, with the pre-verbal nega-tive marker *ne* subsequently and increasingly often being absent from spoken language, especially in interrogatives, by the sixteenth and seventeenth centuries (Harris 1978: 26) and, according to Price (1993: 191), at least, as early as the thirteenth century. In fact, the tendency for bipartite sentential negation to be replaced by single (post-verbal) sentential negation using *pas* is now so strong that, as I argued in chapter 1, in the modern language, the one-time exclusive bearer of sentential negation, pre-verbal *ne*, has lost whatever inherent negativ-ity it had. Whatever negative interpretation can be assigned to this element is now due to its association with some other element marked [+NEG], such as *pas*. The link between *ne* and negation in Modern French is therefore indirect, to say the least. Of course, by virtue of (a) the licensing conditions assumed for *ne* in section 1.2.5, (b) the analysis of *pas* proposed in chapter 2, and (c) the nature of the spec-head relationship inherent in the Neg Criterion proposed in section 3.3, I have the means by which [+NEG] can be transmitted from *pas* to *ne*: movement of *pas* to SpecNegP followed by DA.

I claim that *pas* is the only overt post-verbal "negative" element in the stan-dard modern language to be inherently marked [+NEG]. (See section 3.5.2, for my reasoning.) In contrast, the adverbs I have discussed in this chapter are not marked in this way; the elements *plus, jamais*, and *guère* are not inherently neg-ative, and their co-occurrence does not therefore amount to NC. What I am claiming with respect to negative adverbs is supported by a number of facts, some of which have already been reviewed. First, "negative" adverbs still have some nonnegative uses. For example, *jamais* and *plus* (without *ne*, even in reg-isters not characterized by "*ne*-drop") are stylistic variants of *un jour/en un temps quelconque* 'one day'/'some time or other' or *encore* 'still', respectively (Gaatone 1971: 139, 151). In contrast, no positive use remains for the element *pas*.

(45) a. Je ne crois   pas que cet homme revienne   jamais.
          I *ne* believe *pas* that this man   return-SUBJ *jamais*
          'I don't think that man is ever coming back.'

     b. À jamais
         to *jamais*
         'For ever.'

     c. Si jamais tu   reviens à Paris, . . .
         if *jamais* you return to P.
         'If you're ever back in Paris, . . . '

Second, as illustrated earlier, "negatives" can co-occur without negation being canceled. Third, in the patterns of NC in earlier varieties of French discussed in section 3.5.2, there is reason to believe that the only items entering into NC are *ne* and *pas*, and not the negative adverbs discussed in this chapter or the negative arguments analyzed in chapter 5.

Instead of being lexically marked [+NEG], I claim that the negative interpretation of the adverbs is to be attributed to the fact that they appear in the scope of an inherently [+NEG] operator. Of course, in standard metropolitan Modern French, this inherently [+NEG] operator cannot normally be *pas*; otherwise, some deletion process would need to be invoked to make sure *pas* does not surface in the syntax together with the adverb.[10] However, given the account of sentences such as (43) and (44) proposed in section 1.2.4, and the A'-binding approach to NPI licensing adopted and modified in section 3.4.2, the non-overt counterpart of *pas*, namely Op, is an immediately obvious source of the negative interpretation of these adverbs.[11] To account for the data in (43) and (44) while maintaining the conclusion that *ne* is not inherently negative in the modern language, I attributed the negative interpretation to a non-overt inherently negative operator: Op. Pre-verbal *ne* then acquires the [+NEG] feature from Op as a consequence of the mechanism by which *ne* is formally licensed, namely DA. Op is, of course, identical to *pas*, apart from the fact that it is non-overt. In the next section, I exploit Op and flesh out an analysis of negative adverbs.

4.3.3 Structural analysis

Focusing attention on contexts without pseudopartitive direct objects (but see footnote 12), I assume that negative adverbs are generated in an adjoined

---

10. A deletion-based analysis is in fact proposed for Standard Modern French in Escure (1974).
11. For further discussion of the interaction between verb position and negative adverb position, see Belletti (1990, 1992, 1994a, b) and Zanuttini (1994b, 1995).

position. This was the conclusion I came to in section 2.1, with respect to *pas*, and I see no reason why the same is not the case for the negative adverbs, especially in view of my characterization of the negative adverbs with respect to Di Sciullo and Williams's (1986) distinction between different types of modification; if *pas* produces a composite function with the predicate by adjunction, it seems likely that the negative adverbs do too. (But see Cinque 1995, 1996, 1998 for an analysis of adverbs based on distinct functional projections rather than adjoined positions.)

As mentioned, however, this is not to claim that *pas* and the negative adverbs necessarily occupy identical *surface* positions. While the negative operator *pas* necessarily raises overtly to SpecNegP in order to license *ne* and to mark sentential negation, my claim is that this is crucially not the case for the negative adverbs. This is attributable to the fact that the negative adverbs are not in fact negative, that is, do not bear the feature [+NEG]. They cannot therefore license *ne* or mark sentential negation by raising to SpecNegP. Rather, the negative adverbs co-occur, in the relevant contexts, with Op, the non-overt negative operator. It is therefore *Op* that crucially needs to raise to SpecNegP at S-structure to mark sentential negation. Where the negative adverbs themselves raise to SpecNegP, it is in a sense parasitic on movement of the operator, rather than as a result of any of their own inherent features. For concreteness, I assume the base structure in (46), in which Op and the negative adverbs are adjoined to VP.[12]

(46)

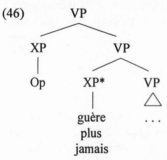

To mark sentential negation, a negative operator has to be in a spec-head configuration with an appropriate functional head, such as Neg°, at S-structure.

---

12. This is something of a simplification. Following Cinque (1995, 1996, 1998), these elements may attach higher in clause structure. This has no implications for the analysis proposed here, which, incidentally, differs from Rowlett (1996c), section 4.4.3. I do not make strong claims about the order of the two VP-adjoined elements in (46). For example, given its interpretation ("always-not" as opposed to "not-always"), it may make sense to assume that *jamais* is base-generated above Op.

As for the licensing of pseudopartitives, as in (i), I assume that Op is generated in SpecNumP and subsequently raised to SpecNegP, as suggested in section 2.2.4, for *pas*. This is illustrated in (ii).

(i)   Julie n' a   jamais lu   de romans.
        J.   *ne* has *jamais* read of novels
        'J. has never read any novels.'

(ii)   . . . n'a [$_{NegP}$ Op (. . .) jamais . . . lu . . . [$_{VP}$ . . . [$_{NumP}$ *t* [de romans]]]]

Failure of *pas* to raise in the relevant contexts was shown in chapter 2 to have two consequences. First, *ne* becomes unavailable. Second, the negation has local scope. In contrast, in the sentences considered here, *ne* is available, and negation has wide scope. I therefore assume that Op has raised to SpecNegP. This is illustrated in (47):

(47)

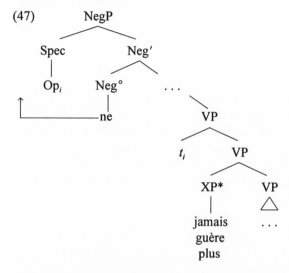

A further possibility, suggested by the examples in (40a) and (41a), would be for Op to be accompanied by the negative adverb (or adverbs—see section 4.3.4.4) as it raises into SpecNegP. This is illustrated for (40a) very schematically in (48):

(48)

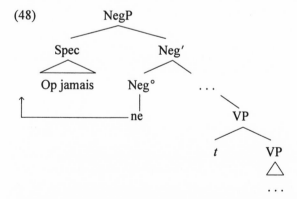

In the second case, the overt adverb in (46) parasitically raises into SpecNegP while, in the first case, it remains in situ in its adjoined position. Given that TP and MoodP intervene between the base VP-adjoined position of the negative adverb and SpecNegP, this analysis has the attraction of predicting that negative adverbs can either precede or follow an infinitive in T°/Mood°. In both scenarios, crucially, Op appears in SpecNegP (as required by the need to mark sentential negation). DA then ensures that *ne* is licensed and endowed with the feature [+NEG]; negation has wide scope and the sentence is negative.

4.3.4 Examples

Some exemplification is perhaps in order at this point, especially since, unlike in chapter 2, where I considered the syntax of *pas*, assumptions about the position of the negative adverbs interact in much more complex fashion with the syntax of infinitives. My assumptions about Verb Movement patterns in Standard French—motivated in chapter 1—were given in (20) and are repeated here:

(49) *Overt Verb Movement patterns in French*:
    a.   All finite verbs move to AgrS°.
    b'. Infinitival auxiliaries (*être, avoir*) freely move to Mood°, T°, or AgrS°.
    b". Infinitival modal verbs (e.g., *pouvoir, devoir*) move to Mood° or T°, *and only exceptionally to AgrS °.*
    b"'. Infinitival lexical verbs move to Mood° or T°, but not as far as AgrS°.

Thus, while tensed verbs always appear in AgrS° at S-structure, infinitivals can, depending on the nature of the verb, appear either in AgrS° (auxiliaries, exceptionally modals, but not lexical infinitives) or in T°/MoodP° (auxiliaries, modals, and lexical verbs). In example 1, the clause is finite, and the verb must therefore move to AgrS°. Examples 2 and 3 contain an auxiliary and a modal infinitive, respectively. The two possible surface orderings of *verb + adverb* and *adverb + verb* are discussed. Finally, in example 4, an infinitival lexical verb co-occurs with two negative adverbs.

4.3.4.1 Example 1

(50) Pierre ne boit   plus.
    P.   *ne* drinks *plus*
    'P. no longer drinks.'

In this example, the clause contains a finite intransitive verb, *boit* 'drinks', which, in line with (49a), raises to AgrS°. The pre-verbal particle *ne* will move along with the finite verb to AgrS°. Op raises to SpecNegP to mark sentential negation. Depending on whether or not *plus* follows Op into SpecNegP, the negative adverb will either remain in situ, VP-adjoined, as in (52), or occupy SpecNegP, as in (51). In either case, the adverb is in post-verbal position.

(51) [Pierre [$_{Agrs'}$ ne boit [$_{NegP}$ [$_{Spec}$ Op plus] [$_{TP}$ t [$_{MoodP}$ [$_{VP}$ ⋯]]]]]]

(52) [Pierre [$_{Agrs'}$ ne boit [$_{NegP}$ [$_{Spec}$ Op] [$_{TP}$ t plus [$_{MoodP}$ [$_{VP}$ ⋯]]]]]]

4.3.4.2 Example 2

(53) ... afin   de ne jamais être sans   argent
            in-order of *ne jamais* be   without money
      ' ... in order never to be without money'

Here, an infinitival clause containing an auxiliary is introduced by a complex complementiser *afin de* 'in order to', whose structure will not be investigated here. Following (49b'), I assume that the verb moves at least as far as Mood°. Given its pre-verbal position, I assume that *jamais* occupies SpecNegP, that is, that it has raised with Op to SpecNegP (as in (48)), and that the verb has not raised above T°.

(54) ... ne [$_{NegP}$ [$_{Spec}$ Op jamais][$_{Neg'}$ [$_{TP/MoodP}$ être [$_{VP}$ *t* [$_{VP}$ sans argent]]]]]

4.3.4.3 Example 3

(55) ... faire preuve de ne vouloir guère que cela soit   le cas
            do   proof of *ne* want   *guère* that that be-SUBJ the case
      ' ... prove that PRO hardly wants that to be the case'

In contrast to example 2, which contains a (nonmodal) auxiliary, the infinitival clause in example 3 contains the modal verb *vouloir* 'to want'. Here, the negative adverb follows the verb, yet precedes the finite CP complement of the verb. Given the nature of the complement of the modal, that is, a finite CP, and the position of the negative adverb, it cannot be claimed that the negative is associated with the CP. (See footnote 8.) I conclude, then, that the "negative" is left-VP-adjoined and that the modal has raised either to Mood° or to T°, as in (56). Sentential negation is marked and *ne* is licensed since Op has raised to SpecNegP.

(56) [$_{AgrS'}$ ne [$_{NegP}$ Op [$_{TP/MoodP}$ vouloir [$_{VP}$ *t* [$_{VP}$ guère [$_{VP}$ [$_{CP}$ ...]]]]]]]

4.3.4.4 Example 4

(57) Dis-lui de ne plus jamais venir.
      say-him of *ne plus jamais* come
      'Tell him/her never to come again.'

In the infinitival clause in example 4, which is the complement of the imperative, the verb is preceded by two negative adverbs, as in (5a–c). However, although I have discussed the possibility of negative adverb concatenation, I have not yet proposed a syntactic analysis of this phenomenon. Given the approach to the examples discussed in section 4.3.3, it seems sensible to assume that multiple negative adverbs are successively adjoined to VP, as in (58), and can both subsequently parasitically raise with Op into SpecNegP, as has presumably happened in (57), given their pre-verbal position.

(58) ... [VP Op [VP plus [VP jamais [VP ...]]]]

Recall that it was observed that these adverbs are not polarity-reversing elements, that is, not inherently specified [+NEG]. In the structure proposed in (46), which, it was suggested, underlies the use of a single negative adverb, the structure receives its negative interpretation by virtue of the presence of Op. What is characteristic, of course, about the interpretation of the structures in (5a-c) and example 4 here is that the apparent negativity of one adverb does not cancel out that of another. (Recall also the discussion in section 4.2.1 and the informal characterization in (10)-(13) of multiple "negatives" in French.) I interpret this fact as suggesting that, in structures containing two or more adverbs, there is only one Op, producing a single instance of negation, as in (58). Given that the relationship between Op and the lexical negative adverb is unselective binding, the ability of two adverbs to "share" a single operator becomes clear. Op can in principle bind any number of suitable items; in this example, it binds two negative adverbs. The surface structure in (57) is a result of short or medium Verb Movement (to Mood°/T°) and movement of both Op and the negative adverbs to SpecNegP, exactly as in previous examples.

The question then arises as to whether it is possible for just one of the two negative adverbs to follow Op into SpecNegP. The example in (59) suggests that this is not ruled out by the grammar.

(59) Elle était contente de ne plus avoir   jamais à faire l' amour avec son
     she was happy   of *ne plus* have-INF *jamais* to do   the love   with her
        mari.
        husband
     'She was glad she didn't ever have to make love to her husband again.'

Here, while *plus* has raised with Op to SpecNegP, *jamais* can remain in situ, as shown by their position with respect to the infinitive. (Of course, it is also possible for *jamais* to raise with *plus* to give the order [ne plus jamais avoir].)

4.4   Explanatory power

In section 4.2, two distributional differences between *pas* and the negative adverbs were discussed. In this section, I demonstrate how the analysis proposed in section 4.3 allows an account of those differences to be given.

4.4.1   Linear ordering of infinitival verbs

The underlying structure in (46) can be used in a relatively straightforward way to explain why, in infinitival clauses, the distribution of the negative adverbs is more flexible than that of *pas*. The table in (60) shows how the analysis of negative adverbs and *pas* proposed or defended here together with the assumptions in (20), can account for the orderings exemplified in the text. What is important to remember is that my analysis predicts that *pas* must appear in Spec-NegP, since this is the only way in which *pas* can mark sentential negation, that is, the only way it can be in the required configuration with a suitable head and the only way *ne* can be licensed. With respect to the negative adverbs, in contrast, two possibilities are open. In the scenario illustrated in (47), lexical *guère*, *plus*, and *jamais* appear in their base position at S-structure; sentential negation is marked, and *ne* is licensed, by Op alone raising to SpecNegP. In the scenario illustrated in (48), lexical *guère*, *plus*, and *jamais* appear in SpecNegP, since they have raised with Op to SpecNegP. Hence, in the table in (60), *pas* must appear in the column headed SpecNegP, while the negative adverbs can appear *either* in the column headed SpecNegP *or* in the column headed VP-adjoined.

(60)

	TEXT EX.	AGRS°	SPECNEGP	T°/ MOOD°	VP-ADJOINED
			POSITION		
a.	(1b)	sera	pas		
b.	(1c-e)	sera	plus/jamais/guère		
c.	(1c-e)	sera			plus/jamais/guère
d.	(21a)		pas/ plus/jamais/guère	être	
e.	(21b)	être	pas/ plus/jamais/guère		
f.	(21b)	(être)		(être)	plus/jamais/guère
g.	(23a)		pas	pouvoir	
h.	(23b)	?pouvoir	pas		
i.	(26a)		plus/jamais/guère	pouvoir	
j.	(26b)			pouvoir	plus/jamais/guère
k.	(38a)		pas	sembler	
l.	(38b)	★sembler	pas		
m.	(38b)			sembler	★pas
n.	(40a)		plus/jamais/guère	sembler	
o.	(40b)			sembler	plus/jamais/guère

In (60a–c), in which the finite verb is in AgrS°, both *pas* and the negative adverbs follow the verb. *Pas* obligatorily occupies SpecNegP, (60a), while the negative adverbs can appear either in SpecNegP, (60b), or, if Op alone raises to SpecNegP, in situ, VP-adjoined, (60c).

In (60d–f), the infinitive is an auxiliary. Following (20b'), the verb can undergo either short, medium, or long Verb Movement and can therefore occupy either Mood°, T°, or AgrS°. Where the adverb is pre-verbal, as in (60d), it must be in SpecNegP, and the verb cannot have raised above T°. Where the adverb is post-verbal, a number of possibilities exist. If the adverb is *pas*, it must be in SpecNegP, and the verb must have risen to AgrS°, as in (60e). However, if the negative is an adverb rather than *pas*, it can be in SpecNegP, in which case the verb must have risen into AgrS°, as in (60e), or in its base position, adjoined to VP, in which case the verb could be in AgrS°, T°, or Mood°, as in (60f).

In (60g–j), the infinitive is a modal. In (60g–h), the verb is negated by *pas*, which must occupy SpecNegP. The most natural order, according to Pollock (1989: 375, 1997b), is for *pas* to precede the infinitival modal. This is illustrated in (60g), where the modal has undergone short or medium Verb Movement to T°/Mood°. The unnaturalness of the reverse ordering is a consequence of the fact that, for such a string to be generated, the infinitival modal would need to undergo long Verb Movement to AgrS°, which is exceptional in line with (20b″). The interesting contrast noted between (23b) and (26b) is illustrated in the table in (60h) and (60j). For, although infinitival modals cannot—without marked stylistic effects—precede *pas*, they can quite naturally precede negative adverbs, not because long Verb Movement becomes more natural when it co-occurs with these adverbs but rather because the adverbs (unlike *pas*) do not have to raise to SpecNegP. Rather, they can remain VP-adjoined, and the modal can precede them without having to raise from T° to AgrS°.

Finally, the situation with respect to full lexical verbs is illustrated in (60k–o). Where a lexical infinitive is negated by *pas*, the verb must follow the negative, as in (60k). This is because *pas* must occupy SpecNegP and the verb cannot raise higher than T°. For the reverse order to be generated, either the verb would have to raise to AgrS°, as in (60l), or the negative would have to remain VP-adjoined, as in (60m). In each case, the string is ungrammatical. In contrast, where the lexical infinitive co-occurs with a negative adverb, both relative orders are equally possible. In each case, the verb appears no higher than T°. Where the adverb is pre-verbal, it has raised with Op to SpecNegP, as in (60n); where it is post-verbal, it remains VP-adjoined, as in (60o).

With respect to (60n) (= (40a)) and (60o) (= (40b)), it was noted on page 151 that the most common order was for the adverb to precede the infinitive as in (60n) (= (40a)). This suggests that, for some reason, yet to be explored, the possibility of parasitic movement, with Op, to SpecNegP, on the part of the negative adverb, is a preferred option. I return to this in the next section.

4.4.2   Co-occurrence restrictions

Within the framework of the structures proposed in (46), the question of why *pas* cannot, in some varieties (including the standard), co-occur with the negative adverbs (without leading to logical DN) is reduced to a consideration of why, on the basis of an underlying configuration such as (61a), the operator bearing the feature [+NEG] cannot be overt, that is, *pas*. Why, instead, must it surface as Op, as in (61b)? And what is it about the grammar of certain nonstandard varieties that allows the operator, optionally, to surface as *pas*, as in (61c)?

(61) a. *Underspecified underlying configuration*:

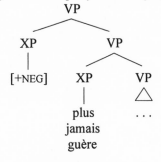

b. *Standard*:

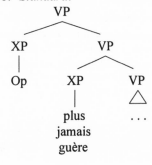

c. *Nonstandard (e.g., Québécois)*:[13]

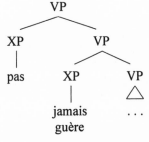

---

13. The absence of *plus* from (61c) follows as a consequence of judgments from native speakers (of Québécois, at least) that the co-occurrence of *pas plus* is not permitted. See (62b).

It is possible to relate the phenomenon illustrated in (61b) to the empirical tendency noted with respect to (60n, o) in section 4.4.1, namely that, where a negative adverb such as *jamais* co-occurs with a lexical infinitive, the preferred order is for the adverb to precede the verb, that is, to raise to SpecNegP with Op (even though the opposite order, in which the adverb remains in situ, is perfectly grammatical). In other words, while negative adverbs do not *have* to raise to SpecNegP with Op, they have a tendency to do so anyway. I attribute the tendency of the negative adverbs to raise to SpecNegP, as well as the non-overt nature of the [+NEG] operator, to an intimate association between the operator and the adverb, an association that can, in turn, probably be attributed to extensive co-occurrence in structures such as those illustrated in section 3.5.2, example (72). (See McMahon 1994: 164.) This seems a plausible approach, given that, as I show in the next section and in section 5.5.2, it is precisely in those syntactic configurations in which the "negative" is increasingly distant from the negative operator that the latter is more likely to surface as *pas* rather that Op. In section 5.5.2, for example, I show that, in the standard language, there are constraints on the necessary intimacy between the "negatives" and the operator and that, where these constraints are not met, the negative operator is overt. In particular, when certain kinds of clause boundary intervene between the surface and underlying position of the negative operator, the operator surfaces as *pas*. In section 4.4.2.1, in which I consider Québécois and other nonstandard varieties of French, I show that negative arguments are generally more likely than negative adverbs to be accompanied by overt *pas* rather than by non-overt Op. This can perhaps be attributed to the fact that the negative arguments cannot raise to SpecNegP with Op. Further, negative arguments are more likely to be accompanied by overt *pas* than by non-overt Op when they are embedded within a PP, that is, syntactically more remote from the negative operator, which, as we saw in section 2.2.4.2, crucially cannot be extracted from within the PP and must therefore originate external to VP. Given that the phenomenon illustrated in (61b) affects both negative adverbs and arguments, I return to it in section 5.5.2. In the next section, I consider varieties of French in which (61b) does not apply.

4.4.2.1 *Québécois*

As suggested earlier with respect to (61c), the relationship between the negative operator and negative adverbs does not force the former to surface as Op in some nonstandard varieties of French, such as Québécois. The examples here (from Marie Claude personal communication [62] and Muller 1991: 262 [63]) show how, in monoclausal contexts, *pas* can co-occur with negative adverbs and, especially, argumental *rien* and *personne*, without inducing DN.

(62) a.   Marie pleure pas jamais.
         M.   cries *pas jamais*
         'M. never cries.'

b. ⋆J'ai   pas plus faim.
    I have *pas plus* hunger
    'I am no longer hungry.'

c. Michel a   pas rien fait.
    M.   has *pas rien* done
    'M. hasn't done anything.'

d. Je vois pas personne.
    I see *pas personne*
    'I can't see anyone.'

(63) a. Le samedi soir . . . , y   a   pas personne en ville à Québec.
         the Saturday evening there has *pas personne* in town at Q.
         'Saturday evenings . . . , there's no-one in the center of Quebec.'

b. J'ai   pas parlé à personne.
    I have *pas* spoken to *personne*
    'I haven't spoken to anyone.'

c. Tu travailles pas rien, tu   risques pas grand-chose . . .
    you work   *pas rien* you risk   *pas* much
    'If you do no work, you don't risk much . . . '

d. Y m' répond pas rien.
    he me answers *pas rien*
    'He doesn't answer me.'

e. Parsonne a   pas l' droit de rien faire pis de rien dire.
    personne has *pas* the right of *rien* do   then of *rien* say
    'No-one has the right to do nothing and say nothing.'

f. Personne n' est pas venu.
    personne ne is *pas* come
    'No-one came.'

Muller's observation about the co-occurrence of *pas* and negative arguments is
confirmed by Moritz and Valois (1994). The following examples are taken from
Daoust-Blais and Kemp (1979: 11–12):

(64) a. Je connais pas personne.
         I know   *pas personne*
         'I don't know anyone.'

b. J'ai   pas vu   personne.
    I have *pas* seen *personne*
    'I haven't seen anyone.'

c. Je vois pas rien.
    I see *pas rien*
    'I can't see anything.'

d. J'en   ai   pas vu   aucun.
    I of-them have *pas* seen *aucun*
    'I haven't seen any of them.'

e. Je sais   pas jamais quand il va   venir.
    I know *pas jamais* when he goes come
    'I never know when he'll come.'

Outside Quebec, Muller (1991: 261) notes a construction in metropolitan French that he suggests is "populaire, dialectal, Moyen-Français, vieilli, rare" and in which *pas* can co-occur with negatives:

(65) a. Toute la   rouscaillure n' y   fera   pas rien.
         all   the moaning   *ne* there do-FUT *pas rien*
         'All the moaning won't make any difference.'

b. J'ai   pas rien trouvé.
    I have *pas rien* found
    'I haven't found anything.'

c. Je connais pas aucun homme.
    I know   *pas aucun* man
    'I don't know any men.'

d. Personne ne sait   pas ce   qu' il y   a   derrière.
    personne ne knows *pas* what that he there has behind
    'No-one knows what's behind it.'

e. ... un parfum qu' aucun artifice ne parvient pas à donner
        a perfume that *aucun* trick *ne* manages *pas* to give
    ' ... a smell that no trick could manage to produce'

Muller notes further that this construction is even more frequent where the negative argument is embedded within a PP (hence the unavailability of negative adverbs, which cannot, for independent reasons, occur in such positions).

(66) a. Il fera   pas d' cadeau [$_{PP}$ à personne].
         he do-FUT *pas* of gift   to *personne*
         'He won't give anyone a present.'

b. Il ne fait   pas de doute [$_{PP}$ pour personne] que ...
    it *ne* does *pas* of doubt   for *personne* that
    'No-one doubts that ... '

c. Je n' ai   pas besoin [$_{PP}$ d' aucune preuve].
    I *ne* have *pas* need   of *aucune* proof
    'I don't need any proof.'

How is one to deal with these data? One possibility is that, unlike in Standard French, *pas* has not become inherently negative in Québécois (and the other relevant varieties). If *pas* were still what Muller (1991) terms a *semi-négation*, that is, a noninherently negative NPI, its co-occurrence properties would be expected. However, this seems unlikely. Denise Daoust-Blais, for example, has argued that, in Québécois as in Standard French, *pas* and not *ne* must be considered the true negative marker (Daoust-Blais 1975; Daoust-Blais and Kemp 1979: 11). Indeed, *ne* is generally omitted in Québécois (Sankoff and Vincent 1977). Such an approach is therefore implausible and unlikely to be able to explain the contrast between the standard and nonstandard varieties. A different approach is therefore needed.

An alternative analysis, one that has been advocated by Moritz and Valois (1994: 679fn12), is to hold that, in Québécois, for example, *pas* has been reanalyzed as Neg°. (Recall, for example, from the discussion of the Negative Cycle in section 3.1.1, especially footnote 6, that the negative marker *non*, an adverb in Latin, has been reanalyzed as the realization of a functional head in the modern Romance languages.) However, as discussed in section 3.1.2, I find this idea implausible for a number of reasons. First, there are no syntactic respects in which *pas* in Québécois behaves like a head. In all respects, most importantly concerning Verb Movement patterns across it, *pas* in Québécois behaves like a maximal projection, a fact adequately reflected in the analysis of this element as the specifier of NegP. Second, there has been no major typological shift in Québécois that might explain why speakers would begin to analyze *pas* as a head rather than as a maximal projection. Third, Québécois is in fact more of a paradigm case of a negative concord language than is Standard French. Given the analysis of the negative adverbs and arguments as non-inherently negative NPIs of one sort or another, I actually *expect* them to co-occur with a negative XP operator. In such terms, it is the "weird" standard language that begs an explanation, rather than the nonstandard varieties. I therefore reject the claim that *pas* in Québécois has been reanalyzed as Neg°.

I return to the relationship between the negative operator and negative adverbs in section 5.5.2, where I develop the approach to (61b, c) sketched in section 4.4.2 for the standard and the nonstandard patterns.

4.5 Summary

In this chapter, I have considered the syntax of the negative adverbs *plus*, *jamais*, and *guère*. In line with the conclusion drawn at the end of chapter 3, namely that Modern French is a non-NC language, I analyzed these elements as nonnegative. I treated them as NPIs, in that their negative interpretation is the result of their co-occurrence with an operator that is inherently negative and that takes scope over them. In the standard language, this operator is non-overt: Op; in some nonstandard varieties, such as Québécois, it can be overt: *pas*. By concluding that the "negative" adverbs of French are not inherently negative themselves, I was able to provide an elegant account for the freer distributions these elements witness in comparison with *pas*. Whereas *pas* must raise to SpecNegP where this position is accessible, since this is the only way in which sentential negation can be marked, the "negative" adverbs do not since sentential negation can be marked if the non-overt Op raises (without taking the lexical adverb with it).

5

Negative Arguments

In this chapter, I move away from negative *adverbs*. My aim is to provide a syntactic analysis of negative *arguments*, which show a number of similarities with the adverbs discussed in chapter 4. They co-occur with each other (and the adverbs) without producing DN; they license *ne*; and they have sentential scope (see (1)). In contrast to the elements discussed in the previous chapter, though, the elements of interest here are argumental rather than adverbial and, consequently, are associated with θ-roles and, presumably, A-positions. The two elements I consider are *personne* 'anyone/no-one' and *rien* 'anything/nothing'. Examples are given in (1):[1]

---

1. While the presence of pre-verbal *ne* is generally optional (see section 1.2.4, and the references in chapter 1, footnote 3, for discussion of the sociolinguistics of "*ne*-drop"), Ashby (1976: 123, 1981: 679) notes in two studies that, where the grammatical subject is *personne* or *rien*, pre-verbal *ne* is never deleted. Prince (1976: 410) gives the same judgment. A couple of comments are in order at this point. First, Escure (1974: 403) disagrees with Ashby and Prince, giving the following data (her (3b) and (4b)):

(i)   Personne vient.
      personne comes
      'No-one is coming.'
(ii) Personne veut   rien.
      personne wants *rien*
      'No-one wants anything.'

Escure's judgments are in no way marginal; my informants also accept (i) and (ii). Second, the fact that *personne* and, in liaison contexts, *rien* both end in an [n] makes it difficult to tell whether or not *ne* has been dropped. The contrast could be reduced to the presence-versus-absence of gemination. Strong categorical claims that *ne* is never dropped in these contexts need therefore to be treated with care. Further, Prince's judgment was based on accepted prescriptivist views rather than observation (personal communication). More reliable contexts in which to test the hypothesis, that is, avoiding phrase-final [n], are suggested in (iii) and (iv):

(iii) Rien du   tout (?n'?)a été   fait.
      rien of-the all   *ne* has been done
      'Nothing at all was done.'
(iv) Personne d' intéressant (?n'?)a été invité à la fête.
      personne of interesting   *ne* has been invited to the party
      'No-one interesting was invited to the party.'

Finally, in recent discussion, and following further fieldwork of the type presented in Ashby (1976, 1981), Bill Ashby (personal communication) reports that he has found instances of *ne*-drop in the presence of *personne* and *rien* in subject position.

(1) a.   Personne ne voit Marie.
         personne ne sees M.
         'No-one can see M.'

    b.   Marie ne soupçonne rien.
         M.   *ne* suspects   *rien*
         'M. suspects nothing.'

    c.   Personne ne fait rien.
         personne ne does *rien*
         'No-one's doing anything.'

Given my conclusion that the negative adverbs considered in chapter 4 are not inherently negative, and in view of the similarities between those items and the negative arguments considered here, I pursue an analysis in which the negative arguments are assumed not to be inherently negative either. Rather, I argue that the negative interpretation which *rien* and *personne* receive is a consequence of their being bound by Op, which *is* inherently negative. The presence of Op is also responsible for conferring sentential scope on the negative arguments and for licensing *ne*.

My approach is supported by the fact that *personne* and *rien* can co-occur with each other, as well as with the negative adverbs discussed earlier, without leading to DN. Given that Jespersen's Generalization predicts that Modern French is a non-NC language, as discussed in section 3.5.2, I do not expect multiple negative XPs to co-occur in the language without leading to DN. Given that *personne* and *rien* can co-occur without leading to DN, they are deemed to be NPIs (nonnegative elements dependent on the presence of a negative operator), rather than negative quantifiers (inherently negative items).

Assuming, then, that *rien* and *personne* are NPIs, I first address the mechanisms responsible for licensing them in clauses. As one might expect, given the noted similarities, these are the same as those responsible for licensing the adverbs discussed in chapter 4, namely local A'-binding by a negative operator at S-structure.

A further aim of this chapter is to account for why, within the standard modern language, the distribution of *rien* does not match that of *personne*, a fact widely recognized in traditional grammars but that, to my knowledge, has been ignored by theoretical syntacticians. (In her recent study of sentential negation, which includes discussion of French, Haegeman 1995: 315–16fn40 decides to leave the precise characterization of these two elements on the research agenda.) For example, in compound perfective verb paradigms, while *personne* must follow the participle, the more natural position for *rien* is between the auxiliary and the participle.[2]

---

2. The symbol # is used in (2b) to indicate that the order is marked. The degree of markedness seems to vary between speakers. For my informants, postparticipial *rien* is emphatic; for Muller (1991: 282) and Viviane Déprez (personal communication), it is ungrammatical.

Muller (1991: 281) points out that, while impossible in the standard language, (3a) is possible in

(2) a.   Jean n' a   vu   personne.
     b.   #Jean n' a   vu   rien.
          J.   *ne* has seen *personne/rien*
          'J. hasn't seen anyone/anything.'

(3) a.   ⋆Jean n' a   personne   vu.
     b.   Jean n' a   rien   vu.
          J.   *ne* has *personne/rien* seen
          (= (2a, b))

This and other parallel distributional mismatches between *personne* and *rien* are discussed in section 5.4.

5.1   Early generative approaches to the syntax of *personne* and *rien*

Early transformational attempts to deal with the syntax of *personne* and *rien* were couched within the terms of LF raising: as quantifiers, these elements were assumed to QR at LF in order to acquire sentential scope. Such LF movement was argued by Kayne (1981, 1984: 24) to account for the contrast in (4):

(4) a.   ⋆Je n' ai   exigé   que personne soit   arrêté.
          I   *ne* have demanded that *personne* be-SUBJ arrested
          'I didn't demand anyone be arrested.'

     b.   ?Je n' ai   exigé   qu' ils   arrêtent   personne.
          I   *ne* have demanded that they arrest-SUBJ *personne*
          'I didn't demand they arrest anyone.'

Kayne argues that the ungrammaticality of (4a) is due to the ECP in (5):

(5) *The Empty Category Principle (ECP)*:
     A (nonpronominal) empty category must be properly governed.

Following QR, Kayne argues that *personne* in (4a) leaves a subject trace that fails to be properly governed; hence the ungrammaticality. Raising of *personne* in (4b) fails to result in ungrammaticality because the trace left after LF movement of *personne* is in object position. Object traces—unlike subject traces—are properly head-governed.[3] Identical facts hold for *rien*, as shown in (6):

---

some nonstandard regional varieties of French (e.g., Genevan French, according to Haegeman 1995: 231 (87b)).
   3. Rizzi (1982: 124 (22) and (26)) shows that the facts for *personne* can be replicated in Italian for *nessuno* (and *niente*):
(i)   Non pretendo   che tu   arresti   nessuno.
      non require-1SG that you arrest-SUBJ *nessuno*
      'I don't require you to arrest anyone.'
(ii) ?⋆Non pretendo   che nessuno ti   arresti.
      non require-1SG that *nessuno* you arrest-SUBJ

(6) a. ★Je n' ai   exigé   que rien soit   fait.
         I *ne* have demanded that *rien* be-SUBJ done
         'I didn't demand anything be done.'

     b. ?Je n' ai   exigé   qu' ils   fassent rien.
         I *ne* have demanded that they do-SUBJ *rien*
         'I didn't demand they do anything.'

A couple of comments are in order here. First, not all speakers of French agree with Kayne's judgments in (4). (See, for example, the comments by Zaring 1985: 160 and the reservations in von Bremen 1986: 230.) This fact could be taken to cast doubt on an ECP approach, since ECP violations usually result in sharp ungrammaticality. Second, it is surprising that the same effects are not found in Spanish at all (see Longobardi 1987). Further, the grammaticality of (7) is problematical for an LF-raising approach to the syntax of *personne/ rien.*[4]

(7) Je ne crois   pas que personne soit   arrivé.   (Prince 1976: 410 (29d))
     I *ne* believe *pas* that *personne* be-SUBJ arrived
     'I don't think anyone has arrived.'

In this example, *personne* appears in the same position as in Kayne's (4a), namely the subject position of the embedded subjunctive clause. The fact that *personne* has matrix scope is clear from the translation of the example as well as the representation in (8).

(8) $\neg\exists x$, person(x), believe(I, (arrived(x)))   (= (7))

In (9), in contrast, the scope of *personne* is restricted to the embedded clause. The meaning of (7) is the opposite of the meaning of (9):

(9) Je ne crois   pas que personne NE soit   arrivé.
     I *ne* believe *pas* that *personne ne* be-SUBJ arrived
     'I don't think no-one has arrived.'
     (= 'I think someone has arrived.')

(10) $\neg$ believe(I, ($\neg\exists x$, person(x), (arrived(x))))   (= (9))

In (9), *personne* has local scope, that is, it is restricted to the embedded clause; the sentence is an example of logical DN, as indicated in (10) by the presence of two logical operators of negation, $\neg$, one of which cancels the other out. In (7),

---

The example in (i) is somewhat better than the equivalent French string in (4b), since the pre-verbal negative marker is sufficient in Italian to mark sentential negation, but not in French. (See section 1.2.4.) The only possible interpretation of the string in (ii)–assuming, anyway, a particular intonational pattern (Rizzi 1982: 175fn12)–is an (irrelevant) DN reading. Hence, (ii) could be glossed as in (iii):
(iii) I don't require that no-one arrest you.   (DN)
   4. The structure illustrated with *croire* 'to believe' in (7) is also possible with other bridge verbs, such as *affirmer* 'to maintain', *prétendre* 'to claim', *penser* 'to think', and *estimer* 'to feel', but not, interestingly, with *dire* 'to say'. Thanks to Odile Cyrille for this information.

in contrast, *personne* has matrix scope, as in (4a); in (8) there is just one negative operator.

Given that Kayne motivates LF raising of *personne* in (4a) on grounds of scope, he would presumably want to do the same in (7). Of course, following Kayne's analysis, by raising out of its surface position, *personne* would leave an ungoverned trace behind. Consequently, (7) should be ungrammatical, yet it isn't. I take this to be further evidence against Kayne's (1981) LF-raising account of *personne* and *rien*.[5]

5.2   The syntax of *personne*

Of the two negative arguments to be discussed here, *personne* is the most straightforward, at least in terms of its distribution. The overt distribution of *personne* is essentially that of any other argument DP (Moritz and Valois 1994: 669).[6] It can be a subject, a direct or indirect object, or the complement of a noun or preposition.[7] Yet, in similar fashion to Kayne (1981), M&V suggest that *personne* raises to SpecNegP at LF. In contrast to Kayne's QR analysis, M&V motivate raising on the basis of the Neg Criterion, repeated in (11): *personne* is deemed to be inherently negative and raises at LF to SpecNegP in order to be in a spec-head configuration with a negative head. In section 5.2.1, I discuss and evaluate the analysis and logic put forward by M&V. General problems with their analysis are raised in section 5.2.2. An alternative proposal—following the line of inquiry pursued in earlier chapters—is made in section 5.2.3.

5.2.1   Moritz and Valois: LF raising
of *personne* to SpecNegP

The syntax of *personne* has been the topic of recent work by Luc Moritz and Daniel Valois (1993, 1994), who assume, following Kayne (1981), that, in

---

5. As I show in section 5.2.2, the grammaticality of (7) is also problematic for Moritz and Valois's (1994) account of the syntax of *personne*.

6. Text references to M&V are to Moritz and Valois (1994).

7. Christine Tellier (personal communication) has drawn my attention to a further distributional possibility exhibited by *personne* in Québécois. In association with a subject or object clitic, *personne* can occupy a right-peripheral position, as in (i)-(ii). The construction is unavailable in Standard French and is ruled out in Québécois with a full NP, as in (iii)-(iv). I leave consideration of this phenomenon to future research.

(i)   Julie les   a   pas vus personne.
       J.   them has *pas* seen *personne*
       'J. hasn't seen any of them.'
(ii)   Ils sont pas venus personne.
       they are *pas* come *personne*
       'None of them came.'
(iii) ⋆Julie a pas vu ses amis personne.
(iv)   ⋆Les invités sont pas venus personne.

contrast to "ordinary" arguments, *personne* (or a larger constituent containing *personne*) undergoes movement at LF. M&V assume that *personne* is inherently negative and suggest that LF raising is to SpecNegP to satisfy Haegeman and Zanuttini's (henceforth, H&Z) (1991: 244 (27)) Neg Criterion in (11):

(11) *The Neg Criterion*:
    a.   Each Neg $X°$ must be in a spec-head relationship with a Neg operator.
    b.   Each Neg operator must be in a spec-head relationship with a Neg $X°$.

If *personne* raises to SpecNegP, the Neg Criterion can be satisfied by virtue of the spec-head configuration between (the constituent containing) *personne* in SpecNegP and (the trace of) *ne* in Neg°. The reader is referred to M&V for the mechanics of how *personne* manages to reach SpecNegP at LF, the exact details of which are irrelevant for my purposes here. Briefly, where possible, *personne* raises alone, directly or successive cyclically to SpecNegP at LF. Where this is not possible, for example, where *personne* is contained within an island XP, M&V suggest that *personne* raises to the highest specifier position within the island. A sequence of Dynamic Agreement (henceforth, DA) between *personne* (in SpecXP) and the head, $X°$, of the island, followed by feature percolation from $X°$ up to XP, guarantees that the [+NEG] feature is borne by the entire XP island constituent, turning it into a negative operator,[8] which then raises to SpecNegP to satisfy the Neg Criterion. M&V call this "LF pied-piping".[9]

To support their LF pied-piping analysis, M&V provide arguments suggesting that movement is involved in sentential negation in French in general, that is, not just in *ne . . . pas* constructions but also in structures containing *ne . . . personne*, and so on. First, albeit tentatively, they refer (p. 671) to Longobardi's (1991) observation of a parallel between rules operating on *wh*-movement and those responsible for scope assignment of negative phrases in Italian, which Longobardi attributes to the fact that negative phrases undergo LF movement. M&V (p. 673) point out that *personne* exhibits some of the properties identified by Longobardi, for example sensitivity to strong islands, providing data that suggest that the distribution of *personne* is sensitive to both the Subject Condition and the Adjunct Condition.[10] However, as M&V acknowledge (p. 674), sensitivity to strong islands is not an undisputed indication of movement. For example, they note that Cinque (1990) challenges this correlation in his (non-movement) analysis of clitic left dislocation constructions in Italian. In Cinque's

---

8. See Haegeman (1996a) for discussion of contexts in English in which an XP becomes a negative operator by virtue of a negative element contained within it.

9. A similar mechanism is used by Ortiz de Urbina (1993) to account for some cases of overt movement in Basque.

10. Subject Condition violations are illustrated in (i), Adjunct Condition violations in (ii) (from M&V, p. 673, (14a) and (16a)):
(i)   *Engager personne n' est permis.
     hire-INF *personne ne* is   allowed
(ii) *Pierre souhaite que Marc ne parte   avant d' engager personne
    P.   wishes that M.   *ne* leave-SUBJ before of hire-INF *personne*
See M&V for discussion.

analysis, sensitivity to strong islands is a condition on "chains" generally, whether created by movement or by base-generation, that is, a condition on chains
and CHAINs. This reservation notwithstanding, M&V (section 4) provide data
that, in their view, constitute direct empirical evidence that, where *personne* is
not higher than SpecNegP at S-structure, it moves to SpecNegP at LF. The first
set of data concerns the licensing of indefinite pseudopartitive direct objects,
that is, with the structure [Ø de NP]. The second concerns the failure of NC between *personne* and *pas*. The data are discussed and the argumentation evaluated in sections 5.2.1.1 and 5.2.1.2, respectively. General problems with M&V's
analysis are raised in section 5.2.2.

5.2.1.1 Pseudopartitive direct objects: [Ø de NP]

In section 2.2, I proposed a derivational A'-binding analysis of pseudopartitives,
which I assumed, following Lyons (1994a), were NumPs: [$_{NumP}$ Ø de NP]. Pseudopartitives are licensed in negative sentences, as in (12a), or by what Battye
(1989, 1995) terms nominal quantifiers in a QàD structure, as in (12b).

(12) a. Jean n' a   pas$_i$ mangé [Ø$_i$ de pain].
         J.   *ne* has *pas* eaten   of bread
         'J. hasn't eaten any bread.'

     b. Jean a   beaucoup$_i$ mangé [Ø$_i$ de pain].
         J.   has lots   eaten   of bread
         'J. has eaten lots of bread.'

What seems to be required is a c-commanding operator (at S-structure) for local
A'-binding of the empty category, Ø, contained within the pseudopartitive (cf.
Kayne 1981). In section 2.2, I claimed that the c-command condition is a consequence of the fact that Ø is the trace of the operator *pas* or *beaucoup*; the operator is generated within the pseudopartitive NumP and subsequently extracted:
Ø = *t*. Since the ECP guarantees that movement is always to a c-commanding
position, the operator will always c-command Ø/*t*. This approach has the desirable consequence that Kayne's c-command condition does not need to be stated,
since it follows from the ECP and the nature of the relationship between the
operator and the empty category. The binding relations in (12) are indicated by
co-indexation. In (12b), the operator is *beaucoup*; in (12a), it is *pas*.

   In addition to the configurations discussed here, M&V (p. 677) point out that
pseudopartitives are licensed when the subject is *personne*, as in (13):

(13) Personne n' a   avalé   de poison.
     personne ne has swallowed of poison
     'No-one swallowed any poison.'

For M&V, who do not assume the derivational analysis of pseudopartitives proposed in chapter 2 (and who cannot therefore explain the unavailability of PP-
embedded pseudopartitives discussed in section 2.2.4.2), the grammaticality of

(13) does not pose a problem: the (S-structure) c-command condition on (the empty category contained within) the pseudopartitive is satisfied if *personne* is analyzed as a potential licenser, that is, if the pseudopartitive in (13) is licensed as in (14).[11]

(14) Personne, n'a avalé [Ø, de poison].

Despite the fact that examples such as (13) are amenable to analysis within the terms of Kayne's *S-structure* c-command condition on licensing pseudopartitives, M&V present data that, according to them, suggest the c-command condition on licensing pseudopartitives should in fact apply at LF. M&V show that pseudopartitives are licensed in the presence of *personne* even when *personne* does not itself c-command the pseudopartitive at S-structure, as in (15) (from M&V, pp. 677-78, (31)), where *personne* is embedded within an indirect object or adverbial PP.[12]

(15) a. Lucie n' a   donné [Ø de livres] [PP à personne].
        L.   *ne* has given   of books   to *personne*
        'L. hasn't given any books to anyone.'

    b. Lucie ne donne [Ø de réceptions] [PP pour personne].
       L.   *ne* gives   of parties   for *personne*
       'L. doesn't throw parties for anyone.'

    c. Lucie n' a   donné [Ø de livres] [PP à l' ami   de personne].
       L.   *ne* has given   of books   to the friend of *personne*
       'L. hasn't given any books to anyone's friend.'

M&V correctly point out that, if nothing else is said about (15), Kayne's c-command condition on licensing pseudopartitives is lost. Given that M&V (quite rightly) do not wish to accept this loss, they assume, instead, that the data represent evidence that *personne* (or the constituent containing *personne*) is a negative operator that undergoes LF movement to a position–SpecNegP in the case of the examples in (15)–from which it c-commands the direct object and that it is from this LF position that the empty category in the pseudopartitive is bound and licensed; the c-command condition is then assumed to hold at that level.[13]

---

11. Note that in (14), the licenser of the empty category in the pseudopartitive [Ø de NP] is not its antecedent: Ø ≠ *t*. For M&V, binding is a representational relationship, not a derivational one. Ø and its licenser form a CHAIN rather than a chain. This, of course, has the weakness of making it necessary to stipulate that the two elements are related by binding at all and, consequently, c-command. In the analysis of pseudopartitives proposed in chapter 2, this stipulation is not necessary. There, pseudopartitives were seen as the result of operator extraction. Since there is independent evidence that antecedents and traces are related, binding (and c-command) do not have to be stipulated.

12. Although in each of the examples in (15), the PP can be argued to c-command the pseudopartitive direct objects, "negative" *personne*, embedded within the PP, clearly cannot. See footnote 14.

13. The shift from S-structure to LF must be stipulated. With respect to (16), since *personne* is contained within an island, *personne* first moves to SpecPP and a sequence of DA and feature percolation turn *the entire PP* into a negative operator which then raises to SpecNegP.

(16)

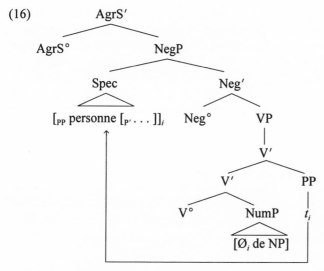

LF raising

Attractive as M&V's proposal may seem on the surface, the logic they adopt to arrive at their conclusion deserves close scrutiny. In particular, their analysis crucially depends on the assumption that Kayne's (1981) c-command condition need not be satisfied until LF. This is clearly a weaker condition than the original formulation (as well as the one adopted here), and it would be nice to have independent empirical evidence motivating such a weakening. Otherwise, one may be left with an account that is in fact too weak. Yet M&V provide no such evidence. Consider in this context the ungrammatical string in (17):

(17) *Lucille a donné de livres à beaucoup.
    L.   has given of books to *beaucoup*
    'L. has given books to lots (of people).'

The string in (17) is identical to (15a) apart from the fact that the complement of the preposition *à* 'to', *personne* in (15a), has been replaced by *beaucoup* 'lots' in (17). As an indefinite quantifier, one might expect *beaucoup* (or the PP *à beaucoup*) to QR at LF. Were this to happen, *beaucoup* would c-command the pseudopartitive [Ø de livres]. As such, and given M&V's LF c-command condition on the licensing of pseudopartitives, one might expect the direct object to be licensed, contrary to fact. The ungrammaticality of (17) therefore casts some doubt on M&V's account of the licensing of pseudopartitives and, more generally, their account of the syntax of *personne*, in particular the claim that *personne* itself is responsible for licensing the pseudopartitives in (13) and (15).[14]

14. Note further that raising as far as SpecNegP is not in fact necessary, even if the c-command condition is applied at LF. In fact, to account for the examples in (15), movement of *personne* to SpecPP followed by DA and feature percolation is arguably all that is needed. Since, with respect to the tree in (16), this would be enough to turn the PP into an operator, and since PP c-commands the empty

Rather than accepting M&V's weaker (= LF) version of Kayne's (1981) c-command condition, I assume that it does indeed apply at S-structure but that an element other than *personne* is responsible for licensing the empty category (as well as *ne*) in the pseudopartitive in, for example, (15). Following the discussion in chapter 4, I argue that *personne* is not inherently negative and, as such, does not need to (and therefore cannot) raise–at S-structure or LF–to SpecNegP. Rather, I assume that *personne* is an NPI, bound by Op, the non-overt negative operator. As argued in chapter 4, I assume that Op occupies SpecNegP at S-structure since sentential negation is marked at that level, and *ne* needs to be licensed at that level. I assume further that it is Op, rather than *personne*, that is responsible for licensing the pseudopartitives. As suggested in chapter 2 for the overt counterpart of Op, *pas*, I assume that Op has been extracted from within the pseudopartitive. (See also chapter 4, footnote 12.) I pursue this analysis in section 5.2.3. Meanwhile, in the next section, I discuss the second empirical argument M&V give to support their LF-raising analysis of *personne*, namely the general unavailability of NC with *pas*.

5.2.1.2   *Unavailability of NC with* pas

M&V argue (pp. 679-81) that the unavailability of an NC interpretation for strings containing *personne* and so on and *pas* supports their LF-raising analysis of *personne* and similar elements. When "negative" phrases such as *personne* and *jamais* co-occur with each other, the resulting interpretation is NC. This is not possible where *personne*, *jamais*, and similar terms co-occur with *pas*.[15] This should be clear from the translations in (18):[16]

(18) a.   Jean n' a   jamais vu   personne.   (NC)
          J.   *ne* has *jamais* seen *personne*
          'J. hasn't ever seen anyone.'

     b.   [*]Jean n' a   pas vu   personne.   (DN)
          J.   *ne* has *pas* seen *personne*
          'J has not seen no-one.'
          (= 'J. *has* seen *some*one.')

category, Ø, in the direct object NumP, the licensing condition of Ø is already satisfied and the Neg Criterion need not be invoked.

15. As has already been seen in numerous places, this is the case in Standard French but not in some nonstandard varieties such as Québécois, as acknowledged by M&V (p. 679fn12), who offer examples such as (i):

(i)   J'ai   pas vu   personne.   (NC)
      I have *pas* seen *personne*
      'I didn't see anyone.'

Haegeman (1995: 302fn15) recognizes that the issue of why NC appears to be impossible between *pas* and *personne* in Standard French is a problem.

16. M&V use the [*] diacritic to indicate that strings such as (18b) containing both *pas* and *personne* are interpreted as instances of DN rather than NC.

M&V suggest that the unavailability of NC in strings like (18b) can be explained by assuming (a) that *pas* occupies SpecNegP (at D-structure–see below) and (b) that SpecNegP cannot then be an LF landing site for *personne* and similar terms. So, while in (18a), both *jamais* and *personne* can raise to SpecNegP at LF,[17] and their respective [+NEG] features can be absorbed,[18] this is not possible in (18b) since, for some unspecified reason, the D-structure presence of *pas* in SpecNegP prevents *personne* from raising to this position at LF.

At this point, one or two words need to be said with regard to M&V's rather confusing stand on the issue of whether *pas* in generated directly in SpecNegP (as in Pollock 1989) or whether it is generated lower in clause structure and subsequently raised into SpecNegP (as I suggest in chapter 2). First, on page 667, M&V suggest movement is always involved in sentential negation. Later, on page 679, M&V claim that *pas* is base-generated in SpecNegP.[19] And, to confuse matters further, in footnote 4 on page 669, M&V are uncommitted on the issue of the base position of *pas*, referring the reader to the discussion in Hirschbühler and Labelle (1992/93) of Rowlett (1992b), an early version of the proposals in chapter 2.

Throughout, M&V (p. 669fn4) claim that nothing in their analysis of *personne* hinges on this particular issue. Nevertheless, it seems to me that there *is* in fact something crucial in M&V's analysis of *personne* that hinges on the issue of where *pas* is generated. It seems to me that their analysis of the unavailability of NC between *personne* and *pas* hinges crucially on *pas* being in Spec-NegP in (18b) *at D-structure*. Indeed, their analysis falls down if the *S-structure* presence of *pas* in SpecNegP could prevent LF raising of *personne* and the NC interpretation. If the presence of *pas* in SpecNegP at S-structure blocked LF raising of *personne*, we would expect the S-structure presence of negative adverbs, such as *jamais*, in SpecNegP to block LF raising of *personne*, too. However, this does not happen, as shown in (18a) as well as (19):

(19) Anne avait peur de ne jamais pouvoir souvent rien faire.
    A.   had   fear of *ne jamais* be-able often   *rien* do
    'A. was afraid she would never be able to do anything often.'

As argued in section 1.1.7.4, it seems that, in the unmarked case, infinitival modals, such as *pouvoir* 'to be able' do not have to move higher than Mood° and that, if they do move any higher, they can freely move only as far as T°. The fact that *pouvoir* appears before the adverb *souvent*, which, following the discussion in chapter 1, I assume is MoodP-adjoined, suggests that, in (19), *pouvoir* has indeed raised into T°. Accordingly, given its pre-verbal position, I assume that *jamais* occupies SpecNegP, as in (20):

---

17. The adverb *jamais* may well occupy SpecNegP as early as S-structure. See the discussion in section 4.4.1. Crucially, though, for M&V's purposes, *jamais* and so on do not occupy SpecNegP at D-structure.

18. Recall that, in contrast to my own analysis, M&V assume these elements are inherently negative. For discussion of absorption, see Higginbotham and May (1981).

19. Moritz and Valois (1993) make the same claim.

(20) [$_{NegP}$ [$_{Spec}$ jamais] [$_{TP}$ pouvoir [$_{MoodP}$ souvent [$_{MoodP}$ rien faire VP]]]]

If M&V's analysis of the unavailability of NC with *pas* and *personne* in (18b) hinges on the *S-structure* presence of *pas* in SpecNegP blocking LF raising of *personne* to that position, then NC should also be unavailable between *personne*/*rien* and *jamais* in (18a) and (19), since *jamais* occupies SpecNegP at S-structure. As the gloss shows, however, this is not the case. The sentences in (18a) and (19) have what might be termed an NC interpretation. Consequently, if M&V's account can be salvaged, it must be the *D-structure* presence of *pas* in SpecNegP that prevents LF raising of *personne*. M&V cannot therefore remain ambivalent and must assume that *pas* is base-generated in SpecNegP, contrary to my proposals in chapter 2. Consequently, they are unable to explain the facts reviewed in sections 2.2.4.2 and 2.1.1, concerning PP-embedded indefinite nominals and negative imperatives. I take this to be somewhat problematic for M&V's proposed analysis of the syntax of *personne*.

This is not the only issue that, it seems to me, needs to be clarified in M&V's proposals. First, if *personne* needs to raise to SpecNegP at LF and if, as M&V suggest, the presence of *pas* in SpecNegP blocks such movement, they would predict that (18b) is ungrammatical. This prediction is, however, not borne out by the data; (18b) is perfectly grammatical but simply does not receive an NC reading. How can *personne* ultimately be licensed without LF movement to SpecNegP? M&V do not answer this question. One might envisage that, in (18b), *personne* fails to qualify as an LF operator in some way, perhaps within the terms of Rizzi's (1996) functional definition of operators. This seems unreasonable, however. Rizzi exploits the functional definition of operators to explain why some constituents appear not to have to raise *at S-structure*. His definition does not apply at LF, where all constituents bearing affective features—*wh*- or negative, for example—are assumed to be operators and, therefore, undergo raising. Certainly, unless some other assumptions are made, Rizzi's functional definition of operators is not going to help M&V explain why *personne* can avoid LF raising in (18b) and maintain grammaticality.

Second, M&V's account of the unavailability of NC in (18b) leads implicitly to a discrepancy between the way the Neg Criterion and the *wh*-criterion work in Modern French.[20] Consider (21), which contains two *wh*-constituents:

(21) Qui a   fait quoi?
     Who has done what
     'Who did what?'

With respect to multiple *wh*-structures such as (21), it is standardly assumed that the *wh*-phrase which remains *in situ* at S-structure raises at LF to adjoin to a higher *wh*-phrase (Huang 1982; Lasnik and Saito 1984) and that absorption of the *wh*-feature takes place at that level (Higginbotham and May 1981). This

---

20. The discrepancy mentioned here is quite independent from the issue of at what level the criteria apply. As is shown in the next section, it is clear that the *wh*-criterion applies at S-structure in French.

approach seems to be suitable for (21).[21] The question that then needs to be answered is the following: Why should a *wh*-phrase in situ (*quoi* 'what' in (21)) be able to raise at LF and adjoin to another *wh*-phrase (*qui* 'who' in (21)) allowing *wh*-absorption, whereas, in the case of negative phrases, *personne* in (18b) cannot LF raise and adjoin to *pas*, allowing absorption of the [+NEG] feature? M&V do not really address this issue, either. They simply note that, while NC is generally available in French, it is unavailable with *pas*. This in no way provides an explanation for the observed facts.

This state of affairs becomes particularly striking when one considers Québécois, in which NC is available in the presence of *pas*, a possibility that M&V tentatively suggest might be dealt with by assuming that, in Québécois, the negative marker *pas* has been reanalyzed as a Neg°-associated element and therefore fails to interfere with LF raising to SpecNegP. (See section 4.4.2 for reasons why I reject such an analysis and for an alternative proposal to deal with this distinction between the standard language and Québécois. See also section 5.5.2 for further discussion, including contexts in the standard language in which NC is also possible with *pas*, as exemplified in (7).)

Third, M&V's analysis of *personne* predicts—wrongly—that NC should be possible between *personne* in subject position and *pas*. M&V suggest that, where *personne* occupies a position within the subject, as in (13) and, presumably, (16), although M&V do not discuss such examples, it does not move to SpecNegP, since this would involve lowering.[22] If *personne* in a subject does not need to move to SpecNegP, the presence of *pas* in SpecNegP should not pose a problem, and NC should be possible. The fact that *pas* and *personne* are in distinct specifier positions is not necessarily a problem for absorption of the [+NEG] feature either, given Haegeman's (1995) analysis of NC in West Flemish. (See section 3.5.1 for discussion.) In West Flemish, negative XPs can move in the syntax to distinct specifier positions. Provided these specifiers are not lower that SpecNegP, NC is possible. In other words, absorption of the feature [+NEG] is possible *even if* the [+NEG]XPs are not in the same specifier position. In Haegeman's analysis, recourse is taken to the notion of extended specifier, following work by Grimshaw (1993): each one of the distinct specifier positions to which concordant [+NEG]XPs move counts as an extended specifier of Neg°. Transferring this notion to French, M&V would predict that *personne* in subject position can co-occur with *pas* in SpecNegP with an NC reading, contrary to fact:[23]

---

21. See Plunkett (1996) for an alternative view.

22. Acquaviva (1993: 17–21) discusses Quantifier Lowering, for example, LF lowering of "negatives" from the subject position to SpecNegP, and concludes that it is implausible. See also Rizzi (1990).

23. To counter my objection here, M&V might argue that *personne* needs to pass through SpecNegP in its way to SpecAgrSP and that the D-structure presence of *pas* in SpecNegP prevents it from doing so.

(22) Personne n' est pas venu.   (DN)
      personne ne is *pas* come
      'No-one *didn't* come.'
      (= 'Everyone came.')

Fourth, M&V's account of NC in terms of multiple adjunction to SpecNegP followed by [+NEG] absorption makes erroneous predictions for (admittedly highly marked) strings such as (23):

(23) a. ??Personne n' a   pas rien fait.
          personne ne has *pas rien* done
          'No-one didn't do anything.'

     b. ??Je n' ai   pas rien donné à personne.
          I *ne* have *pas rien* given to *personne*
          'I didn't give nothing to anyone.'

M&V predict that the presence of *pas* in SpecNegP in the examples in (23) prevents the other negatives from entering into NC (with *pas* and with each other). Given that both examples in (23) contain three negatives, this means that each should have net negative polarity. That is to say, the strings in (23) should be synonymous with (24), which they are not:

(24) a. Personne n' a   rien fait.
          personne ne has *rien* done
          'No-one has done anything.'

     b. Je n' ai   rien donné à personne.
          I *ne* have *rien* given to *personne*
          'I haven't given anyone anything.'

In other words, despite the "blocking" presence of *pas* in SpecNegP in (23), *personne* and *rien* are still able to enter into NC with each other (which is, of course, subsequently canceled by *pas*). The issue that M&V fail to address is how *personne* and *rien* manage to do this, given that they cannot converge on SpecNegP for [+NEG] absorption.

The same point can be made in the context of "true" negative imperatives. These were discussed in chapter 2, where it was argued that they are characterized by the absence of a number of functional projections in clausal architecture, including NegP. Given the absence of NegP in such structures, there is obviously no SpecNegP for multiple negative phrases to LF raise to for [+NEG] absorption. Assuming M&V's analysis of *personne*, NC should not be possible in these configurations. Yet, as shown in (25), NC is indeed possible:

(25) Donne- lui jamais rien.
      give-IMP him *jamais rien*
      'Never give him anything.'

Here, two negative phrases, *jamais* and *rien*, occur in a true imperative clause. That the clause contains a true imperative and, consequently, no NegP projection is clear from the post-verbal position of the indirect object clitic pronoun and the unavailability of pre-verbal *ne*. Yet, as is clear from the translation, NC is available, contrary to M&V's prediction.

Finally, by arguing that the (D-structure) presence of *pas* in SpecNegP prevents LF raising of *personne* and similar elements, M&V are unable to account for the interpretation of (7), repeated here:

(26) Je ne crois   pas que personne soit   arrivé.   (Prince 1976: 410 (29d))
    I *ne* believe *pas* that *personne* be-SUBJ arrived
    'I don't think anyone has arrived.'

As is clear from the translation, the interpretation of (26) is one of NC. *Personne* therefore has wide/matrix scope. Given the assumptions that M&V make (cf. Kayne 1981), this means that *personne* raises at LF to the matrix SpecNegP. However, M&V's analysis predicts that (26) should be interpreted as DN, since the presence of *pas* in the matrix clause should prevent LF raising of *personne* from the embedded clause into the matrix SpecNegP.

5.2.2 Summary: what's wrong with Moritz and Valois's analysis?

Having discussed the logic that M&V use to support their proposed analysis, I now summarize what I see as the fundamental flaws. I differ from M&V (a) on the nature of the negative phrase that raises to SpecNegP and (b) on the level at which raising takes place. With respect to (a), M&V assume that it is either *personne* itself or some larger constituent containing *personne* that raises to SpecNegP. With respect to (b), they assume that movement to SpecNegP is delayed until LF. I disagree on both these points.

First, given that M&V motivate raising of *personne* to SpecNegP in terms of the Neg Criterion in (11), the fact that this movement does not take place until LF means that M&V are effectively concluding that, in Modern French, the Neg Criterion need not be satisfied until LF.[24] This conclusion arouses immediate suspicion in the light of the evidence presented here, in chapters 1 and 2 in particular, which clearly suggests that sentential negation has to be marked at S-structure in Modern French. Furthermore, the conclusion that the Neg Criterion does not apply until LF in Modern French is problematic when one considers the *wh*-criterion. It has been argued (see Rizzi 1996; Haegeman 1995: 101–2 and references there) that the following data from embedded clauses show that the *wh*-criterion applies at S-structure in Modern French:

---

24. This is in fact in line with H&Z's (1991: 244) suggestion that the level of application of the Neg Criterion could be parametrized and Haegeman's (1992a) claim that the value for the parameter is indeed set to LF in French.

(27) a. Je me demande qui$_i$ ils ont invité t$_i$.   (Haegeman 1995:
         I me ask   who they have invited   101 (70c, d))
         'I wonder who they invited.'

    b. *Je me demande (que) ils ont invité qui.

Movement of the *wh*-phrase is compulsory in selected embedded *wh*-clauses, arguably to satisfy the *wh*-criterion. If M&V's analysis of *personne* is right, these data imply a divergence between the *wh*-criterion on the one hand and the Neg Criterion on the other. This is problematic if the *wh*-criterion and Neg Criterion are nothing more than construction-specific instantiations of the more general AFFECT criterion, as discussed in section 1.3. In contrast, if both criteria are assumed to apply at S-structure, as I have been arguing throughout, there is no such divergence.

Before I leave the issue of the level at which raising to SpecNegP takes place, consider the contrast in (28):

(28) a. Jean n' est sorti   avec personne.
         J.   *ne* is gone-out with *personne*
         'J. didn't go out with anyone.'

    b. %Jean (*n')est sorti   avec pas d' argent.
         J.   *ne* is gone-out with *pas* of money
         'J. went out without any money.'

In (28a), *ne* is licensed. Within M&V's account, *ne* is licensed by virtue of the fact that *personne* raises to SpecNegP (by pied-piping its containing PP) at LF. As for (28b), the string is grammatical (if frowned upon by prescriptivists) if *ne* is absent but universally rejected if *ne* is present. The issue of relevance to us here is the ungrammaticality of (28b) with *ne*. If, in (28a), raising of a negative XP to SpecNegP at LF is sufficient to license *ne* at S-structure, why is it not possible to assume that *pas* pied-pipes to SpecNegP at LF in order to license *ne* in (28b)? Given M&V's analysis of *personne*, and given that the surface position of *pas* in (28b) is licit, I see no reason why a parallel derivation should not be possible for (28b) with *pas*. The fact, therefore, that *ne* is *not* licensed in (28b) casts doubt on the validity of any analysis in which *ne* is licensed by the *LF* presence of an operator in SpecNegP in (28a). What seems to be the case, rather, is that "negative" *ne* is licensed by the *S-structure* presence of an operator in SpecNegP. Indeed, this is what I have assumed since chapter 1 and what, in the next section, I suggest is true in the case of *personne*. Before I go on to do that, I consider the second fundamental objection I have to M&V's analysis of *pas*, namely the issue of whether *personne* is specified [+NEG].

M&V assume that *personne* is inherently negative. Although they claim (p. 669fn5) that they do not wish to take a stand on the issue of whether *personne*-like elements are real (negative) quantifiers or NPIs, they go on (p. 690) to claim that *personne* "inherently bears the [+NEG] feature", which does rather suggest that they have made their minds up on the issue. Further, their analysis in fact crucially depends on *personne* bearing the feature [+NEG]. First, movement of *personne* to SpecNegP (at any level of representation) cannot be motivated by the Neg Criterion in (11) unless *personne* is [+NEG]. Second, in the context of structures in which *personne* is embedded in an island constituent from which it cannot be extracted, M&V suggest that the island constituent as a whole pied-pipes to SpecNegP. The pied-piping mechanism that M&V posit depends upon a feature, namely [+NEG], associated with *personne* alone underlyingly, being transferred to the entire island constituent as discussed briefly in section 5.2.1. It is clear that this mechanism relies on *personne* being marked [+NEG].

Given Jespersen's Generalization and the discussion in chapter 3, this is not a conclusion I am happy to make about elements like *personne* in Modern French. Indeed, in chapter 4, I was able to provide an elegant account of the distributional differences between *plus, jamais,* and similar elements on the one hand and *pas* on the other on the basis of an analysis whereby the former are *not* inherently negative, while the latter is. For these reasons, I reject M&V's assumption that *personne* and so on are inherently negative and that *personne* (or a larger XP constituent containing *personne*) raises to SpecNegP at LF.

5.2.3   An alternative proposal

As an alternative to the analysis proposed by M&V, I suggest that the conclusions reached in previous chapters about sentential negation in French lend themselves immediately to an account of the syntax of *personne*. In what follows, I will assume, in line with Jespersen's Generalization, that *personne* is not inherently negative and does not therefore need to raise to SpecNegP in order to satisfy the Neg Criterion. Rather, I argue that *personne* is an NPI, licensed in situ by binding from the (non-overt) negative operator, Op, which, in contrast, *does* raise to SpecNegP. From this position, Op licenses *ne* and marks sentential negation, ensuring that *personne* has wide scope. I base my discussion on the example in (29), taken from M&V (p. 670, (5)):

(29) Jules n' a   vu   personne.
    J.   *ne* has seen *personne*
    'J. hasn't seen anyone.'

I assume that *personne* is interpreted negatively in (29) by virtue of being unselectively bound by Op. Further, I assume that the sentential scope of *personne* is due to the position of Op (Acquaviva 1993: 25). Given that Op is seen as a non-overt counterpart to *pas*, I assume it can be base-generated adjoined to the constituent over which it takes scope: VP (see section 2.1). The binding relationship in (30) is indicated by co-indexation.[25]

(30) [$_{VP}$ Op$_j$ [$_{VP}$ voir personne$_j$]]

25. Haegeman (1995: 193, 230) suggests that Op here is in fact nonnegative, that is, an expletive null polarity operator.

Given that Op is marked [+NEG] and that sentential negation has to be marked at S-structure, I assume that Op raises overtly to SpecNegP. The relevant parts of the (S-)structure of (29) are given in (31):

(31) $[_{AgrSP} \ldots ne_i \ldots [_{NegP} Op_j [_{Neg'} t_i [_{TP} \ldots [_{VP} t_j [_{VP} \ldots personne_j \ldots]]$

The spec-head relationship between Op and (the trace of) *ne* in Neg° serves to license *ne* by trasmitting the [+NEG] feature by DA. The clause is therefore negative: $i = j$.

As for the way in which *personne* seems able to license pseudopartitives without c-commading them at S-structure, consider again the example from M&V given in (15a), repeated here.

(32) Lucie n' a   donné [Ø de livres] [_{PP} à personne].
     L.   *ne* has given   of books   to *personne*
     'L. hasn't given any books to anyone.'

In section 2.2.3, I argued that, where pseudopartitive NumPs are licensed by *pas* (the overt counterpart of Op), the empty category within the nominal is in fact the trace of *pas*, which has been extracted and raised to SpecNegP. Given that Op in (31) fulfills the same function as overt *pas* in the structures discussed in chapter 2, I argue that the parallel should be extended further and that Op should be generated in SpecNumP within the pseudopartitive in (32) and raised to SpecNegP whence (in addition to marking sentential negation and licensing *ne*) it can bind *personne*. The relevant difference between the structure of (32)– given in (33)–and the representation in (31) is therefore the extraction site of Op. Whereas, in (31) it is VP-adjoined, in (33) it is within NumP. In both cases, it unselectively A′-binds *personne* at S-structure.

(33) $[_{AgrSP} \ldots ne_i \ldots [_{NegP} Op_j [_{Neg'} t_i [_{TP} \ldots [_{VP} [_{NumP} t_j [de NP]] [\ldots$
                                                                         personne_j ...]]

In (32) and (33), the pseudopartitive is therefore licensed in the usual way, by extraction of an operator from SpecNumP. (The trace of) *ne* in Neg° is licensed by its (DA) relationship with Op in SpecNegP.

That Op is extracted from within the pseudopartitive NumP in (32) is supported by the ungrammaticality of (34):

(34) ⋆Je ne sortirais   [_{PP} avec [_{NumP} Ø de filles]][_{PP} pour personne au   monde].
     I *ne* go-out-COND with   of girls   for *personne* to-the world
     'I wouldn't go out with girls for anyone in the world.'

In the same way that *pas* cannot license a PP-embedded pseudopartitive, as discussed in section 2.2.4.2, it seems that Op cannot do so, either. In the former case, the constraint was analyzed with respect to the island status of the PP in

French. In order for *pas* to license a PP-embedded pseudopartitive, it would need to be generated within the PP and subsequently extracted, which it can't do. The ungrammaticality of (34) suggests that a parallel analysis is required for Op. I conclude, therefore, that, in (32), Op originates within the pseudopartitive and is raised to SpecNegP at S-structure, just like *pas*. Of course, given that I am assuming that Op is the non-overt equivalent of *pas*, this is exactly what I would like to do, anyway.

5.3   The distribution of *rien*

Despite the semantic parallel between *rien* and *personne*-the fact that they are both NPIs of some sort-there are clear distributional differences between the two. While *personne* essentially has the distribution of a DP, *rien* behaves like the universal quantifier *tout* 'everything'. The differences are illustrated in the following examples:

(35) a.   Jean n' a   vu   personne.
   b.   #Jean n' a   vu   rien.
       J.   *ne* has seen *personne*/*rien*
       'J. hasn't seen anyone/anything.'

   c.   #Jean a   vu   tout.
       J.   has seen everything
       'J. has seen everything.'

(36) a.   ⋆Jean n' a   personne   vu.
   b.   Jean n' a   rien   vu.
       J.   *ne* has *personne*/*rien* seen
       (= (35a, b))

   c.   Jean a   tout   vu.
       J.   has everything seen
       (= (35c))

The examples in (35a) and (36a) show that, where *personne* is the direct object of a verb taken from a compound perfective paradigm, that is, one with an auxiliary and a past participle, *personne* must appear in post-verbal position (for most speakers—see footnote 2); it cannot intervene between auxiliary and past participle. In contrast, (35b) and (36b) show that, in the unmarked case, *rien* raises to such a position between the auxiliary and the past participle. (Given the argumental/thematic nature of *rien* in these examples, I assume that it is base-generated within an A-position and subsequently moved.) The word *rien* can appear in postparticipial position (for some speakers—see footnote 2), but only with a marked emphatic reading. Examples (35c) and (36c) show that, in this respect, the distribution of *rien* parallels that of *tout*.

It is not just in the context of compound perfective paradigms that the distributions of *rien* and *tout* coincide (and diverge from *personne*). Parallels can also be drawn in the case of infinitives, as shown in (37) and (38):

(37) a.   N' aimer personne,   c'est un crime.
   b.   #N' aimer rien,   c'est un crime.
       ne love   *personne/rien* it is   a   crime
       'Not loving anyone/anything is a crime.'

   c.   #Aimer tout,   c'est un crime.
       love   everything it is   a   crime
       'Loving everything is a crime.'

(38) a.   ★Ne personne   aimer, c'est un crime.
   b.   Ne rien   aimer, c'est un crime.
       ne personne/rien love   it is   a   crime
       (= (37a, b))

   c.   Tout   aimer, c'est un crime.
       everything love   it is   a   crime
       (= (37c))

Within the topicalized infinitival clauses, *personne* must follow the verb. In contrast, in the unmarked case, *rien* precedes the infinitive and can follow the infinitive only with emphatic stress. Once again, *tout* parallels *rien*.

Finally, the examples in (39)–(41) show how, when the direct object of a lexical infinitive is embedded under a modal infinitive, *rien/tout* can—in the unmarked case—precede either the lexical infinitive or both the modal and the lexical infinitive, while *personne* must follow the lexical infinitive:

(39) a.   Afin   de ne DEVOIR   VOIR   personne, . . .
   b.   #Afin   de ne DEVOIR   VOIR   rien, . . .
       In-order of *ne* have-to-INF see-INF *personne/rien*
       'In order not to have to see anyone/anything, . . . '

   c.   #Afin   de DEVOIR   VOIR   tout, . . .
       In-order of have-to-INF see-INF *tout*
       'In order to have to see everything, . . . '

(40) a.   ★Afin   de ne DEVOIR   personne   VOIR, . . .
   b.   Afin   de ne DEVOIR   rien   VOIR, . . .
       In-order of *ne* have-to-INF *personne/rien* see-INF
       (= (39a, b))

   c.   Afin   de DEVOIR   tout VOIR, . . .
       In-order of have-to-INF *tout* see-INF
       (= (39c))

(41) a.   *Afin   de ne personne   DEVOIR   VOIR, . . .
     b.   Afin   de ne rien   DEVOIR   VOIR, . . .
           In-order of *ne personne/rien* have-to-INF see-INF
           (= (39a, b))

     c.   Afin   de tout DEVOIR   VOIR, . . .
           In-order of *tout* have-to-INF see-INF
           (= (39c))

The possibilities are schematized in (42), where MI stands for modal infinitive, LI for lexical infinitive:

(42) a.   *personne* MI *personne* LI   *personne*
     b.   *tout/rien* MI   *tout/rien* LI #*tout/rien*

So, in the unmarked case, *rien* occupies a position further to the left (= higher) than the position occupied by *personne*.

Of course, I have no reason to assume that the positional differences illustrated in these examples are not also manifested in structures in which the nature of verb syntax means that the differences cannot be seen. In other words, given that I can see from these examples that *rien* generally occupies a higher position than *personne*, the null hypothesis must be that these two elements also occupy different positions in (43), even though the difference does not lead to distinct word orders. This is represented schematically in (44).

(43) a.   Marie ne voit personne.
     b.   Marie ne voit rien.
          M.   *ne* sees *personne/rien*
          'M. can't see anyone/anything.'

(44) a.   Marie ne voit$_i$ t_i personne
          |_____|

     b.   Marie ne voit$_i$ rien$_j$ t_i t_j
          |_____|

The absence of contrasting word orders in (43a, b) falls out naturally if I assume that finite verbs raise higher than participial or infinitival forms, high enough at any rate to mask the effect of *rien*-raising. (See the discussion of Verb Movement patterns in section 1.1.7.)

What is particularly interesting about the data reviewed in this section is the fact that the distribution of *rien* matches that of *tout* in a number of significant respects. This means that, in addition to explaining why *rien* behaves differently from *personne*, my analysis must also explain why *rien* patterns with *tout*. In the next section, I propose an analysis of *rien* that takes these points into account. At the heart of the proposal is the observation that *rien* and *tout* (unlike *personne*) are both unrestricted universal quantifiers.

5.4   The formal differences between *personne* and *rien*

Before considering *rien* itself, I look at work on *tout* and the related *tutto* in Italian. Early generative work on *tout* was carried out by Kayne (1975) under the rubric of L-*tous* (leftward movement of *tous* or some morphologically related item, such as *tout*, *toute*, and *toutes*, to an adverbial position). Kayne's observation was that, generally speaking, "bare" *tout* is susceptible to leftward movement (= raising), while "non-bare" *tout* is not. Thus, in addition to the movement possibilities illustrated in (36c), (38c), (40c), and (41c), in which *tout* is clearly bare, Kayne notes the possibility in (45a), in which it is not immediately clear whether *tout* has raised with–(45b)–or without–(45c)–the non-overt category associated with the clitic,[26] but that minimally contrasts with (46):

(45) a.   Elle l' a   tout lu.
          she it has *tout* read
          'She has read it all.'

     b.   Elle l$_i$'a [tout t_i]$_j$ lu t_j.

     c.   Elle l$_i$'a tout$_j$ lu t_j t_i.

(46) a.   Elle a   lu   tout le livre.
          she has read *tout* the book
          'She has read all the book.'

     b.   ★Elle a tout lu t le livre.

     c.   ★Elle a [tout le livre]$_i$ lu t_i.

More recently, Cinque (1992) has suggested that the distribution of both French *tout* and Italian *tutto* is the result of movement to an A' scope position (Kayne's 1975 adverbial position). I accept this basic analysis and generalize it to French *rien*. Two questions arise from this. The first is considered by Cinque, who was concentrating on *tout/tutto*: What is the A' scope position these elements occupy? The second is more relevant to my concerns about *rien*: Why is it that *rien* moves to such an A' scope position, while *personne* does not? In other words, why is it that whatever triggers/allows movement of *rien* fails to trigger/allow movement of *personne*. I take these questions in turn in the next sections.

----

26. I remain agnostic over whether the non-overt category associated with the clitic is raised before or after L-*tous* takes place. But see footnote 27 for a constraint on L-*tous* that suggests it might take place after cliticization.

   With respect to the mechanism involved in cliticization, while it has no relevance for the point at hand, I assume Sportiche's (1992) analysis, in which a non-overt XP is generated in the canonical position and subsequently raised into the specifier of some functional projection, either a Voice Phrase or an Agr phrase, which is headed by the clitic itself.

5.4.1   The position of *tout/rien*

First, I consider the position occupied by *tout/rien* in, for example, (36b, c). Following Rizzi (1996), I assume that an A' scope position is an A' left-peripheral specifier or adjoined position, that is, an XP position. That I am dealing with an XP position can be demonstrated quite straightforwardly. First, *rien* can be modified, even in pre-verbal position, as in (47a). Second, a very restricted kind of "non-bare" *tout* can move, as in (47b), to which I return later.[27] Both these facts suggest I am dealing with XP movement.

(47) a.   Anne n' a   [absolument [rien]] mangé.
       A.   *ne* has absolutely   *rien*   eaten
       'A. ate absolutely nothing.'

     b.   Il nous a   [tous les deux] invités.   (Kayne 1975: 14 (24b))
       he us   has *tous* the two   invited
       'He invited us both.'

So, under the further (uncontroversial, I think) assumption that *tout/rien* are generated in the θ-position with which they are associated (witness the marginal acceptability of (35c), (37c), and (39c)), I suggest that [$_{XP}$ tout/rien] moves from this A-position to the relevant A'-position. Consider (48), in which *pas* necessarily precedes *tout*:

(48) Jean n' a   pas tout lu.
     J.   *ne* has *pas tout* read
     'J. hasn't read everything.'

Since chapter 1, I have been assuming that the canonical position of the negative marker *pas* is SpecNegP. Assuming further that examples such as (48) are in fact monoclausal, an assumption supported by the position to which the clitic moves in (49a) in contrast to the situation in the biclausal (49b), I conclude that *tout* occupies a position below SpecNegP in (48).

(49) a.   Jean ne (LES) a   pas (⋆LES) lu.
       J.   *ne* them has *pas*   them read
       'J. hasn't read (them).'

     b.   Jean ne (⋆LES) veut   pas (LES) lire.
       J.   *ne*   them wants *pas* them read
       'J. doesn't want to read (them).'

27. The movement of non-bare *tout* illustrated in (b) is parasitic upon cliticization. Witness the ungrammaticality of (i):
(i)   ⋆Il a   [tous les deux] invités.
      he has *tous* the two   invited

Given the parallel distributions of *tout* and *rien* illustrated in the previous section, an additional conclusion I draw at this point is that *rien* is also lower than SpecNegP in (50).

(50) Jean n' a   rien mangé.
     J.   *ne* has *rien* eaten
     'J. hasn't eaten anything.'

The conclusion that *pas* and *rien* occupy different surface positions is supported by the distribution of the adverbs *encore* 'yet/still' and *souvent* 'often' in the examples in (52)–(53). While the distribution of *encore* is admittedly fairly free, a number of speakers have a preferred position for this element. It seems that this preferred position is between those occupied by *pas* and *rien*. Consider first (51). Here, *pas* and *rien* intervene between the auxiliary and the past participle.

(51) a.   Jean n' a   rien   mangé.
     b.   Jean n' a   pas   mangé.
          J.   *ne* has *rien/pas* eaten
          'J. hasn't eaten (anything).'

On the basis of these data alone, one might be tempted to conclude (contrary to my assumptions here) that *rien* and *pas* occupy the same position, that is, Spec-NegP. Were this the correct conclusion, one would predict that any given adverb would occupy the same linear position with respect to both *rien* and *pas*. This prediction is, however, not borne out by the data in (52) and (53). In (52), the sentences from (51) have been modified by the adverb *encore*. While *encore* can either precede or follow both *rien* and *pas*, the unmarked order is for *encore* to precede *rien* but follow *pas*.[28] Under the assumption that *encore* occupies the same position in both (52a) and (52b), I conclude that *pas* and *rien* occupy different positions.

(52) *Unmarked position of* encore *in (51)*:
     a.   Jean n' a   encore rien mangé.
     b.   Jean n' a   pas encore   mangé.
          J.   *ne* has *(pas)* encore *(rien)* eaten
          'J. hasn't eaten (anything) yet.'

Turning now to the less flexible *souvent*, the data in (53) show even more clearly that *pas* occupies a higher position than *rien*. In both examples, the embedded infinitival clause is modified by the adverb *souvent*. If *pas* and *rien* occupy the same position, one would expect *souvent* either to precede both or to follow both. However, as shown by (53a), *encore* must precede *rien*, while (53b) shows that *souvent* must follow *pas*.[29]

28. Thanks to Odile Cyrille for pointing out the relevance of these facts.
29. Thanks to Sylvain Larose for confirming the relevance of these data.

(53) a.   . . . afin   de ne pas souvent   manger.
     b.   . . . afin   de ne   souvent rien manger.
              in-order of *ne (pas) souvent (rien)* eat
          ' . . . in order to not often eat (anything).'

So, I conclude (a) that *encore* and *souvent* have a unique (unmarked) S-structure
position and (b) that *pas* occupies a higher position than *rien*. While *pas* is in
SpecNegP (see chapter 2), *rien* is not. The unmarked position of *encore/souvent*
can then be assumed to be between the S-structure positions of *pas* and *rien*. As
a working hypothesis, I assume that *rien/tout* raise and adjoin to MoodP, below
encore/souvent, which I assume are adjoined to TP (i.e., below SpecNegP).

This state of affairs is significant, since it seriously weakens any argument
that the overt movement that *rien* undergoes, in (36b) for example, has anything
to do with negation. If negation were a factor in *rien*-raising, we would expect
overt raising to be to SpecNegP, to satisfy the Neg Criterion/license *ne*/mark
sentential negation, in much the same way that *pas* is obliged to raise to Spec-
NegP. Given that *rien* is very adept at raising out of its base position to A'
scope positions, I see no reason why it would not raise as far as SpecNegP *if it
had to*. The fact that it does not raise that far, I argue, clearly shows that it does
not have to, a consequence of the fact that it is not actually negative. What is
clear from this discussion is that whatever motivates movement of *rien* out of its
base position has nothing to do with negation.

If *rien*-raising is not then due to negation, it can only be related to the quantificational properties of *rien*. In other words *rien*-raising must be a consequence of the fact that *rien* is a universal quantifier, as in (54a), a welcome conclusion, given that the distribution of *rien* matches so closely that of *tout*, which
is also a universal quantifier, as in (54b).

(54) a.   X *ne* verb *rien*: $\forall x, \neg(\text{verb}'(X,x))$ (e.g., Jean ne mange rien)
     b.   X verb *tout*: $\forall x, \text{verb}'(X,x)$ (e.g., Jean mange tout)

So much for the S-structure position occupied by *tout/rien*. In the next section, I
turn to a characterization of the formal differences between *rien* and *personne*.

5.4.2   Why doesn't *personne* behave like *rien*?

In the previous section, I concluded that the XP elements *rien* and *tout* raise to
an A' scope position at S-structure, possibly adjoined to MoodP. The data discussed so far suggest that, in contrast, *personne* does not. I have not explained
why this should be so. Haegeman (1995: 231) suggests that the (quasi-obliga-
tory) movement of *rien* is triggered by a "strong intrinsic quantifier feature" that
forces the operator to attain an A' scope position at S-structure and that the
same applies to *tout*. While this seems plausible, given that *tout* and *rien* are
both universal quantifiers (more plausible certainly, given our conclusions about
the surface position of *rien* in the previous section, than an analysis that motivates *rien*-raising on the basis of any negative feature it might bear), the

questions that need to be answered are the following. First, why does *personne* (in most varieties) not have the same feature? (Alternatively, what *additional* feature does *personne* bear that prevents it from raising in similar fashion to *rien/tout*?) Second, what are the structural consequences of the feature mismatch between *rien* and *personne*? Third, how is the feature mismatch overridden when *tout/rien* are emphasized, as in (37b), for example, which is acceptable for some speakers?

In what follows, I adopt an analysis whereby the contrast between *rien/tout* and *personne* with respect to mobility is attributed to the structural configurations in which the items are generated. I argue that "mobile" *rien* and *tout* are generated as bare QPs in a specifier position within the argument nominal construction. To be precise, I argue that they appear in SpecNumP and function as cardinality markers for NumP. In contrast, "immobile" *personne* is generated as the head noun of the argument nominal construction. With respect to why *rien* and *personne* should function differently, I follow Haegeman (1995: 231) (to some extent) and Cinque (1992) and attribute this to feature specification: while *rien* is an absolute or universal quantifier in an intuitive sense, *personne* is not (in that, minimally, it also bears the feature [+HUMAN]). I therefore assume that this feature specification is sufficient to prevent *personne* from functioning as a cardinality marker and, consequently, being generated as a bare QP in Spec-NumP. Emphatic *tout/rien* is assumed to bear an additional syntacticopragmatic feature that overrides the "strong intrinsic quantifier feature" and prevents S-structure A'-movement (L-*tous/rien*-raising) from taking place in the sense that emphatic *tout/rien* is not deemed to be "bare" in the relevant way. Such an approach opens the door to an account of the possibility of L-*tous* in (47b). Here, the entire constituent [tous les deux] functions as a cardinality marker in Spec-NumP. It is thus deemed to be "bare" in the relevant sense and can raise. (But see the constraint discussed in footnote 27.)

I turn now to the analysis, where my discussion begins with the contrast between (55) and (56):

(55) a.   Jeanne a   déjà   fait tout son travail.
     b.   *Jeanne a   déjà   tout$_j$ fait t_j son travail.
          J.   has already (all) done (all) her work
          'J. has already done all her work.'

(56) a.   Jean a   déjà   fait tout de ce   qu' on lui a   donné.
     b.   Jean a   déjà   tout$_j$ fait t_j de ce   qu' on lui a   donné.
          J.   has already (all) done (all) of what that one him has given
          'J. has already done all he's been given.'

In (55a), the direct object of the verb is the constituent [tout son travail]. The ungrammaticality of (55b) indicates that *tout* cannot undergo L-*tous* from its base position. (See also (46b).) In (56a), in contrast, the direct object of the verb is [tout [$_{PP}$ de . . .]] containing *tout* and a partitive structure headed by *de* 'of'. From such a base structure, raising of *tout* is possible, as shown in (56b). How can one account for the fact that raising of *tout* is possible in one case but not in the other?

I first consider the structure of the direct object in (55a). One might assume that these French examples have a parallel structure to the Italian structures discussed by Cinque (1992), who suggests (p. 4), following Giusti (1991) and Bianchi (1992), that Italian *tutto* (= French *tout*) is a head, Q°, whose complement in (57) is a DP:

(57) a. [$_{QP}$ tutto [$_{DP}$ il   libro]]
      b. [$_{QP}$ tutti [$_{DP}$ i   libri]]
           all   the book(s)

What is relevant if this analysis of Italian *tutto* is adopted for *tout* is that *tout* is a complement-taking head: Q°. If this is the correct analysis, the immobility of *tout* in (55b) is expected. Movement of *tout* out of its base position within the direct object (without taking its complement DP with it) over V to a position outside VP would require long head movement, which would violate Travis's (1984) HMC. Further, even if Q° could be extracted from VP, given the Structure Preservation Hypothesis, one would not expect it to be possible to move it to the type of XP position that, in the previous section, I suggested *tout*/*rien* occupies at S-structure, namely MoodP-adjoined. Finally, as was shown in (47), *tout*/*rien* movement has all the marks of XP movement, rather than head movement.

Consider now (56). Here, the direct object of the verb comprises *tout* and the partitive, as in (56a), a base configuration from which *tout* can be extracted, as in (56b). This suggests that *tout* does not have the same status within the direct object in (55) as it does in the direct object in (56). Given that the pre-verbal A' scope position is an XP position, the grammaticality of (56b) suggests that *tout* is an XP within the direct object rather than a head. So, while structures such as Cinque's (57) may be suitable for (55) and may provide the basis of the unacceptability of (55b), Cinque's structure in (57) will clearly not do for the direct object in (56). Rather than being a *complement-taking* Q°, like *tutto* in (57), I assume instead that *tout* in (56) is a *bare* Q° and that QP functions as a cardinality marker in SpecNumP (following the discussion in section 2.2), as in (58).

(58)

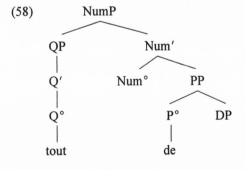

As was the case in my discussion of pseudopartitives licensed by *pas* in section 2.2.3, in which *pas* was deemed to be generated as a bare XP in SpecNumP, I assume that *tout* in SpecNumP is well placed to determine the cardinality of the entire NumP by virtue of its spec-head relationship with Num°. With such a structure underlying (56), the freedom of movement of *tout*, as in (56b), can be dealt with in the same way as quantifier movement in QàD structures, discussed in section 2.2.3. Crucially, *tout* can be extracted from (Spec)NumP in (58) as a maximal projection, QP; head movement is not required; the HMC does not apply.

Returning now to *rien*, note that the freedom illustrated in (56) with respect to *tout* also applies to *rien*:

(59) a. Jean n' a   toujours   fait   rien de ce   qu' on lui a   donné.
     b. Jean n' a   toujours rien fait   de ce   qu' on lui a   donné.
     J.   *ne* has always *(rien)* done *(rien)* of what that one him has given
     'J. still hasn't done any of what he's been given.'

I assume that the same base structure underlies the movement possibilities in both (56) and (59):

(60)

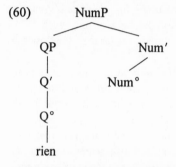

Like *tout* in (58) (=(56a)), *rien* in (60) (=(59a)) is a bare quantifier heading a QP in SpecNumP, which can be extracted in (59) because it is a maximal projection.[30] In both cases, movement to an A′ scope position is triggered by the "strong intrinsic quantifier feature".

Turning finally to *personne*, given that this element does not demonstrate the same mobility as *rien/tout* (see (36a), (38a), (40a), and (41a)), and given that I attributed this mobility to the fact that *rien/tout* occupy SpecNumP in (58) and (60), I must assume that *personne* cannot appear in SpecNumP. Instead, I assume that "negative" *personne* is analyzed by speakers as a noun and, consequently, generated as the ultimate head of the indefinite nominal expression, NumP, in which it appears.

---

30. In many ways, this structural analysis of *rien* as a specifier echoes the suggestion by Acquaviva (1995: 9) that *rien* is a determiner.

(61)   NumP

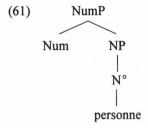

    Num   NP

              N°

        personne

The question that immediately poses itself is why *rien* and *personne* should be analyzed in such divergent ways by speakers of the language. I have suggested that *rien/tout* occupy SpecNumP in (58) and (60) because they function as cardinality markers for NumP. The real question to be answered therefore is why *personne* (in contrast to *tout, rien, tous les deux*, and so on) cannot function as a cardinality marker for NumP. It seems to me that there are two potential ways of explaining this. First, one might assume that the different categorial/ structural analyses are determined by feature specification. The two contrasting elements being considered here (*personne* versus *rien*) are identical but for one feature. While *personne* bears the feature [+HUMAN], *rien* does not. *Rien* and *tout* are both unrestricted universal quantifiers, as in (54a, b); in contrast, *personne* has an inherent restriction, namely the set of human beings, as in (62):

(62) X *ne* verb *personne*: $\forall x, x([+\textit{HUMAN}]), \neg\text{verb}'(X,x)$

                                        (e.g., Jean ne voit personne)

It could be that this is sufficient to prevent speakers from analyzing *personne* like *rien/tout*, namely as a bare cardinality marker, QP. Under such an approach, the elements *rien/tout* are readily susceptible to analysis by acquirers as quantifiers because of their impoverished feature matrix.

The second way one might envisage explaining the fact that speakers analyze *personne* differently from *rien/tout* derives from the fact that the lexical noun, *la personne*, from which the negative argument being discussed here was derived, is retained in the modern language. The existence of this lexical item may be enough to ensure that "negative" *personne* is treated as a noun. In fact, Cinque (1992) himself pursues a similar line in terms of categorial feature poverty. In his terms, *tutto/tout/rien* can move into an A' scope position, which, as Kayne (1975) observes, is essentially an adverbial position, because they are unspecified for the features [±N] and [±V]. Given that *personne* is clearly a lexical noun elsewhere in the grammar, its lack of mobility as a "negative" item can arguably be attributed to its categorial feature specification: [+N, −V].

Finally, note that the analysis I have pursued here, in particular the grounds for the structural distinction between *rien* and *personne*, suggests that other negative arguments in the language are unlikely to be analyzed as quantifiers like *rien/tout* if they are restricted universal quantifiers like *personne* or if there exist parallel nonnegative lexical items. While there are only a few other negative arguments in Modern French, the ones that exist bear out this prediction, as shown in (63):[31]

(63) a. Marie n' a   pipé *mot*.
         M.   *ne* has piped word
         'M. didn't say a word.'

     b. *Marie n'a *mot* pipé.

(64) a. n' y   voir *goutte*
         ne there see   drop
         'to not see a thing'

     b. *n'y *goutte* voir

In summary, then, I conclude that the diverging distributions of *personne* and *rien* are best dealt with in terms of the underlying configurations in which these elements appear. The fundamental distinction to be captured is that *rien* can be generated as a bare quantifier (QP) that can function as a cardinality marker within an indefinite NumP. With such a function, [$_{QP}$ rien] appears in Spec-NumP and is afforded the same movement possibilities as the nominal quantifiers discussed in chapter 2. In particular, and as a consequence of some strong intrinsic quantifier feature, *rien* can move out of SpecNumP and adjoin to MoodP. In contrast, *personne* is analyzed as a lexical noun, even in its "negative" use. As a lexical head, movement to an essentially adverbial position such as the MoodP-adjoined position is unavailable.

5.5   Residual issues

Here, I deal with one issue that has yet to be addressed and another that was discussed in section 4.4.2. First, in section 5.5.1, given that I have assumed that *personne* and *rien* are NPIs, I consider why their distribution differs from that of the *any*-NPIs in English. Then, in section 5.5.2, I consider once again contexts in which NC is possible with *pas*, and not just in nonstandard varieties.

5.5.1   French versus English

Why is it that *personne* and *rien* can occupy the subject position while the *any*-series of NPIs in SE cannot?

(65) a. Personne ne vient.
         personne ne comes
         'No-one is coming.'

31. My thanks to John-Charles Smith for pointing this out.

b. ⋆Anyone isn't coming.[32]

Further, why is it that *personne* and *rien* can function as one-word answers to constituent questions while *any*-NPIs in English cannot?

(66) A: Qu'est-ce que tu fais?
     B: *Rien.*

(67) A: What are you doing?
     B: ⋆*Anything.*

While it is indeed the case that the *any*-NPIs cannot function as one-word answers or as the subject of matrix negative clauses in SE, the contrast with French can be attenuated if one recalls that the licenser of *rien/personne* is non-overt, that is, Op. One might assume that, in (65a) and (66), respectively, *personne* and *rien* are in the scope of Op. In (65a), this would mean that Op is adjoined either to *personne* in SpecAgrSP or to AgrSP itself. In such a position, Op would count as an extended specifier of AgrS° and, consequently, would license *ne* from that position, which, given the assumptions we have made throughout, will have raised to AgrS°. (Note that the Neg Criterion obliges a negative operator and head to be in a spec-head configuration at S-structure; it does not specify that this must take place at the NegP level. Note also that the fact that *ne* is licensed in a slightly less direct way in these examples than in the contexts considered so far might explain why a number of authors have claimed that *ne*-deletion is impossible in these cases—see footnote 1.) In (66), Op is adjoined directly to *rien*. In both cases, Op has scope over the negative argument, thus accounting for its interpretation. The suggestion being made here echoes an early analysis of *no*-XPs given in Klima (1964). If, as Klima argues, a *no*-XP is assumed to be the surface form of an underlying combination of *not* plus an *any*-XP, then the grammatical response to the constituent question in (67) (*nothing*) is, underlyingly, [not [anything]], that is, exactly parallel to the [Op [rien]] sequence I am positing for the French (66). Whereas [Op [rien]] in French surfaces as *rien*, the sequence [not [anything]] in English is converted into *nothing*.

5.5.2 NC with *pas*

In section 4.4.2, I addressed the unavailability of NC between negative adverbs and *pas*, concluding that the empirical domain was best dealt with in the following way: after prolonged co-occurrence and structural proximity between the

---

32. But see Duffield (1993) on Hiberno-English, where *any*-NPIs are licensed in "subject" position. Duffield (1993: 222 (15b–e)) gives the following Hiberno-English examples that are ungrammatical in SE:

(i) a. %Any country couldn't stand it.
     b. %Any fellow wouldn't bother joining if he wasn't interested enough to try.
     c. %Anything is no sin.
     d. %Anybody don' seem to like to live in Russia.

underlying position of the negative operator and the negative adverb(s), the former can be identified by the latter and is required to surface phonologically null. In other words, the association between the operator and adverb(s) is so intimate that the former is necessarily non-overt. Given that the unavailability of NC with *pas* applies to negative arguments in more or less the same way as it does to negative adverbs, one might assume that the same approach is appropriate in the case of negative arguments too.

In section 4.4.2, I argued that this approach is attractive given that, within nonstandard varieties of French, the tendency for the negative operator to surface as overt *pas* increases as the syntactic distance between the underlying positions of the operator and the negative increases. For example, in Québécois, the negative operator is more likely to appear as *pas* rather than as its null equivalent (Op) in contexts containing negative arguments like *personne* than in contexts containing negative adverbs like *jamais* (Muller 1991). Given that negative arguments contrast with negative adverbs in that the former are generated VP-internally whereas the latter are generated outside or adjoined to VP, the structural approach to the unavailability of NC with *pas* seems well placed to deal with the empirical facts. Indeed, as mentioned in section 4.4.2.1, Muller notes further that PP-embedded negative arguments are in turn more likely to co-occur with *pas* than non-PP-embedded negative arguments. Once again, given that PP-embedded negative arguments are even more syntactically distant from the VP-adjoined negative operator, a structural approach to the ban on NC with *pas* seems appropriate. Within the varieties in question, then, the hierarchy in (68), in which *jamais* represents the class of negative adverb discussed in chapter 4 and *personne* represents the class of negative argument analyzed in this chapter, seems to be operative. The more deeply embedded the negative adverb/argument is, the more likely the negative operator is to surface as *pas* rather than Op.

(68) a.   ... [$_{VP}$ [+NEG] [$_{VP}$ jamais [$_{VP}$ ...]]]

     b.   ... [$_{VP}$ [+NEG] [$_{VP}$ ... personne ...]]

     c.   ... [$_{VP}$ [+NEG] [$_{VP}$ ... [$_{PP}$ personne] ...]]

This structural approach to the absence of NC with *pas* also finds support in the standard language. It is, for example, not the case that NC is *never* available with *pas* in Standard French.[33] Indeed, an example of NC with *pas*, from Prince (1976: 410 (29d)), was given in (7), and is repeated here for convenience as

---

33. See also the discussion of the Haitain Creole contrast in (i) and (ii), discussed by Déprez (1992: 38) and DeGraff (1993b: 79 (20)).

(i)   Mwen pa kwè   pèsonn ap   vini.
     1sg   *pa* believe no-one IRREAL come
     'I don't think that anyone will come.'

(ii)   Mwen pa kwè   pèsonn pa ap   vini.
     1sg   *pa* believe no-one *pa* IRREAL come
     'I don't think that no-one will come.'
     (i.e., the opposite of (i))

(69a), along with a second example, which I came across in the writing of the linguist Gilbert Lazard (Lazard 1994: 41), in (69b), and a third, from von Bremen (1986: 238 (37)), in (69c); (69d) is from Kayne (1984: 40). In all these examples, *pas* occurs with a negative argument without leading to logical DN:

(69) a. Je ne crois   PAS que PERSONNE soit   arrivé.
         I   *ne* believe *pas* that *personne*   be-SUBJ arrived
         'I don't think anyone has arrived.'

     b. Elle n' indique PAS que le chien ait   RIEN fait   pour voir
         it   *ne* says   *pas* that the dog   have-SUBJ *rien* done for   see-INF
             l' évêque.
             the bishop
         'It doesn't say that the dog did anything to see the bishop.'

     c. Je ne crois   PAS que Pierre ait   vu   PERSONNE.
         I   *ne* believe *pas* that P.   have-SUBJ seen *personne*
         'I don't believe that P. has seen anyone.'

     d. Je ne veux PAS que PERSONNE vienne.
         I   *ne* want *pas* that *personne*   come-SUBJ
         'I don't want anyone to come.'

The same phenomenon is also attested with the negative adverbs discussed in chapter 4:

(70) Jean ne croit   PAS qu' il ait   JAMAIS fait   d' erreur.
     J.   *ne* believes *pas* that he have-SUBJ *jamais* done of error
     'J. doesn't think he has ever made a mistake.'

The problem is that, given what is known about the interaction between *pas* and, for example, the negative adverbs in Standard French, discussed in section 4.4.2, (69) and (70) are expected to mean the opposite of what they actually do mean. And this is also what is predicted by the approaches to the licensing of negative items such as *personne* proposed by Rizzi (1981, 1984) and Moritz and Valois (1993, 1994). Given that negative arguments pattern with negative adverbs, Rizzi and Moritz and Valois expect the *pas* that occurs in the matrix in (69) and (70) to be independent of the non-overt Op, which is assumed to bind *personne*. In other words, they expect *personne* to have local scope, which it does not.

In contrast, the data in (69) and (70) are *not* a problem for the analysis of these "negative" items proposed here. The claim that these items are NPIs rather than negative quantifiers deals with their co-occurrence possibilities in a non-NC language like French. The structural approach to the ban on NC with *pas* in turn arguably sheds light on the unexpected interpretations of the examples in (69) and (70). I suggest that what distinguishes the examples in (69) and (70) from the one in (18b) is the fact that, in (69) and (70), a (subjunctive) clause boundary intervenes between *pas* and the negative arguments. It is the nature of the embedded CP shell that lies at the heart of any solution to the problem, and the relationship between *pas* and the negative arguments/adverbs in (69) and (70). Intuitively, it seems that the relationship between *personne/rien/jamais* in the embedded clauses in (69) and (70) and the operator in the matrix SpecNegP (which determines the scope of the "negatives") is not close or direct enough to allow the operator to be non-overt, which is why it must surface as *pas* rather than Op.

Consider first what is in fact being negated in (69a) (= (7)). Specifically, consider whether the verb *croire* 'to think' is within the scope of the negation. Arguably, it is not. The example is at the very least ambiguous, and the most natural reading is one of NEG-raising in which the negation originates within the embedded clause and has raised into the matrix. (See chapter 4, footnote 36, for references to discussion of NEG-raising.) The scope relations in (69a) are then as in (71a) rather than (71b), in which *x* represents the embedded clause:

(71) a. $\text{croire}(\neg(x))$
     b. $\neg(\text{croire}(x))$

If it is in fact reasonable to interpret strings like (69a) in this way, one might propose that the base position of *pas* is lower than the VP-adjoined position in the matrix clause. Two possibilities immediately come to mind. First, one could imagine that *pas* originates in the specifier position of the embedded CP and raises into SpecNegP from there. A second possibility is to follow the tack of numerous researchers, including Prince (1976), in assuming that *pas* is base-generated within the embedded IP domain (i.e., VP-adjoined in my analysis) and raised into the matrix domain. Here, too, one can assume that *pas* passes through the specifier position of the embedded CP. In both scenarios, then, one expects the embedded SpecCP position to be involved in mediating in the A'-binding relationship between *pas* in the matrix SpecNegP and *personne* in the embedded clause in (69a).

To be precise, where, in the examples discussed so far, the A'-binding relationship between the negative operator and the NPI is direct, that is, clause-bounded or across an infinitival clause boundary, in (69a) it is indirect in the sense that it crosses a subjunctive clause boundary and is mediated by SpecCP. In chapter 4, the *non-overt* nature of the operator in SpecNegP that licenses negative adverbs was attributed to the fact that the relationship between the operator and the adverb was local. In (69a), in contrast, the operator in the matrix SpecNegP binds its trace in SpecCP, while the trace in SpecCP unselectively binds the NPI. In other words, it is nonlocal. This, I argue, must be at the root of any explanation of why the operator in SpecNegP cannot itself be non-overt. The relationship between the operator in the matrix SpecNegP and the NPI in the embedded clause is "indirect", and the operator cannot be identified. Consequently, it cannot be non-overt and must be spelt out as *pas*, the overt equivalent of Op. In a sense, then, the hierarchy in (72) mirrors the one in (68): the likelihood that the operator is overt is determined by the contiguity between it and the NPI it binds.

(72) a.   [... [$_{NegP}$ Op$_i$ [$_{Neg'}$ ... [... personne$_i$ ...]]]]   (Direct A'-binding)

b.   [... [$_{NegP}$ pas$_i$ [$_{Neg'}$ ... [$_{CP}$ t_i [$_{C'}$ ... personne$_i$ ...]]]]][34]
(Indirect A'-binding)

In both scenarios, crucially, *personne* is an NPI, and the operator in SpecNegP is inherently negative irrespective of whether or not it is overt, as predicted by Jespersen's Generalization in chapter 3. That the embedded SpecCP is involved in the binding relationship between the matrix operator and the embedded NPI is supported by the following contrast. In (73a), the [+WH] argument *qui* is extracted from the embedded domain. Given that the embedded clause contains *personne* with matrix scope, I assume, by hypothesis, that *personne* is bound indirectly by the negative operator, *pas*, in the matrix SpecNegP. Further, this relationship is assumed to be mediated by the embedded SpecCP position, which is, consequently, unavailable as an intermediate landing site for *wh*-movement; hence the ungrammaticality of the example. In (73b), in contrast, *personne* in the embedded clause has (relatively) local scope. No binding relationship is therefore posited with the matrix SpecNegP position, and the embedded SpecCP is not involved. Instead, *personne* is bound by the negative operator in the embedded SpecNegP (a relationship that allows the operator to be non-overt). Consequently, the embedded SpecCP is available as an intermediate landing site for *wh*-movement, and the example is grammatical:

(73) a.   ★Qui ne croyais- tu   pas que personne ait   invité t ?
who *ne* believed you *pas* that *personne* have-SUBJ invited

b.   Quel livre croyais- tu   que Jean n' avait prêté t à   personne?
what book believed you that J.   *ne* had   lent   to *personne*
'Which book did you think J. hadn't lent to anyone?'

Finally, I consider the obligatory subjunctive morphology in the embedded clauses in the examples dealt with in this section. One might assume that this is the consequence of the fact that a negative operator has transited through the embedded SpecCP. Assuming that some sort of abstract DA might occur at that level, the subjunctive morphology would amount to indirect selection from C°. Consider in this respect the contrast between (74a) and (74b):

(74) a.   Nous pensons qu' il est   là.
we   think   that he be-IND there
'We think he's there.'

b.   Nous ne pensons pas qu' il soit   là.
we   *ne* think   *pas* that he be-SUBJ there
'We don't think he's there.'

---

34. The fact that the embedded C°, *que*, is overt can be taken as evidence to support the argument that the embedded SpecCP is filled with no more than t. In null operator structures in Standard French, C° is non-overt. Given that C° here is in fact overt suggests strongly that the SpecCP position is not occupied by a null operator (at S-structure).

In both examples, the matrix predicate is *penser* 'to think'. Yet, in a number of varieties, as in (74a), the selected embedded clause must contain an indicative verb, while in (74b) it must be subjunctive. The difference must lie in the presence of the negation in the matrix clause in (74b). Note, though, that (74b) is a case of NEG-raising. In other words, what (74b) actually means is, 'We think he isn't there'. The negation has "raised" out of the embedded clause and is marked overtly in the matrix domain. Arguably, "raising" has taken place via the embedded SpecCP. Indeed, one might claim that the fact that a negative operator has transited through the embedded SpecCP is the reason that the embedded verb in (74b) is subjunctive (rather than the indicative as in (74a)). Further, if a suitable context could be found in which to interpret something like (74b) as if NEG-raising had *not* taken place, one would expect the selected embedded clause to contain an indicative verb. In fact, this is exactly what occurs:

(75) Nous ne pensons pas qu' il est   là,   nous le savons.
     we   *ne* think   *pas* that he be-IND there we   it know
     'We don't *think* he's there, we *know* he is.'

5.6   Summary

In this final chapter, I have focused on the negative arguments *rien* and *personne*. I have pursued the line of thinking discussed in chapters 3 and 4 and provided an analysis of the negative arguments as NPIs, rather than as inherently negative quantifiers. This parallel analysis is justified by the fact that negative arguments can freely co-occur with each other and negative adverbs. In this respect, they are identical to the negative adverbs discussed in chapter 4. Any divergent analysis I might propose would therefore be difficult to justify.

The analysis proposed here differs crucially from suggestions made, for example, by Kayne (1981, 1984) and Moritz and Valois (1993, 1994) in that I have not posited LF raising. While all these authors have assumed that *personne* and similar elements raise at LF for one reason or other (QR for Kayne, the Neg Criterion for Moritz and Valois), I have argued that S-structure is the level at which the scopal properties of negative arguments are determined and the Neg Criterion is satisfied. In this respect, I have followed suggestions by Brody (1995) with respect to in situ *wh*-constructions and work on negation by Haegeman (1995). Rather than posit LF raising, I have suggested that the scopal properties of *personne* and *rien* are determined by the S-structure position of Op, namely SpecNegP. Op in SpecNegP serves to license *ne* and mark sentential negation by DA; it confers a negative intepretation on *personne* and *rien* via A'-binding. In pursuing my analysis, I have two significant advantages over earlier proposals. First, I have avoided the mismatch between the level at which the *wh*-criterion and the Neg Criterion apply in French. There is clear empirical evidence to suggest that the former applies at S-structure. Yet Moritz and Valois's (1994) analysis of *personne* depends on the latter not applying until LF. This divergence is undesirable if the two criteria are ultimately to be viewed as a single AFFECT criterion, as assumed in section 1.3. Second, my analysis of negative arguments allows me to maintain a unitary account of pseudopartitives. In section 2.2, I considered the syntax of these indefinites and concluded that their distribution was best dealt with in terms of S-structure operator extraction. While this was appropriate for the data discussed in chapter 2, it was questioned by Moritz and Valois's (1994) analysis of *personne*. For Moritz and Valois, *personne* licenses the empty category contained within a pseudopartitive by A'-binding after LF raising to SpecNegP. LF raising was necessary since *personne* doesn't necessarily c-command the empty category at S-structure. By assuming, as I have done, that it is a non-overt negative operator (rather than *personne*) that raises (at S-structure rather than LF) to SpecNegP, I am able to maintain my original analysis of pseudopartitives. In other words, rather than being licensed by *personne* itself, pseudopartitives are licensed by Op (in the same way that they are licensed by *pas*, *beaucoup*, and so on), namely by S-structure operator extraction out of (Spec)NumP.

The analysis fleshed out here unites a number of the conclusions drawn in earlier work by other researchers. For example, I follow Muller (1984, 1991) in treating *rien* and *personne* (as well as adverbs such as *plus*, *jamais*, and *guère*, discussed in chapter 4) as NPIs (in the scope of a non-overt, underlyingly negative operator), rather than as inherently negative items. I also follow Kayne (1981), Rizzi (1982), Hornstein (1984), and Zaring (1985) in assuming that the adverbs/arguments (associated with the operator in SpecNegP) are quantifiers. Finally, along with Milner (1979) and Aoun (1986), I assume that the negative adverbs/arguments are "anaphoric" in the sense that they are licensed by virtue of being A'-bound by an "antecedent", namely the negative operator, Op/*pas*.

Having concluded that *personne* and *rien* are both NPIs bound by a negative operator and licensed at S-structure, I went on to ask why these two elements do not have matching distributions. Here, the crucial observation, dating back at least to Kayne (1975), was that, rather than matching *personne*, *rien* matches the other universal quantifier, namely *tout*. On the basis of work by Cinque (1992) on Italian *tutto*, it was suggested that *rien* and *tout* (at least in its "mobile" version) are generated as bare quantifiers heading a QP in the specifier of an argument NumP. As a maximal projection, the QP containing bare *rien/tout* is afforded the syntactic mobility needed to allow it to raise to an A' scope position, a movement triggered by a "strong intrinsic quantifier feature" common to them both. In contrast, it was argued that the lack of movement possibilities of *personne* suggest that this element does not occupy such a specifier position. Rather, I suggested that *personne* is a head noun and that this naturally accounted for its immobility.

References

Abney, Steven P. (1987) "The English noun phrase in its sentential aspect." Ph.D. diss., MIT.

Acquaviva, Paolo (1992) "The representation of negative 'quantifiers'," *Rivista di Linguistica*, 4: 319–381.

—— (1993) "The Logical Form of negation: a study of operator-variable structures in syntax." Ph.D. diss., Scuola Normale Superiore, Pisa.

—— (1994) "The representation of operator-variable dependencies in sentential negation," *Studia Linguistica*, 48: 91–132.

—— (1995) "Operator composition and the derivation of negative concord." MS, University College Dublin.

—— (1997) *The Logical Form of negation: a study of operator-variable structures in syntax.* (Outstanding Dissertations in Linguistics.) New York: Garland.

Adams, Marianne P. (1987) "From Old French to the theory of *pro*-drop," *Natural Language and Linguistic Theory*, 5: 1–32.

—— (1988a) "Embedded *pro*," *Proceedings of NELS*, 18: 1–21.

—— (1988b) "Les effets V2 en ancien et en moyen français," *Revue Québécoise de Linguistique Théorique et Appliquée*, 7: 13–39.

Agard, Frederick B. (1984) *A course in Romance linguistics.* Vol. 1: *A synchronic view.* Vol. 2: *A diachronic view.* Washington, D. C.: Georgetown University Press.

Anderson, John M. and Charles Jones (eds.) (1974) *Historical linguistics 1: syntax, morphology, internal and comparative reconstruction.* (Proceedings of the First International Conference on Historical Linguistics.) New York: North Holland.

Aoun, Joseph (1986) *Generalized binding: the syntax and logical form of* wh-*interrogatives.* (Studies in Generative Grammar, 26.) Dordrecht: Foris.

Arnold, Doug, Martin Atkinson, Jacques Durand, Claire Grover, and Louisa Sadler (eds.) (1989) *Essays on grammatical theory and Universal Grammar.* Oxford: Clarendon Press.

Ashby, William J. (1976) "The loss of the negative morpheme *ne* in Parisian French," *Lingua*, 39: 119–137.

—— (1981) "The loss of the negative particle *ne* in French: a syntactic change in progress," *Language*, 57: 674–687.

—— (1988) "The syntax, pragmatics and sociolinguistics of left- and right-dislocations in French," *Lingua*, 75: 203–229.

—— (1991) "When does linguistic change indicate change in progress?" *Journal of French Language Studies*, 1: 1–19.

Ashby, William J., Marianne Mithun, Giorgio Perissinotto, and Eduardo Raposo (eds.) (1993) *Linguistic perspectives on the Romance languages.* (Selected papers from the

21st Linguistic Symposium on Romance Languages.) (Current Issues in Linguistic Theory, 103.) Amsterdam: John Benjamins.

Attal, Pierre (1971) "Négation de phrase et négation de constituant," *Langue Française*, 12: 98–111.

—— (1979) "Négation et quantificateurs." Ph.D. diss., Université de Paris 8.

—— (ed.) (1994) *La négation.* (Actes du colloque de Paris X–Nanterre, 12–14 novembre 1992.) Numéro spécial de *Linx.* Nanterre: Centre de Recherches Linguistiques, Université de Paris X–Nanterre.

Ayer, Cyprien (1882) *Grammaire comparée de la langue française*, 3rd ed. Paris: Georg.

Baciu, Ioan (1978) *Précis de grammaire roumaine.* Lyons: L'Hermès.

Baker, Mark C. (1985) "The mirror principle and morphosyntactic explanation," *Linguistic Inquiry*, 16: 373–415.

—— (1988) *Incorporation: a theory of grammatical function changing.* Chicago: University of Chicago Press.

Ball, Martin J. (ed.) (1993) *The Celtic languages.* London: Routledge.

Barbaud, Philippe (1991) "Subjunctive and ECP," in Wanner and Kibbee (eds.), pp. 125–144.

Barker, Chris and David R. Dowty (eds.) (1992) *Proceedings of the second conference on semantics and linguistic theory.* (Ohio State University Working Papers in Linguistics, 40.) Columbus: Ohio State University.

Battye, Adrian C. (1987) "Quantificatori nominali in francese," in Cordin (ed.), pp. 9–27.

—— (1989) "Reflections on nominal quantification in three Romance varieties: French, Italian, and Genoese," *York Papers in Linguistics*, 14: 101–121.

—— (1990) "La quantificazione nominale: il veneto e l'italiano a confronto con il genovese e il francese," *Annali di ca' Foscari*, 29: 27–44.

—— (1991) "Partitive and pseudo-partitive revisited: reflections on the status of *de* in French," *Journal of French Language Studies*, 1: 21–43.

—— (1995) "Aspects of quantification in French in its regional and diachronic varieties," in Smith and Maiden (eds.), pp. 1–35.

Battye, Adrian C. and Marie-Anne M. J. Hintze (1992) *The French language today.* London: Routledge.

Battye, Adrian C. and Ian G. Roberts (eds.) (1995) *Clause structure and language change.* (Oxford Studies in Comparative Syntax.) Oxford: Oxford University Press.

Belletti, Adriana (1990) *Generalized Verb Movement: aspects of verb syntax.* Turin: Rosenberg and Sellier.

—— (1992) "Verb positions, NP positions: evidence from Italian." MS, Université de Genève/Scuola Normale Superiore, Pisa.

—— (1994a) "Verb positions: evidence from Italian," in Lightfoot and Hornstein (eds.), pp. 19–40.

—— (1994b) "*Pas* vs. *più*: a note," in Cinque et al. (eds.), pp. 25–34.

Belletti, Adriana, Luciana Brandi, and Luigi Rizzi (eds.) (1981) *Theory of markedness in generative grammar.* (Proceedings of the 1979 GLOW conference.) Pisa: Scuola Normale Superiore.

Belletti, Adriana and Luigi Rizzi (eds.) (1996) *Parameters and functional heads: essays in comparative syntax.* (Oxford Studies in Comparative Syntax.) New York: Oxford University Press.

Bénac, Henri (1976) *Guide de l'expression écrite.* Paris: Hachette.

Benmamoun, Ellabas (1991) "Negation and verb movement," *Proceedings of NELS*, 21: 17–31.

Bennis, Hans, Frits H. Beukema, and Marcel den Dikken (1995a) "Verb placement." Paper presented to the Comparative Germanic Syntax Workshop, Brussels, Belgium.

—— (1995b) "Getting verb placement." Paper presented to the LAGB spring meeting, Newcastle-upon-Tyne.

—— (1997) "Getting verb placement," *Linguistics*, 35: 1003–1028.

Benveniste, Émile (1966) *Problèmes de linguistique générale*. Vol. 1. Paris: Gallimard.

Bernot, Denise (1980) *Le prédicat en birman parlé*. Paris: SELAF.

Besten, Hans den (1986) "Double negation and the genesis of Afrikaans," in Muysken and Smith (eds.), pp. 185–230.

—— (1989) *Studies in West Germanic syntax*. Amsterdam: Rodopi.

Beukema, Frits H. (1994) "The development of negation in English: a government and binding perspective." Paper presented to the conference on Negation in the History of English, Leiden, The Netherlands.

Bianchi, Valentina (1992) "Sulla struttura funzionale del sintagma nominale italiano," *Rivista di Grammatica Generativa*, 17: 1–26.

Bickerton, Derek (1981) *Roots of language*. Ann Arbor: Karoma.

Bloom, Lois (1970) *Language development: form and function in emerging grammars*. Cambridge, Mass.: MIT Press.

—— (1991a) *Language development from two to three*. Cambridge: Cambridge University Press.

—— (1991b) "Sentence negation," in Bloom (1991a), pp. 143–207. Reprinted from Bloom (1970), pp. 148–165, 170–220.

Bok-Bennema, Reineke and Roeland van Hout (eds.) (1992) *Linguistics in the Netherlands 1992*. (AVT Publications, 9.) Amsterdam: John Benjamins.

Boysson-Bardies, Bénédicte de (1976) *Négation et performance linguistique*. (Connaissance et Langage, 4.) Paris: Mouton.

Bremen, Klaus von (1986) "Le problème des forclusifs romans," *Lingvisticæ Investigationes*, 10: 223–265.

Brody, Michael (1990) "Some remarks on the focus field in Hungarian," *UCL Working Papers in Linguistics*, 2: 201–225.

—— (1995) *Lexico-logical form: a radically minimalist theory*. (Linguistic Inquiry Monographs, 27.) Cambridge, Mass.: MIT Press.

Burridge, Kate (1993) *Syntactic change in Germanic: aspects of language change in Germanic with particular reference to Middle Dutch*. (Current Issues in Linguistics, 89.) Amsterdam: John Benjamins.

Burton, Strang and Jane Grimshaw (1992) "Coordination and VP-internal subjects," *Linguistic Inquiry*, 23: 305–313.

Byrne, Francis and John Holm (eds.) (1993) *Atlantic meets Pacific: a global view of pidginization and creolization*. (Creole Language Library, 11.) Amsterdam: John Benjamins.

Cardinaletti, Anna and Maria Teresa Guasti (1992) "Negation in small clauses." Paper presented to Going Romance 6, Utrecht, The Netherlands.

Casagrande, Jean (1968) "On negation in French." Ph.D. diss., Indiana University.

Choi, Soonja (1988) "The semantic development of negation: a cross-linguistic longitudinal study," *Journal of Child Language*, 15: 517–531.

Chomsky, Noam (1955) *The logical structure of linguistic theory*. New York: Plenum. Reprinted 1975/77.

—— (1981) *Lectures on government and binding*. (Studies in Generative Grammar, 9.) Dordrecht: Foris.

—— (1986a) *Knowledge of language: its nature, origin and use*. New York: Praeger.

—— (1986b) *Barriers*. (Linguistic Inquiry Monographs, 13.) Cambridge, Mass.: MIT Press.

—— (1991) "Some notes on economy of derivation and representation," in Freidin (ed.), pp. 417-454. Also in Laka and Mahajan (eds.), pp. 43-75 and Chomsky (1995b), pp. 129-166.

—— (1993) "A minimalist program for linguistic theory," in Hale and Keyser (eds.), pp. 1-52. Original version published in 1992 as *MIT Occasional Papers in Linguistics*, 1. Also in Chomsky (1995b), pp. 167-217.

—— (1995a) "Bare phrase structure," in Webelhuth (ed.), pp. 383-439. Original version published in 1994 as *MIT Occasional Papers in Linguistics*, 5. Also to appear in H. Campos and P. Kempchinsky (eds.), *Evolution and revolution in linguistic theory: essays in honor of Carlos Otero*. Washington, D. C.: Georgetown University Press.

—— (1995b) *The minimalist program*. (Current Studies in Linguistics, 28.) Cambridge, Mass.: MIT Press.

Chomsky, Noam and Howard Lasnik (1977) "Filters and control," *Linguistic Inquiry*, 8: 425-504.

—— (1993) "The theory of principles and parameters," in Jacobs et al. (eds.), vol. 1, pp. 506-569. Also in Chomsky (1995b), pp. 13-127.

Cinque, Guglielmo (1990) *Types of A' dependencies*. (Linguistic Inquiry Monographs, 17.) Cambridge, Mass.: MIT Press.

—— (1992) "On leftward movement of *tutto* in Italian," *University of Venice Working Papers in Linguistics*, CLI - 92.I.6.

—— (1995) "Adverbs and the universal hierarchy of functional projections," *GLOW Newsletter*, 34: 14-15.

—— (1996) "Adverbs and the universal hierarchy of functional projections." MS, University of Venice.

—— (1998) *Adverbs and functional heads: a cross-linguistic perspective*. Oxford: Oxford University Press.

Cinque, Guglielmo, Jan Koster, Jean-Yves Pollock, Luigi Rizzi, and Raffaella Zanuttini (eds.) (1994) *Paths towards Universal Grammar: studies in honor of Richard S. Kayne*. (Georgetown Studies in Romance Linguistics.) Washington, D. C.: Georgetown University Press.

Cole, Peter (ed.) (1978) *Pragmatics*. (Syntax and Semantics, 9.) New York: Academic Press.

Cordin, P. (ed.) (1987) *Ipotesi ed applicazioni di teoria linguistica dal XIII incontro di grammatica generativa*. Trento: Università di Trento.

Corne, Chris and Pierre-Marie J. Moorghen (1978) "Proto-créole et liens génétiques dans l'Océan Indien," *Langue Française*, 37: 60-75.

Cornulier, Benoît de (1973) "Sur une règle de déplacement de négation," *Le Français Moderne*, 41: 43-57.

—— (1974) "La négation anticipée: ambiguïté lexicale ou effet de sens," *Le Français Moderne*, 42: 206-216.

Coveney, Aidan (1989) "Variability in interrogation and negation in spoken French." Ph.D. diss., University of Newcastle-upon-Tyne.

—— (1990) "The omission of *ne* in spoken French," *Francophonie*, 1: 38-43.

—— (1996) *Variability in spoken French: a socio-linguistic study of interrogation and negation*. (Elm Bank Modern Language Studies.) Exeter: Elm Bank Publications.

Cristea, Teodora (1971) *La structure de la phrase négative en français contemporain*. Bucharest: Société Roumaine de Linguistique Romane.

Croft, William (1991) "The evolution of negation," *Journal of Linguistics*, 27: 1-27.

Culicover, Peter W. (1992) "Polarity, inversion, and focus in English," in Westphal et al. (eds.), pp. 46–68.

Culicover, Peter W., Thomas Wasow, and Adrian Akmajian (eds.) (1977) *Formal syntax.* New York: Academic Press.

Da Cruz, Maxime (1992) "Contribution à l'étude de la négation en fɔ̀ngbè." MS, Université du Québec à Montréal.

Dahl, Östen (1979) "Typology of sentence negation," *Linguistics*, 17: 79–106.

Damourette, Jacques and Édouard Pichon (1911–40) *Des mots à la pensée: essai de grammaire de la langue française.* Paris: Collection de Linguistes Modernes (1930–56).

D'Ans, André-Marcel (1968) *Le créole français d'Haïti : étude des unités d'articulation, d'expansion, et de communication.* (Janua Linguarum, 106.) The Hague: Mouton.

Daoust-Blais, Denise (1975) "L'influence de la négation sur certains indéfinis en français québécois." Ph.D. diss., Université de Montréal.

Daoust-Blais, Denise and William Kemp (1979) "*Pour pas que ça se perde*: *pour* as a 'quantifier-raising' subordinator in Quebec French." MS.

DeGraff, Michel F. (1992) "Creole grammars and acquisition of syntax." Ph.D. diss., University of Pennsylvania.

—— (1993a) "Is Haitian Creole a *pro*-drop language?" in Byrne and Holm (eds.), pp. 71–90.

—— (1993b) "A riddle on negation in Haitian," *Probus*, 5: 63–93.

—— (1997) "Verb syntax in, and beyond, creolization," in Haegeman (ed.) (1997a), pp. 64–94.

—— (ed.) (forthcoming) *Creolization, language change, and language acquisition.* Cambridge, Mass.: MIT Press.

De Haan, Ferdinand (1997) *The interaction of modality and negation: a typological study.* (Outstanding Dissertations in Linguistics.) New York: Garland.

Déprez, Viviane M. (1992) "Is Haitian Creole really a *pro*-drop language?" *Travaux de Recherche sur le Créole Haïtien*, 11.

—— (1995) "French and Haitian Creole n-words united in their differences." Paper presented to the conference on Negation: Syntax and Semantics, Ottawa, Canada.

—— (forthcoming) "The roots of negative concord in French and French-based creoles," in DeGraff (ed.).

Déprez, Viviane M. and Amy E. Pierce (1993) "Negation and functional projections in early grammar," *Linguistic Inquiry*, 24: 25–67.

Di Sciullo, Anna-Maria and Mireille Tremblay (1993) "Négation et interfaces," *Toronto Working Papers in Linguistics*, 12: 75–89.

Di Sciullo, Anna-Maria and Mireille Tremblay (1996) "Configurations et interprétation: les morphèmes de négation," *Recherches Linguistiques de Vincennes*, 25: 27–52.

Di Sciullo, Anna-Maria and Edwin S. Williams (1986) *On the definition of word.* (Linguistic Inquiry Monographs, 14.) Cambridge, Mass.: MIT Press.

Donadze, N. (1981) "Quelques remarques concernant les constructions négatives dans les langues romanes," *Quaderni di Semantica*, 2: 297–301.

Duffield, Nigel G. (1993) "On Case-checking and NPI licensing in Hiberno-English," *Rivista di Linguistica*, 5: 215–244.

Dupuis, Fernande, Monique Lemieux, and D. Gosselin (1992) "Conséquences de la sous-spécification des traits de Agr dans l'identification de *pro*," *Language Variation and Change*, 3: 275–299.

Emonds, Joseph E. (1976) *A transformational approach to English syntax: root, structure-preserving, and local transformations.* New York: Academic Press.

—— (1978) "The verbal complex V′-V in French," *Linguistic Inquiry*, 9: 151–175.

Englebert, Annick (1985) "L'opposition *ne/ne . . . pas* en ancien français," *Revue de Linguistique Romane*, 49: 365–378.

—— (1993) "Le statut grammatical de DE," *Journal of French Language Studies*, 3: 127–144.

Engver, K. (1972) *Place de l'adverbe déterminant un infinitif dans la prose du français contemporain*. Stockholm: Almqvist and Wiksell.

Epstein, Samuel D. (1976) "Investigations in pragmatic theory." Ph.D. diss., University of California at San Diego.

Ernst, Thomas (1992) "The phrase structure of English negation," *Linguistic Review*, 9: 109–144.

Escure, Geneviève (1974) "Negation and dialect variation in French," *Papers in Linguistics* (Edmonton, Alberta, Canada), 7: 403–435.

Espinal, Maria-Teresa (1991a) "Negation in Catalan: some remarks with regard to *no pas*," *Catalan Working Papers in Linguistics*, 1: 33–63.

—— (1991b) "On expletive negation: some remarks with regard to Catalan," *Lingvisticæ Investigationes*, 15: 41–65.

—— (1992) "Expletive negation and logical absorption," *Linguistic Review*, 9: 333–358.

—— (1993) "Two squibs on modality and negation," *Catalan Working Papers in Linguistics*, 3: 113–138.

Ewert, Alfred (1943) *The French language*. London: Faber.

Fillmore, Charles J. (1963) "The position of embedding transformations in a grammar," *Word*, 19: 208–231.

Fodor, Jerry A. and Jerrold J. Katz (eds.) (1964) *The structure of language: readings in the philosophy of language*. Englewood Cliffs, N. J.: Prentice Hall.

Forest, Robert (1983) "«Négation promue», insularité, performatifs, et empathie," *Bulletin de la Société Linguistique de Paris*, 77: 77–97.

Forget, Danielle, Paul Hirschbühler, France Martineau, and María-Luisa Rivero (eds.) (1997) *Negation and polarity: syntax and semantics*. Amsterdam: John Benjamins.

Freidin, Robert (ed.) (1991) *Principles and parameters in comparative grammar*. (Current Studies in Linguistics, 20.) Cambridge, Mass.: MIT Press.

Gaatone, David (1971) *Étude descriptive du système de la négation en français contemporain*. (Publications Romanes et Françaises, 114.) Geneva: Droz.

Gabbay, Don M. and Julius Moravcsik (1978) "Negation and denial," in Guenthner and Rohrer (eds.), pp. 251–265.

Galet, Yvette (1971) *L'évolution de l'ordre des mots dans la phrase française de 1600 à 1700: la place du pronom personnel complément d'un infinitif régime*. Paris: Presses Universitaires de France.

Gallagher, John D. (1993) Review of Peter Rickard (1989), *Journal of French Language Studies*, 3: 119–121.

Giusti, Giuliana (1991) "The categorial status of quantified nominals," *Linguistische Berichte*, 136: 438–452.

Gougenheim, Georges, Paul Rivenc, René Michéa, and Aurélien Sauvageot (1964) *L'élaboration du français fondamental (1er degré)*. Paris: Didier.

Green, John N. (1988) "Romance creoles," in Harris and Vincent (eds.), pp. 420–475.

Green, John N. and Wendy Ayres-Bennett (eds.) (1990) *Variation and change in French: essays presented to Rebecca Posner on the occasion of her sixtieth birthday*. (Croom Helm Romance Linguistics.) London: Routledge.

Greenberg, Joseph H. (ed.) (1978) *Universals of human language*. 4 vols. Stanford: Stanford University Press.

Grevisse, Maurice (1986) *Le bon usage*, 12th ed, rev. by André Goosse. Paris: Duculot.

Grimshaw, Jane (1993) "Minimal projection, heads, and optimality." MS, Rutgers University.

Gross, Maurice (1978) *Méthodes en syntaxe*. Paris: Hermann.

Guasti, Maria Teresa (1991) "The *faire -par* construction in Romance and in Germanic," *Proceedings of WCCFL*, 9.

Guéron, Jacqueline and Jean-Yves Pollock (eds.) (1991) *Grammaire générative et syntaxe comparée*. Paris: CNRS.

Guenthner, Franz and Christian Rohrer (eds.) (1978) *Studies in formal semantics: intensionality, temporality, and negation*. (North Holland Linguistic Series, 35.) Amsterdam: North Holland.

Haase, Alfred (1969) *Syntaxe française du XVIIe siècle*, 7th ed., trans. and rev. by M. Obert. Paris: Delagrave.

Haegeman, Liliane M. V. (1991) "Negative heads and negative operators." MS, Université de Genève.

—— (1992a) "Sentential negation in Italian and the Neg Criterion," *GenGenP*, 0: 10-26.

—— (1992b) "Negation in West Flemish and the Neg Criterion," *Proceedings of NELS*, 22.

—— (1993) "Introduction: the syntax of sentential negation," *Rivista di Linguistica*, 5: 183-214.

—— (1994a) *Introduction to government and binding theory*, 2nd ed. (Blackwell Textbooks in Linguistics, 1.) Oxford: Blackwell.

—— (1994b) "Developments in government and binding theory." GLOW International Summer School in Linguistics, Girona, Spain.

—— (1995) *The syntax of negation*. (Cambridge Studies in Linguistics, 75.) Cambridge: Cambridge University Press.

—— (1996a) "Negative inversion, the Neg criterion and the structure of CP." MS, University of Geneva.

—— (1996b) "The syntax of N-words and the Neg Criterion," *GenGenP*, 4: 1-14.

—— (ed.) (1997a) *The new comparative syntax*. (Longman Linguistics Library.) London: Longman.

—— (ed.) (1997b) *Elements of grammar: a handbook of generative syntax*. (Kluwer International Handbooks of Linguistics.) Dordrecht: Kluwer.

Haegeman, Liliane M. V. and Raffaella Zanuttini (1991) "Negative heads and the Neg Criterion," *Linguistic Review*, 8: 233-251.

—— (1996) "Negative concord in West Flemish," in Belletti and Rizzi (eds.), pp. 119-181.

Hale, Kenneth and Samuel J. Keyser (eds.) (1993) *The view from building 20: essays in linguistics in honor of Sylvain Bromberger*. (Current Studies in Linguistics, 24.) Cambridge, Mass.: MIT Press.

Harris, James (1991) "The exponence of gender in Spanish," *Linguistic Inquiry*, 22: 27-62.

Harris, Martin B. (1978) *The evolution of French syntax: a comparative approach*. (Longman Linguistics Library, 22.) London: Longman.

Harris, Martin B. and Nigel B. Vincent (eds.) (1988) *The Romance languages*. (Croom Helm Romance Linguistics/Routledge Language Family Descriptions.) London: Croom Helm/Routledge.

Heldner, Christina (1981) *La portée de la négation, examen de quelques facteurs sémantiques et textuels pertinents à sa détermination dans des énoncés authentiques*. Stockholm: Norstedts Tryckeri.

Henry, Alison (1995) "Dialect variation and minimalist syntax." Paper presented to the LAGB autumn meeting, Essex.

Higginbotham, James and Robert May (1981) "Questions, quantifiers, and crossing," *Linguistic Review*, 1: 41-79.

Hirschbühler, Paul and Marie Labelle (1992a) "Négation, clitiques, et position du verbe dans l'histoire du français." Paper presented to the Université de Paris 7.

—— (1992b) "Changes in verb position in French negative infinitival clauses." Paper presented to the Second Diachronic Generative Syntax Conference, Pennsylvania.

—— (1992/93) "Le statut de (*ne*) *pas* en français contemporain," *Recherches Linguistiques de Vincennes*, 22: 31-58.

—— (1993) "From *ne V pas* to *ne pas V* and the syntax of *pas*." MS, University of Ottawa/Université du Québec à Montréal.

—— (1994a) "Changes in verb position in French negative infinitival clauses," *Language Variation and Change*, 6: 149-178.

—— (1994b) "L'évolution des propositions infinitives négatives en français," in Attal (ed.), pp. 59-90.

Hopper, Paul J. and Elizabeth C. Traugott (1993) *Grammaticalization*. (Cambridge Textbooks in Linguistics.) Cambridge: Cambridge University Press.

Horn, Laurence R. (1978a) "Some aspects of negation," in Greenberg (ed.), vol. 4: Syntax, pp. 127-210.

—— (1978b) "Remarks on Neg-raising," in Cole (ed.), pp. 129-220.

—— (1989) *A natural history of negation*. Chicago: University of Chicago Press.

Hornstein, Norbert (1984) *Logic as grammar*. Cambridge, Mass.: MIT Press.

Hualde, José Ignacio and Jon Ortiz de Urbina (eds.) (1993) *Generative studies in Basque linguistics*. Amsterdam: John Benjamins.

Huang, C-T. James (1982) "Logical relations in Chinese and the theory of grammar." Ph.D. diss., MIT.

Huang, C-T. James and Robert May (eds.) (1991) *Logical structure and linguistic structure*. (Studies in Linguistics and Philosophy, 40.) Dordrecht: Kluwer.

Hulk, Aafke C. J. and Ans van Kemenade (1995) "Verb-second, *pro*-drop, functional projections, and language change," in Battye and Roberts (eds.), pp. 227-256.

Hyams, Nina (1986) *Language acquisition and the theory of parameters*. Dordrecht: Reidel.

Iordanskaja, Lidija (1986) "Propriétés sémantiques des verbes promoteurs de la négation en français," *Lingvisticæ Investigationes*, 10: 345-380.

Jacobs, Joachim, Arnim von Stechow, Wolfgang Sternefeld, and Theo Vennemann (eds.) (1993) *Syntax: an international handbook of contemporary research*. Berlin: Walter de Gruyter.

Jaeggli, Osvaldo and Kenneth J. Safir (eds.) (1989) *The null subject parameter*. (Studies in Natural Language and Linguistic Theory, 15.) Dordrecht: Kluwer.

Jespersen, Otto (1917) *Negation in English and other languages*. Copenhagen: Host.

—— (1924) *The philosophy of grammar*. London: Allen and Unwin.

Joseph, Brian D. and Irene Philippaki-Warburton (1987) *Modern Greek*. (Croom Helm Descriptive Grammars.) London: Croom Helm.

Kahrel, Peter and René van den Berg (eds.) (1994) *Typological studies in negation*. (Typological Studies in Language.) Amsterdam: John Benjamins.

Kalik, A. (1971) "La caractérisation négative," *Le Français Moderne*, 39: 128-146.

Kampers-Manhe, Brigitte (1992) "The French subjunctive and the ECP," in Bok-Bennema and van Hout (eds.), pp. 137-148.

Kayne, Richard S. (1975) *French syntax: the transformational cycle*. (Current Studies in Linguistics, 6.) Cambridge, Mass.: MIT Press.

—— (1981) "Two notes on the NIC," in Belletti et al. (eds.), pp. 317-346. Reprinted in Kayne (1984), pp. 23-46.

—— (1984) *Connectedness and binary branching.* (Studies in Generative Grammar, 16.) Dordrecht: Foris.

—— (1990) "Romance clitics and PRO," *Proceedings of NELS*, 20: 255–302.

—— (1991) "Romance clitics, verb movement and PRO," *Linguistic Inquiry*, 22: 647–686.

—— (1992) "Italian negative imperatives and clitic climbing," in Tasmowski-De Ryck and Zribi-Hertz (eds.), pp. 300–312.

—— (1994) *The antisymmetry of syntax.* (Linguistic Inquiry Monographs, 25.) Cambridge, Mass.: MIT Press.

Kitagawa, Yoshihisha (1986) "Subjects in Japanese and English." Ph.D. diss., University of Massachusetts at Amherst.

Klima, Edward S. (1964) "Negation in English," in Fodor and Katz (eds.), pp. 246–323.

Kok, Ans de (1985) *La place du pronom personnel régime conjoint en français: une étude diachronique.* Amsterdam: Rodopi.

Koopman, Hilda (1984) *The syntax of verbs: from verb-movement rules in the Kru languages to Universal Grammar.* (Studies in Generative Grammar, 15.) Dordrecht: Foris.

—— (1994) "Licensing heads," in Lightfoot and Hornstein (eds.), pp. 261–296.

Koopman, Hilda and Dominique Sportiche (1982/83) "Variables and the Bijection Principle," *Linguistic Review*, 2: 139–160.

—— (1991) "The position of subjects," *Lingua*, 85: 211–258.

Körner, Karl-Hermann (1987) *Korrelative Sprachtypologie: die zwei Typen romanischer Syntax.* Stuttgart: Franz Steiner.

Kornfilt, Jaklin (1990) "Remarks on headless partitives and case in Turkish," in Mascaró and Nespor (eds.), pp. 285–303.

Labov, William (1972a) "Negative attraction and negative concord," in Labov (1972c), pp. 130–196.

—— (1972b) "Negative attraction and negative concord in English grammar," *Language*, 48: 773–818.

—— (1972c) *Language in the inner city: studies in the Black English Vernacular.* Philadelphia: University of Pennsylvania Press.

Ladusaw, William A. (1992) "Expressing negation," in Barker and Dowty (eds.), pp. 237–259.

—— (1993) "Negation, indefinites, and the Jespersen cycle," *Proceedings of BLS*, 19: 437–446.

Laka, Itziar (1990) "Negation in syntax: on the nature of functional categories and projections." Ph.D. diss., MIT.

—— (1993a) "Negative fronting in Romance: movement to Σ," in Ashby et al. (eds.), pp. 315–333.

—— (1993b) "Negation in syntax: the view from Basque," *Rivista di Linguistica*, 5: 245–273.

Laka, Itziar and Anoop Kumar Mahajan (eds.) (1989) *Functional heads and clause structure.* (MIT Working Papers in Linguistics, 10.) Cambridge, Mass.: MIT.

Lakoff, Robin T. (1969) "A syntactic argument for negative transportation," in *Chicago Linguistic Society*, 5: 145–165.

Larrivée, Pierre (1995) "La sémantique du cumul des négations." MS, Université de Laval.

Lasnik, Howard and Mamoru Saito (1984) "On the nature of proper government," *Linguistic Inquiry*, 15: 235–289.

Lazard, Gilbert (1994) *L'actance.* (Linguistique Nouvelle.) Paris: Presses Universitaires de France.

Lebeaux, David (1988) "Language acquisition and the form of the grammar." Ph.D. diss., University of Massachusetts at Amherst.

Lightfoot, David and Norbert Hornstein (1994a) "Verb movement: an introduction," in Lightfoot and Hornstein (eds.), pp. 1-17.

—— (eds.) (1994b) *Verb movement*. Cambridge: Cambridge University Press.

Longobardi, Guiseppe (1987) "Parameters of negation in Romance dialects." Paper presented to the GLOW Dialectology Workshop, Venice.

—— (1991) "In defense of the correspondence hypothesis: island effects and parasitic constructions in Logical Form," in Huang and May (eds.), pp. 149-196.

Lonzi, Lidia (1991) "Il sintagma avverbiale," in Renzi and Salvi (eds.), vol. 2, pp. 341-412.

Lupu, Coman and Glanville Price (eds.) (1994) *Hommages offerts à Maria Manoliu-Manea*. Bucharest: Editura Pluralia/Editura Logos.

Lyons, Christopher G. (1994a) *Movement in "NP" and the DP hypothesis*. (Working Papers in Language and Linguistics, 8.) Salford: University of Salford European Studies Research Institute.

—— (1994b) "Definiteness and person." Paper presented to the LAGB autumn meeting, Middlesex.

Maiden, Martin and M. Mair Parry (eds.) (1996) *The dialects of Italy*. London: Routledge.

Martineau, France (1990) "La montée du clitique en moyen français: une étude de la syntaxe des constructions infinitives." Ph.D. diss., Université d'Ottawa.

—— (1994) "Movement of negative adverbs in French infinitival clauses," *Journal of French Language Studies*, 4: 55-73.

Mascaró, Joan and Maria Nespor (eds.) (1990) *Grammar in progress: GLOW essays for Henk van Riemsdijk*. (Studies in Generative Grammar, 36.) Dordrecht: Foris.

May, Robert (1985) *Logical form: its structure and derivation*. (Linguistic Inquiry Monographs, 12.) Cambridge, Mass.: MIT Press.

McMahon, April M. S. (1994) *Understanding language change*. Cambridge: Cambridge University Press.

McNally, Louise (1992) "VP coordination and the VP-internal subject hypothesis," *Linguistic Inquiry*, 23: 336-341.

Meillet, Antoine (1912a) *Linguistique historique et linguistique générale*. Paris: Champion.

—— (1912b) "L'évolution des formes grammaticales," in Meillet (1912a), pp. 131-148.

Meisel, Jürgen M. (ed.) (1992) *The acquisition of verb placement, functional categories, and V2 phenomena in language acquisition*. (Studies in Theoretical Psycholinguistics, 16.) Dordrecht: Kluwer.

Milner, Jean-Claude (1978) "Cyclicité successive, comparatives, et cross-over en français (première partie)," *Linguistic Inquiry*, 9: 673-693.

—— (1979) "Le système de la négation en français et l'opacité du sujet," *Langue Française*, 44: 80-105. Slightly modified version in Milner (1982), pp. 186-223.

—— (1982) *Ordres et raisons de langue*. Paris: Éditions du Seuil.

Morgan, Raleigh Jr. (1959) "Structural sketch of Saint Martin Creole," *Anthropological Linguistics*, 1: 820-824.

—— (1976) "The Saint Martin Creole copula in relation to verbal categories," in Snyder and Valdman (eds.), vol. 1, pp. 147-165.

Moritz, Luc (1989) "Aperçu de la syntaxe de la négation en français et en anglais." Mémoire de licence, Université de Genève.

Moritz, Luc and Daniel Valois (1993) "French sentential negation and LF pied-piping," *Proceedings of NELS*, 22: 319-333.

—— (1994) "Pied-piping and specifier-head agreement," *Linguistic Inquiry*, 25: 667-707.

Muller, Claude (1984) "L'association négative," *Langue Française*, 62: 59-94.

—— (1991) *La négation en français: syntaxe, sémantique et éléments de comparaison avec les autres langues romanes*. (Publications Romanes et Françaises, 198.) Geneva: Droz.

Muysken, Pieter and Norval Smith (eds.) (1986) *Substrata versus universals in creole genesis*. (Creole Language Library, 1.) Amsterdam: John Benjamins.

Newson, Mark (1994) "Negation, double negation, and optimality theory," *Even Yearbook 1994*, pp. 87-136.

Obenauer, Hans-Georg (1983) "Une quantification non-canonique: la quantification à distance," *Langue Française*, 58: 66-88.

—— (1984) "On the identification of empty categories," *Linguistic Review*, 4: 153-202.

Ortiz de Urbina, Jon (1993) "Feature percolation and clausal pied-piping," in Hualde and Ortiz de Urbina (eds.), pp. 189-219.

Ouhalla, Jamal (1990) "Sentential negation, relativised minimality, and the aspectual status of auxiliaries," *Linguistic Review*, 7: 183-231.

—— (1991) *Functional categories and parametric variation*. (Theoretical Linguistics.) London: Routledge.

—— (1993a) "Subject-extraction, negation, and the anti-agreement effect," *Natural Language and Linguistic Theory*, 11: 477-518.

—— (1993b) "Negation, focus, and tense: the Arabic *maa* and *laa*," *Rivista di Linguistica*, 5: 275-300.

Parry, M. Mair (1996) "Negation," in Maiden and Parry (eds.), pp. 179-185.

Payne, John R. (1985) "Negation," in Shopen (ed.), vol. 1: Clause structure, pp. 197-242.

Pearce, Elizabeth (1990) "An analysis of negated infinitives in Middle French," *Wellington Working Papers in Linguistics*, 2: 31-45.

—— (1991) "Tense and negation: competing analyses in Middle French," Parasession on negation, *Chicago Linguistic Society*, 27: 218-232.

—— (1993) "Diachronic change and negation in French," *Rivista di Linguistica*, 5: 301-328.

Phinney, Marianne (1981) "Children's interpretation of negation in complex sentences," in Tavakolian (ed.), pp. 116-138.

Pierce, Amy E. (1992) *Language acquisition and syntactic theory: a comparative analysis of French and English child grammars*. (Studies in Theoretical Psycholinguistics, 14.) Dordrecht: Kluwer.

Pinchon, J. (1972) *Les pronoms adverbiaux* en *et* y: *problèmes généraux de la représentation pronominale*. Geneva: Droz.

Platzack, Christer and Anders Holmberg (1989) "The role of Agr and finiteness," *Working Papers in Scandinavian Syntax*, 43: 51-76.

Plunkett, Bernadette (1993) "Subjects and specifier positions." Ph.D. diss., University of Massachusetts at Amherst.

—— (1994) "The minimal approach to *wh*-movement." MS, University of York.

—— (1996) "Situating *que*," *York Papers in Linguistics*, 17: 265-298.

Pohl, Jacques (1968) "*Ne* dans le français parlé contemporain: les modalités de son abandon," *Actes du XIe congrès international de linguistique et philologie romanes*. Vol. 3. Madrid.

—— (1975) "L'omission de *ne* dans le français parlé contemporain," *Le Français dans le Monde*, 111: 17-23.

Pollock, Jean-Yves (1989) "Verb Movement, Universal Grammar, and the structure of IP," *Linguistic Inquiry*, 20: 365-424.

—— (1991) "Sur quelques différences de comportement entre arguments et circonstants: îlots adverbiaux et extractibilité," in Guéron and Pollock (eds.), pp. 83-106.

—— (1997a) *Langage et cognition: introduction au programme minimaliste de la grammaire générative*. (Psychologie et Sciences de la Pensée.) Paris: Presses Universitaires de France.

—— (1997b) "Notes on clause structure," in Haegeman (ed.), pp. 237-279.

Posner, Rebecca R. (1984) "Double negatives, negative polarity, and negative incorporation in Romance: a historical and comparative view," *Transactions of the Philological Society*, 82: 1-26.

—— (1985a) "Post-verbal negation in Non-standard French: a historical and comparative view," *Romance Philology*, 39: 170-197.

—— (1985b) "L'histoire de la négation et la typologie romane," in *Linguistique comparée et typologie des langues romanes (Actes du XVIIème congrès international de linguistique et philologie romanes)*. Vol. 2. Aix-en-Provence: Université de Provence, pp. 265-271.

—— (1996) *The Romance languages*. (Cambridge Language Surveys.) Cambridge: Cambridge University Press.

Price, Glanville (1962) "The negative particles *pas*, *mie*, and *point* in French," *Archivum Linguisticum*, 14: 14-34.

—— (1978) "L'interrogation négative sans *ne*," *Studii și Cercetări Lingvistice*, 29: 599-606.

—— (1984) *The French language: past and present*. London: Grant and Cutler.

—— (1986) "Aspects de l'histoire de la négation en français," in *Morphosyntaxe des langues romanes (Actes du XVIIème congrès international de linguistique et philologie romanes)*. Vol. 4. Aix-en-Provence: Université de Provence, pp. 569-575.

—— (1990) "The origins and syntax of *ne . . . goutte*," in Green and Ayres-Bennett (eds.), pp. 201-209.

—— (1993) "*Pas (point)* without *ne* in interrogative clauses," *Journal of French Language Studies*, 3: 191-195.

—— (1994) "Old French *de sa fame ne voit mie*–an explanation rehabilitated," in Lupu and Price (eds.), pp. 149-157.

—— (1995) "A possible Celtic influence in Romance syntax." MS, University of Wales, Aberystwyth.

Prince, Ellen F. (1976) "The syntax and semantics of Neg-raising, with evidence from French," *Language*, 52: 404-426.

Progovac, Ljiljana (1988) "A binding approach to polarity sensitivity." Ph.D. diss., University of Southern California.

—— (1991) "Polarity in Serbo-Croatian: anaphoric NPIs and pronominal PPIs," *Linguistic Inquiry*, 22: 567-572.

—— (1992a) "Nonnegative polarity licensing must involve Comp," *Linguistic Inquiry*, 23: 341-347.

—— (1992b) "Negative polarity: a semantico-syntactic account," *Lingua*, 86: 271-299.

—— (1993a) "Negative polarity: entailment and binding," *Linguistics and Philosophy*, 16: 149-180.

—— (1993b) "Negation and Comp," *Rivista di Linguistica*, 5: 329-347.

—— (1994) *Negative and positive polarity: a binding account*. (Cambridge Studies in Linguistics, 68.) Cambridge: Cambridge University Press.

Puskàs, Genoveva (1994) "Sentential negation in Hungarian," *Rivista di Linguistica*, 6.

Quer, Josep (1993) "The syntactic licensing of negative items." M. A. diss., Universitat Autònoma de Barcelona.

Quirk, Randolph, Sidney Greenbaum, Graham Leech, and Jan Svartvik (1985) *A comprehensive grammar of English*. London: Longman.

Radford, Andrew (1989) "The status of exclamative particles in modern spoken French," in Arnold et al. (eds.), pp. 223–284.

—— (1990) *Syntactic theory and the acquisition of English syntax: the nature of early child grammars of English*. Oxford: Blackwell.

—— (1997) *Syntactic theory and the structure of English: a minimalist approach*. (Cambridge Textbooks in Linguistics.) Cambridge: Cambridge University Press.

Ramat, Paolo (1987) *Linguistic typology*. Berlin: Mouton de Gruyter.

Ramat, Paolo, Piera Molinelli, and Guiliano Bernini (1987) "Sentence negation in Germanic and Romance languages," in Ramat, pp. 165–187.

Renzi, Lorenzo and Giampaolo P. Salvi (eds.) (1991) *Grande grammatica italiana di consultazione*. Bologna: Il Mulino.

Rickard, Peter (1989) *A history of the French language*, 2nd ed. London: Routledge.

Ritz, Marie-Ève (1993) "La sémantique de la négation en français," *Langue Française*, 98: 67–78.

Rivero, María-Luisa (1991) "Long head movement and negation: Serbo-Croatian vs. Slovak and Czech," *Linguistic Review*, 8: 319–351.

—— (1994) "Negation, imperatives, and Wackernagel effects," *Rivista di Linguistica*, 6.

Rivero, María-Luisa and Arhonto Terzi (1995) "Imperatives, V-movement, and logical mood," *Journal of Linguistics*, 31: 301–332.

Rizzi, Luigi (1982) *Issues in Italian syntax*. (Studies in Generative Grammar, 11.) Dordrecht: Foris.

—— (1990) *Relativized minimality*. (Linguistic Inquiry Monographs, 16.) Cambridge, Mass.: MIT Press.

—— (1996) "Residual verb second and the *wh*-criterion," in Belletti and Rizzi (eds.), pp. 63–90. Original version published in 1991 as *Technical Reports in Formal and Computational Linguistics*, 2, Faculté des Lettres, Université de Genève.

—— (1997) "The fine structure of the left periphery," in Haegeman (ed.) (1997b), pp. 281–337.

Robbers, Karin (1992) "Properties of negation in Afrikaans and Italian," in Bok-Bennema and van Hout (eds.), pp. 223–234.

Roberts, Ian G. (1992) *Verbs and diachronic syntax: a comparative history of English and French*. (Studies in Natural Language and Linguistic Theory, 28.) Dordrecht: Kluwer.

—— (1994) "Two types of head movement in Romance," in Lightfoot and Hornstein (eds.), pp. 207–242.

Roeper, Thomas (1991) "Acquisition architecture: from triggers to trees in the realization of IP and CP." MS, University of Massachusetts at Amherst.

Rooryck, Johan (1992) "Romance enclitic ordering and Universal Grammar." MS, Indiana University.

Ross, John Robert (1967) "Constraints on variables in syntax." Ph.D. diss., MIT. Published in (1986) as *Infinite syntax!* Norwood, N. J.: Ablex.

Rottet, Kevin J. (1992) "Functional categories and Verb Movement in Louisiana Creole," *Probus*, 4: 261–289.

Rowlett, Paul (1992a) "On the D-structure position of negative sentence adverbials in French." Paper presented to the XVIII Incontro di Grammatica Generativa, Ferrara, Italy.

—— (1992b) *On the D-structure position of negative sentence adverbials in French*. (Working Papers in Language and Linguistics, 12.) Salford: University of Salford Department of Modern Languages.

—— (1993a) "On the syntactic derivation of negative sentence adverbials," *Journal of French Language Studies*, 3: 39–69.

—— (1993b) "A derivational approach to sentential negation in French: what can it explain?" Paper presented to the Seminari de Sintaxi i Semàntica, Grup de Gramàtica Teòrica, Universitat Autònoma de Barcelona, Spain, and the Parametric Variation Seminar, Centre for Cognitive Science, Edinburgh.

—— (1993c) Pas de deux: *further thoughts on the syntax of sentential negation in French*. (Working Papers in Language and Linguistics, 18.) Salford: University of Salford Department of Modern Languages.

—— (1993d) "Remarks on sentential negation in French," *Catalan Working Papers in Linguistics*, 3: 153–169.

—— (1994a) "The Doubly-Filled Comp Filter meets the Neg Criterion in Quebec." Paper presented to the XXII Romance Linguistics Seminar, Cambridge.

—— (1994b) "Why doesn't *ne . . . plus* behave like *ne . . . pas?*" Paper presented to the Staff-PG seminar, Department of Language and Linguistic Science, York.

—— (1994c) *The Negative Cycle, negative concord and the nature of spec-head agreement*. (Working Papers in Language and Linguistics, 7.) Salford: University of Salford European Studies Research Institute.

—— (1994d) Review of Claude Muller (1991), *Journal of French Language Studies*, 4: 120–122.

—— (1995a) "Negative concord and A'-binding." Paper presented to the LAGB spring meeting, Newcastle-upon-Tyne.

—— (1995b) "Jespersen, negative concord, and A'-binding." Paper presented to the conference on Negation: Syntax and Semantics, Ottawa, Canada.

—— (1996a) "On the difference between *rien* and *personne*." Paper presented to the XXIV Romance Linguistics Seminar, Cambridge.

—— (1996b) "Negation in French." Paper presented to the Oxford Linguistics Circle, Oxford.

—— (1996c) "Negative configurations in French." Ph.D. diss., University of York. Distributed as *Negative configurations in French*. (Working Papers in Language and Linguistics, 11.) Salford: University of Salford European Studies Research Institute.

—— (1996d) Review of Liliane M. V. Haegeman (1995), *Journal of Linguistics*, 32: 188–193.

—— (1996e) *On French* personne. (Working Papers in Language and Linguistics, 12.) Salford: University of Salford European Studies Research Institute.

—— (1996f) "A non-overt negative operator in French." Paper presented to Going Romance 10, Utrecht, The Netherlands.

—— (1997) "Jespersen, negative concord, and A'-binding," in Forget et al. (eds.), pp. 323–340.

—— (1998a) "The syntax of negation." Paper presented to the workshop on *New Perspectives in French and English Linguistics*, Toulouse-Le Mirail, France.

—— (1998b) "A non-overt negative operator in French," *Probus*, 10: 83–104.

Sankoff, Gillian (1980) *The social life of language*. Philadelphia: University of Pennsylvania Press.

Sankoff, Gillian and Diane Vincent (1977) "L'emploi productif du *ne* dans le français parlé à Montréal," *Le Français Moderne*, 45: 243–256. English version published as "The productive use of *ne* in spoken Montreal French," in Sankoff (1980).

Schafer, Robin (1994) "Negation and verb second in Breton," *Natural Language and Linguistic Theory*, 13: 135–172.

Scheitlin, Walter (1962/72) *Il pled puter: grammatica ladina d'Engiadin'ota*. Samedan, Switzerland: Edizium da l'Uniun dals Grischs.

Schwegler, Armin (1983) "Predicate negation and word-order change: a problem of multiple causation," *Lingua*, 61: 297–334.

—— (1988) "Word-order changes in predicate negation strategies in Romance languages," *Diachronica*, 5: 21–58.

—— (1991) "Negation in Palenquero: synchrony," *Journal of Pidgin and Creole Languages*, 6: 165–214.

Selkirk, Elisabeth O. (1977) "Some remarks on the noun phrase structure," in Culicover et al. (eds.), pp. 285–316.

Shlonsky, Ur (1989) "A note on Neg Raising," *Linguistic Inquiry*, 19: 710–17.

Shopen, Timothy (ed.) (1985) *Language typology and syntactic description.* 3 vols. Cambridge: Cambridge University Press.

Smith, John-Charles and Martin Maiden (eds.) (1995) *Linguistic theory and the Romance languages.* (Current Issues in Linguistic Theory, 122.) Amsterdam: John Benjamins.

Snyder, Émile and Albert Valdman (eds.) (1976) *Identité culturelle et francophonie dans les Amériques.* Quebec: Presses de l'Université de Laval.

Speas, Margaret (1991a) "Functional heads and the mirror principle," *Lingua*, 84: 181–214.

—— (1991b) "Functional heads and inflectional morphemes," *Linguistic Review*, 8: 389–417.

Sportiche, Dominique (1988) "A theory of floating quantifiers and its corollaries for constituent structure," *Linguistic Inquiry*, 19: 425–449.

—— (1992) "Clitic constructions." MS, UCLA.

—— (1993) "Subject clitics in French and Romance: complex inversion and clitic doubling." MS, UCLA.

Stephens, Janig (1993) "Breton," in Ball (ed.), pp. 349–409.

Suñer, Margarita (1993) "NPIs, island effects, and resumptive *no*." MS, Cornell University.

Tanase, Eugène (1986) "Sur les origines de la négation à deux termes du français," in *Morphosyntaxe des langues romanes (Actes du XVIIème congrès international de linguistique et philologie romanes).* Vol. 4. Aix-en-Provence: Université de Provence, pp. 579–590.

Tasmowski-De Ryck, Liliane and Anne Zribi-Hertz (eds.) (1992) *Hommages à Nicolas Ruwet.* (Communication and Cognition.) Ghent.

Tavakolian, Susan L. (ed.) (1981) *Language acquisition and linguistic theory.* Cambridge, Mass.: MIT Press.

Tellier, Christine (1995) *Éléments de syntaxe du français: méthodes d'analyse en grammaire générative.* Montreal: Presses de l'Université de Montréal.

Torrego, Esther (1996) "On quantifier float in control clauses," *Linguistic Inquiry*, 27: 111–126.

Travis, Lisa de Mena (1984) Parameters and effects of word order variation. Ph.D. diss., MIT.

Uriagereka, Juan (1995) "Aspects of the syntax of clitic placement in Western Romance," *Linguistic Inquiry*, 26: 79–123.

Vennemann, Theo (1974) "Topics, subjects, and word order: from SXV to SVX via TVX," in Anderson and Jones (eds.), pp. 339–376.

Verrips, Maaike and Jürgen Weissenborn (1992) "Routes to verb placement in early German and French: the independence of finiteness and agreement," in Meisel (ed.), pp. 283–331.

Vikner, Carl (1978) "Les auxiliaires négatifs: fonction et position," *La Revue Romane*, 13: 88–109.

Vinet, Marie-Thérèse (1996) "Adverbes de quantification, négation et phénomènes d'accentuation," *Recherches Linguistiques de Vincennes*, 25: 129–140.

Wanner, Dieter and Douglas A. Kibbee (eds.) (1991) *New analyses in Romance linguistics.* Amsterdam: John Benjamins.

Wartburg, Walther von (1967) *Évolution et structure de la langue française*, 8th ed. Berne: Éditions A Francke.

Watanabe, Akira (1991) "*Wh*-in-situ, subjacency, and chain formation." MS, MIT.

Webelhuth, Gert (ed.) (1995) *Government and binding theory and the minimalist program.* (Generative Syntax.) Oxford: Blackwell.

Weissenborn, Jürgen, Maaike Verrips, and Ruth Berman (1989) "Negation as a window to the structure of early child language." MS, Max-Planck-Institut für Psycholinguistik/Tel Aviv University.

Westphal, Germán F., Benjamin Ao, and Hee-Rahk Chae (eds.) (1992) *Proceedings of ESCOL 1991.* Columbus: Ohio State University.

Wexler, Kenneth (1994) "Optional infinitives, head movement, and the economy of derivations," in Lightfoot and Hornstein (eds.), pp. 305–350.

Williams, Edwin S. (1994a) "A reinterpretation of evidence for verb movement in French," in Lightfoot and Hornstein (eds.), pp. 189–205.

—— (1994b) *Thematic structure in syntax.* (Linguistic Inquiry Monographs, 23.) Cambridge, Mass.: MIT Press.

Winters, Margaret E. (1987) "Innovations in French negation: a cognitive grammar account," *Diachronica*, 4: 27–52.

Wode, Helen (1977) "Four early stages in the development of L1 negation," *Journal of Child Language*, 4: 87–102.

Wouden, Anton van der (1994) "Negative contexts." Ph.D. diss., University of Groningen.

Wouden, Anton van der and Frans Zwarts (1992) "Negative concord," *Language and Cognition*, 2: 317–331.

Yaeger-Dror, Malcah (1997) "Contraction of negatives as evidence of variance in register-specific interactive rules," *Language Variation and Change*, 9: 1–36.

Yvon, Henri (1948) "*Pas* et *point* dans les propositions négatives," *Le Français Moderne*, 61: 19–35.

Zanuttini, Raffaella (1990) "Two types of negative markers," *Proceedings of NELS*, 20: 517–530 (vol. 2).

—— (1991) "Syntactic properties of sentential negation: a comparative study of Romance languages." Ph.D. diss., University of Pennsylvania.

—— (1994a) "Speculations on negative imperatives," *Rivista di Linguistica*, 6: 119–142.

—— (1994b) "Re-examining negative clauses," in Cinque et al. (eds.), pp. 427–451.

—— (1995) "The structure of negative clauses." Paper presented to the conference on Negation: Syntax and Semantics, Ottawa, Canada.

—— (1996) "On the relevance of tense for sentential negation," in Belletti and Rizzi (eds.), pp. 183–209.

—— (1997a) "Negation and Verb Movement," in Haegeman (ed.) (1997a), pp. 214–245.

—— (1997b) *Negation and clausal structure: a comparative study of Romance languages.* (Oxford Studies in Comparative Syntax.) New York: Oxford University Press.

Zaring, Laurie (1985) "The syntactic role of verbal inflection in French and Brazilian Portuguese." Ph.D. diss., Cornell University.

Zribi-Hertz, Anne (1994) "The syntax of nominative clitics in Standard and Advanced French," in Cinque et al. (eds.), pp. 453–472.

Zwart, C. Jan-Wouter (1993) "Dutch syntax: a minimalist approach." Ph.D. diss., University of Groningen.

Zwicky, Arnold M. and Geoffrey K. Pullum (1983) "Cliticization vs. inflection: English *n't*," *Language*, 59: 502–513.

Index